To Donë –

D0199704

Thirsting *for* GOD

GARY L. THOMAS

The peace of Christ,

Gary Thomas

HARVEST HOUSE PUBLISHERS

EUGENE, OREGON

THIRSTING FOR GOD
Copyright © 1999/2011 by Gary Thomas
Published by Harvest House Publishers
Eugene, Oregon 97402
www.harvesthousepublishers.com

Library of Congress Cataloging-in-Publication Data
Thomas, Gary (Gary Lee)
Thirsting for God / Gary L. Thomas.
    p. cm.
Augmented ed. of: Seeking the face of God. c1999.
Includes bibliographical references.
ISBN 978-0-7369-2890-8 (pbk.)
1. Spiritual life—Christianity. I. Thomas, Gary (Gary Lee) Seeking the face of God. II. Title.
BV4501.3.T47155 2011
248.409—dc22
                                                                2010015989

In Memory of Dr. Klaus Bockmuehl

Dr. Bockmuehl was a man of great faith and intellect.
Though he never lived to see my writing ministry, he spoke
matter-of-factly about it years before he had any earthly
reason to do so. Plenty of students were much more deserving
of his attention than I was, but Dr. Bockmuehl's gracious
contribution and encouragement has left a lasting impression.
The memory of his life continues to call me forward in Christ.

Author's Preface

Thirsting for God is a completely rewritten and updated version of *Seeking the Face of God*, which I wrote in 1994. The subjects are the same (except for three entirely new chapters), but I've reworked the old material and added new, including more than 125 new quotes from a variety of Christian classics. I wrote *Seeking the Face of God* when I was in my early thirties, and though I'm pleased at how well the themes have held up (not that surprising, considering that the book is based on the timeless wisdom of the classics), rewriting it just shy of my fiftieth birthday reflects almost two additional decades of living with, reflecting on, and applying these truths.

The format has also been changed extensively. As I continued my journey of reading and rereading the classics, I noticed the helpfulness of savoring smaller nuggets of truth, which is why this volume has 48 short chapters. Yes, part of the additional number of chapters is to accommodate more material, but it also marks a different approach to devotional reading. I hope it will make your reading a gentler, more meditative, and more life-changing encounter.

I believe that even if you have read *Seeking the Face of God*, reading *Thirsting for God* will feel like an entirely new experience. I offer this new version of my first book to the church, and to God's service, with prayers that it will further our lives of devotion and remind us of the vast amounts of wisdom from which we can continue our journey in the twenty-first century.

Contents

PART I

Soul Advancement: The Art *and* Discipline *of* Spiritual Training

The Journey of Faith:
Knowing God More Intimately

With one simple sentence, Franklin Graham, president of Samaritan's Purse, instantly put me on the edge of my seat. "Maybe I should take Gary with me to see Daddy," he said. "We can work while we fly, have dinner with Daddy and Mama, and then work on the way back."

I could hardly believe my ears. *A personal dinner with Billy Graham!*

Billy Graham had no choice but to become one of the least accessible people in the world. *Everybody* wanted to meet the aging patriarch of evangelicalism, but Billy—despite his age and failing health—determined to preach until his strength literally gave out. If he spent 15 hours a day meeting people, he wouldn't have had the strength to preach. Being unavailable for personal appointments is much more realistic than laboriously filtering through the literally thousands of requests he receives. Those who love him dearly have been forced to become understandably protective.

And yet I was looking at the possibility of a private dinner! Of course, I'd have to make some adjustments in my schedule, and airlines seem to enjoy exploiting desperate travelers. "Oh, you need to change your day of departure? Sure, we can do that for a mere $800 more."

You know what? I didn't care what it would cost me.

I would also have to cancel some appointments, but none of that mattered either. I thought I could look any of my friends in the eyes and say, "Hey, it was you or Billy Graham, and I went with Billy." They would have thought me foolish not to take advantage of the opportunity.

As it turned out, the dinner never took place. During the long journey home, I reflected on how excited I'd been at the prospect of meeting this great man, how willing I was to undergo any difficulty to make it happen, and how quick I was to accept any discomfort the visit might bring to other areas of my life. All the while, every day, One who is infinitely greater than Billy Graham cries out, "Where is the man or woman who will devote himself or herself to be close to Me?"

The true cry of our hearts is to worship, know, and love the God who created us. But let's be honest. This relationship can, at first glance, seem incredibly difficult to enter into. How can we, encased in flesh and imprisoned in time, relate to a God who is spirit and eternal? How do we, with finite minds scarcely able to think above our sinful passions, commune with a God who is infinite in all His holy glory and in whose mind no sin has ever dwelled?

Surely no relationship has been less equal than the one Christ calls us to when He says, "Come, follow Me." Our occasional lack of wonder at the absolute inequality of the relationship is evidence enough that we do not fully comprehend the greatness of the God who speaks and the humility of us who listen.

This relationship calls us to the chief goal of humankind, "to glorify God, and enjoy Him forever," as the Westminster Shorter Catechism says. But this itself presents a problem. What does *enjoy God* mean? How do we relate to One we can't see, whose voice we cannot audibly hear?

For centuries, that has been the ultimate question of women and men whose hearts have burned with the passion of a pure and all-consuming love for their God. In many traditions, in many lands, teenagers, young adults, middle-aged and elderly people, and even children have heard the call of God and made their hearts receptacles of His grace. A.J. Russell wrote, "The story of every live church is the story of a continuous war for spirituality."[1]

As I sought guidance for devoting myself to becoming close to God, I soon found that many contemporary writers on the spiritual life answer questions that are different from the ones I was asking. One writer seemed to be searching for relevance, another sought a collection of formulas and recipes for successful living, and others seemed mesmerized by spiritual experiences. All these pursuits seemed decidedly sterile compared with the journey I felt called to make—to devote myself to becoming close to God.

Then I opened a book that was written 1500 years ago, an Eastern

Christian classic by John Climacus called *The Ladder of Divine Ascent*. I felt as if something that had atrophied inside me was suddenly being nursed to life. I soon found myself meeting new friends, spiritual soul mates who were on the same search, like John of the Cross and Teresa of Avila, who joined forces in the sixteenth century to bring renewal to a stale religious order. I met the early eighteenth-century Anglican William Law and a brilliant seventeenth-century Puritan named John Owen, who gave some of the most practical advice for facing temptation I had ever read. Next, I met François Fénelon, a mystic whose writings to the French upper class in the eighteenth century are remarkably applicable to today's North American middle class. I met a wise spiritual director named Francis de Sales, who did something stunning for the seventeenth century—he directed his book on spirituality toward laypeople. His wisdom and practical advice for combining family life with spirituality was nothing short of astonishing. And then I met Henry Drummond, who helped me look at love and the will of God as I had never looked at either before.

Over time, as I read classic after classic, I began to realize some common themes. I went back to the classics I had read earlier and made notes in the margins, comparing their thoughts with the classics I read later. I was amazed that though the Anglican William Law had a radically different view of the nature of the church than did John Climacus, they agreed passionately and both had some very insightful things to say about the awareness of death being an aid to the Christian's spiritual life. Lorenzo Scupoli, who worked in the Counter-Reformation in the seventeenth century, can often sound suspiciously like John Calvin, the brilliant innovator of the Reformed system of thought, when both talk about relating to God, growing in character, or cultivating the life of Christ in our souls.

So many of our theological discussions today highlight issues upon which we profoundly and often vehemently disagree. But as I met these writers throughout church history, I soon witnessed a beautiful tapestry of common truth that gave stunning witness to the accepted faith of the wider church—elements of the Christian life on which zealots and thoughtful adherents spoke in virtual unanimity.

I realized that though these saints were from different times, places, and Christian traditions, they agreed on so very much. They faced the same struggles and arrived at many of the same answers. They certainly weren't spouting simple formulas or ten easy steps. And their conclusions never promised instant joy or earthly bliss. In fact, they often spoke of a spiritual desert or a dark night of the soul, and I knew, at a deep, instinctual level, that they were speaking the truth.

I would like to introduce you to some precious Christian brothers and sisters who have walked this life before us. I want to introduce you to their struggles and their insights, their victories and their defeats. Most of all, I want us to capture not only their wisdom and practical advice but also their passion for God. Though I'll tell some of their stories, I'll primarily focus on what they taught and discover the rich legacy of the classical Christian life.

Enemies or Friends?

Some may ask, why go back to the classics? Didn't some of these authors embrace traditions that are substantially different from what most evangelicals believe today?

Admittedly, quoting from these writers can be controversial. After I preached at one church, an earnest young man came up to me and said, "What you shared is so important for the church to hear; it was truly inspired. But why did you have to quote enemies of the gospel to make your point?"

I sighed. I had quoted Francis of Assisi and an Eastern Orthodox monk.

"Francis couldn't very well have been a Calvinist, now could he," I said, "because Calvin wasn't even born until Francis had been dead for almost 300 years. And though evangelicals certainly have disagreements with certain points of Eastern Orthodox theology, do you really want to simply and completely write off all the wisdom this wing of the church has gained over the past two millennia? The Orthodox claim to historicity is as strong as, if not stronger than, any other branch of the church!"

My final admonition was this: "Do you truly want to limit your reading to the 'three Johns'—Calvin, MacArthur, and Piper? I have enormous respect for each one of them, but I have gained so very much from reading widely. Different generations and different Christian perspectives have broadened my understanding of the journey of faith."

I believe we would be silly to avoid the classic devotional writings of Roman Catholics (many of whom wrote before the Reformation) or Eastern Orthodox Christians. This book does not split theological hairs. Rather, it examines the seasons, stages, and characteristics of the soul's pursuit of God and response to Him, themes on which various Christian traditions enjoy wide agreement.

The Cry of Our Hearts

Some people may hesitate to read the Christian classics not only for sectarian reasons but also because they doubt that someone writing hundreds or thousands of years ago could have anything relevant to say to Christians today. Admittedly, the classic devotional writers probably couldn't have conceived of the 20,000 member megachurches we see today, with paved parking lots and parking attendants in orange vests. They may not have anticipated the football stadiums packed with seekers waiting to hear Billy Graham, satellites carrying Christian programming all over the world, or John Piper and Rick Warren sending out four or five inspirational tweets every day.

But has the human heart changed? Is jealousy any less destructive today than it was a thousand years ago? Does God's silence cause any fewer doubts in Christian souls today than it did in the Middle Ages?

Perhaps the faith of the saints is more relevant than much of what is being preached today. In our race for advances in technology, many of us may be losing touch with the individual human soul and the transcendent God who made us. Some of these precious saints of ages past knew the ache of humanity and the glory of God like few since. They discovered the fundamental issues of life and had an amazing capacity to see through all the trappings that confuse so many of us today.

We can read all the bookstores' volumes on emotional wholeness, marital and family relationships, financial responsibility, and other pressing issues, and well we should, but every book worth reading recites one familiar refrain: The foundational issue is our relationship to God. If we center our life on Him, every other area will fall into place as well. The men and women who wrote the Christian classics were masters at understanding the spiritual life. We may not accept every single doctrine they teach, but perhaps we can recognize the love of God in them, learn how that love was kindled, and see how they learned to enjoy God.

They taught basic Christian spirituality. Unfortunately, the whole notion of spirituality is becoming problematic today, and the noble pursuit of it can lead us down the wrong path if we're not careful. Therefore, let's spend just a few moments defining Christian spirituality.

2

Good Intentions

Alan Thornhill, a British playwright, tells a true story about his mother, who lived in the early part of the twentieth century. When Mrs. Thornhill learned that some young acquaintances in another country were getting married, she sent them a congratulatory telegram (the normal form of international communication at that time). Being a godly woman, Mrs. Thornhill liked to put Bible verses at the end of her letters, but because she was sending a telegram—and each word added to the price—she settled on including a biblical reference: 1 John 4:18.

First John 4:18 is an appropriate enough verse for a newlywed couple— "Perfect love casts out fear"—but unfortunately, the telegram operator misunderstood Mrs. Thornhill and dropped the *1*, making the reference John 4:18. If you're familiar with John 4, which includes the story of the woman at the well, you can imagine what happened. Instead of reading, "Perfect love casts out fear," the new bride, with her husband looking over her shoulder, opened up her Bible and read, "You have had five husbands, and the man you now have is not your husband."

Good intentions, wrong result.

That sums up much of today's interest in spirituality—good intentions, wrong result. Out of good intentions, the materialistic eighties gave way to the spiritual nineties. Madonna, the quintessential material girl two decades ago, has now joined other Hollywood celebrities in the Jewish mystical teachings of Kabbalah. Many popular television shows have joined the spirituality craze, and young adult novels with a spiritualistic twist routinely top the bestseller lists. Gregorian chants have taken their place on many an iPod. At the dawn of the twenty-first century, depictions of vampires and wizards are all but taking over popular culture.

Given this rampant and often undiscerning interest in spirituality, we need to clarify what we mean by *Christian* spirituality.

Focused on God, Not Man

True Christian spirituality is not a search to discover ourselves or to be enlightened or even to add a new dimension to our lives. No. Christian spirituality is a relationship with God. This search is initiated by God, empowered by God, and made possible by God. He is our desire. Not power, not experience, not the supernatural...but God, revealed to us in Jesus Christ.

Therefore, Christian spirituality has more to do with what we receive than what we achieve. Our potential and activity depend entirely on God's work in our lives. If we set out to be achievers rather than receivers, we have not begun to follow God. Achievers call attention to themselves, whereas receivers lead others to appreciate the Giver. If we insist on being achievers, seeking God so that others might admire our faith, our commitment, or our dedication, we become God's competitors, trying to steal some of His glory.

Too often, contemporary spirituality is spoken of as humans pursuing God and the riches we find in Him. But the wisdom of the Christian classics reminds us that *God* wants to be in a relationship with *us*. In other words, these authors were motivated more by empathy toward God, who desires to know us, than by our own self-interested desire to know God. Julian of Norwich, author of the earliest Christian classic written by a woman, reminds us. "[God] wants to be seen and he wants to be sought; he wants to be waited for and he wants to be trusted...Seeking with faith, hope and love pleases our Lord."[1]

Built on Objective Truth, Not Subjective Experience

More than a hundred years ago, Henry Drummond, a Scottish leader in the early YMCA movement and a trusted friend of D.L. Moody, warned, "There is probably nothing in the world so disorderly and slipshod as personal spiritual experience."[2]

The very word *spirituality* can sound hopelessly subjective, spooky, esoteric, mysterious. Many of us might think it is best left to those who would prefer to float above the earth, who have no more use for logic or reason than a baby has for a motorcycle.

This is not Christian spirituality, which is anchored in biblical truth and expressed in the corporate church. We might think of ourselves as pioneers, but we are so only in the sense of those pioneers who followed the deep wagon ruts of the Oregon Trail. Others have preceded us. Others have faced the same temptations. Others have reached the same understandings.

Every spiritual journey is unique, but each one also shares experiences with those who have gone before. And every spiritual journey has the same goal—to know God. To that end, spiritual pilgrims study, chart, and map the stages, experiences, and themes of the Christian life.

Seeking Others' Good, Not Our Own

One of the chief aims of Christian spirituality, second only to knowing God, is to enter other people's lives, pain, doubts, and joys—to be other-centered. Consider this contrast. The Pharisees sought to make themselves holy; Jesus, on the other hand, delivered others from the unholy things that held them captive.

We glamorize evangelism, and indeed, evangelism is a holy, necessary, and primary calling. We would do well, however, to also prioritize "soul surgery"—the ability to work with God to bring back to health those who are suffering from spiritual problems.

Every spiritual problem has an individual genesis and requires an individual exodus. Generalized preaching is crucial to the Christian community, but individual needs call for individual attention. Most believers have had their fill of simplistic answers and general platitudes that leave people impressed but still broken. Instead, they want and need someone to be with them, to encourage them to continue on in the journey. Thus the need for maturity, to become surgeons of the soul.

We do not need to be mature to reach heaven. We can experience salvation just minutes after being enthusiastic heathens. God answers our simple prayer for help, which expresses the true cry of our hearts, and immediately ushers us into the eternal kingdom. However, without maturity, we will have neither the motivation nor the ability to get involved in other people's lives.

God must do a work *in* us before He can work *through* us. That is why a lack of growth is so dangerous. We live in a world of wasted human lives. Part of the problem has to do with sin, and much of it has to do with complacency as lives are slowly wasting away in front of television sets, in gossip sessions, and in other means of escape.

True fulfillment comes as we receive God's love and respond to it by loving others. This is the essence of Christian spirituality.

An Intentional Pursuit:
The Development of Spiritual Goals

Cheryl was a gifted and motivated young gymnast. The competition to qualify for the Olympic team was fierce, but Cheryl knew what she wanted to do, and she was willing to pay the price to achieve it. Her diet, her social life, her education, and her sleep all revolved around her training. At night she fell asleep thinking about the next competition. In the morning she was consumed with getting the kinks out of a particular move.

After months of preparation for a qualifying competition, Cheryl didn't score high enough to continue on to the national event. She decided she was too old to continue and retired from gymnastics at 16. As a result, Cheryl experienced a radical transformation in her schedule, her thoughts, and her actions. Her life as a gymnast was completely different from her new life.

Goals move us. In business, sports, politics, and even the Christian life, goals often make the difference between moving forward or going around in circles.

Limping to Heaven?

Unfortunately, contemporary Christian spirituality often starts at the finish line. In this spirituality, the goal of the Christian life is salvation, which is received the instant one becomes a Christian. Because many evangelicals also believe that salvation cannot be lost, the new believer has already attained the goal of Christianity, which he or she can't lose, just seconds after being a complete unbeliever. We've started at the finish line. All that is left to do is to hold on and wait for the awards ceremony to begin.

This has had a brutal effect on evangelicals' spirituality. Historically, we have functioned more like an evangelistic club than a place where people can grow deep. Many evangelicals have looked outside the evangelical tradition for books and sermons that talk about a growing spirituality.

When I was a young campus pastor, people often asked me, "Can I lose my salvation?" Why did so few people ask, "How can I grow?" We seem to have an overwhelming desire to drag ourselves into heaven in the same way a hero barely survives at the end of a movie. We'll limp into heaven bruised and bleeding with buildings burning all around us, our clothes ripped and torn, our faces scratched, sweaty, and dirty, and our hair moving every which way in the smoke-filled air.

The focus on our ultimate salvation rather than persistent growth has been a convenient but spiritually depleting lapse. Growth is painful. It is most frequently the result of enduring difficulty and pain. Unless we are strongly motivated to grow, the effort required will be too great, and we'll excuse ourselves from the obligation by saying, "Jesus already did it for me." In such a context, this is not a statement of faith; it's a statement of slothfulness. Scripture is bursting with references urging us to grow.[1]

Other traditions took these verses seriously in a way that we don't. Writing from the Orthodox perspective, John Climacus describes fellow monks gathering around a brother's deathbed, almost as if they were watching a modern-day athletic event. These monks *ache* for a sign—a smile just before death, a vision of light, a greeting from God, a pleasant smell—anything that might signal that their brother (after years of fasting, prayer vigils, sexual abstinence, and oftentimes violent penance) was entering heaven. Even after living lives of heroic asceticism, few had any assurance of salvation, and this humble uncertainty fueled their efforts at piety.

I'm not celebrating the unhealthy extent of these monks' asceticism, but I am moved by their willingness to give their lives over to achieving spiritual maturity. In one sense, this could be seen as a selfish preoccupation from which the gospel of grace saves us. On the other hand, does our relative indifference to spiritual disciplines and spiritual growth honor the gift of this grace, or is it rather an indication that we are taking God's mercy for granted?

Our spiritual ancestors followed the apostle Peter's advice and urged us to do the same: "Make every effort to add to your faith..." (2 Peter 1:5). Thomas à Kempis wrote, "Our fervor and progress should increase daily: but now it is accounted a great matter, if a man can retain but some part of his first zeal."[2] He was telling us our Christian growth should progress daily. Even centuries ago, apparently, Christians were more concerned about not "falling away" than about developing a mature and abiding faith.

John Climacus went a step further when he exhorted, "Regarding every vice and every virtue, we must unceasingly scrutinize ourselves to see what point we have reached, a beginning, a middle or the end."[3] Notice he says this about *every* vice and *every* virtue. From this perspective, we should pay attention to our progress in conquering fear, growing in gentleness, overcoming sloth and gluttony, increasing in kindness. Without due attention, Climacus warns, we'll have no idea whether we are stuck at the beginning, complacent at the middle, or making progress toward the end.

Thomas à Kempis and John Climacus are just two examples of Christian saints who urged the church of their day to shun complacency. Historical Christianity reserves spiritual retirement for heaven. In many cases, the uncertainty of entering heaven provoked Christians to train and guard their hearts and minds to an almost neurotic degree. We don't want to go back to that, but we can learn from the urgency of their faith. As we explore the classics of Christian literature and spirituality, we will see that those who had a particularly vibrant walk with God first had a clear picture of what they wanted to become in *this* world, not just the next.

A Clear Goal

Our first step in rediscovering an authentic Christian spirituality is to gain a clear picture of a mature Christian. If we ignore this question, spiritual growth will be random and accidental. God has His way of making us grow regardless of circumstances, but when He is forced to move without our cooperation, growth becomes haphazard and slower than it need be.

Christians have adopted many goals through the ages. These goals may not all fit within a traditional evangelical framework, but becoming familiar with them may help you develop some spiritual goals of your own.

Climacus sought to draw believers to what he called "dispassion." This is not a passion*less* existence but a redirecting of worldly passions into heavenly longings. "Many have been speedily forgiven their sins," he said. "But no one has rapidly acquired dispassion, for this requires much time and longing, and God."[4] Such a state required years of submission, spiritual training, growth in detachment, and earnest prayer. Eventually, the soul was set on desiring only what God desires and was unmoved by anything displeasing to God.

John of the Cross, a monk who lived in the sixteenth century, spoke often of "divine union," a sort of spiritual marriage one experiences only after traveling through the "dark night of the soul," a particularly difficult stage of the spiritual journey. The divine union calls for the renunciation of everything else so one may be completely and utterly devoted to God. The union is not achieved in a day or even in a decade, wrote John. It requires a lifetime of service and dedication, and even then its achievement is not guaranteed.

The primary difficulty of these two goals for me (apart from fully understanding them) is that they assume one is living in a religious community. They still challenge me, however, for if these people, who devoted virtually every waking moment to seeking intimacy with God, needed to establish clear goals, how much more do I—having to face the daily distractions of a job, a family, and modern society—need to keep a clear goal in focus if I'm to stay on the narrow way.

John Wesley, of whom I'm a big fan, had the audacious goal of what he called "Christian perfection." Understandably, this phrase elicited quite a bit of controversy. But here's how he defended it in a letter "to a pious and sensible woman":

> By Christian perfection, I mean, 1. Loving God with all our heart. Do you object to this? I mean, 2. A heart and life all devoted to God. Do you desire less? I mean, 3. Regaining the whole image of God. What objection to this? I mean, 4. Having all the mind that was in Christ. Is this going too far? I mean, 5. Walking uniformly as Christ walked. And this surely no Christian will object to. If anyone means anything more or anything else by perfection, I have no concern with it.[5]

The glory of Wesley's approach is that he wanted himself and all believers to truly become like Christ—not just *believe* in Christ, but to actually be Christlike. This is a refreshing message for contemporary believers who are quick to claim, "I rest in God's grace, who loves me just as I am" when actually they are simply complacent. Yes, He loves us, and His grace is the source of our lives. But because of His love and grace, He wants us to grow and experience the benefits and blessings of spiritual maturity.

The benefit of having a goal became especially clear to me when I encountered Teresa of Avila, a famous woman of prayer who was a contemporary and acquaintance of John of the Cross in the sixteenth century. In high school and college (before I had a job, a mortgage, and kids), I used to think the only measure of a maturing prayer life was increasing the amount of time I spent in prayer. Thus I reasoned if I regularly prayed 30 minutes a day and wanted to grow, I'd have to pray 45 minutes a day and then 60 minutes a day—and throw in some all-night vigils and on and on.

That's why I found Teresa's writings so intriguing. She carefully guided readers through six stages of prayer until they finally reached the seventh stage, the ultimate goal, which she called the "interior castle." Her writings establish a mature standard of prayer. Teresa's goal moved me to drop my punch-card prayer goals and focus instead on increasing *intimacy*, something that can't be measured by a clock.

These writers—John Climacus, John of the Cross, John Wesley, and Teresa of Avila—had one thing in common: a clear goal that shaped their Christian lives. Climacus worked his way up a well-defined "ladder," John of the Cross and Teresa of Avila both sought mature contemplative experiences, and Wesley focused on experiential growth that resulted in improved character and Christian service. Each goal was different, but each individual could taste, see, and smell the goal. In this they are like modern athletes who are driven to complete another workout as they dream of one day winning a gold medal. They can't afford to lose sight of the prize.

Notice that all these goals can be obtained and are sought within our earthly bodies, prior to our being taken up to heaven. In the opinion of the classics, heaven's final goal needn't preclude having earthly goals. In fact, we are clearly acting somewhat without precedent when we imply that heaven is our only goal.

Where does this leave us today? Suggesting sanctification (holiness) as a goal is helpful only insofar as people understand what sanctification is and why it is necessary. Many Christians I have talked with have only the most general notion of what true sanctification entails. This often creates soft Christians who are unwilling to face the pain that comes with growth. And who can blame them? We know we don't have to fast to be saved, so why endure the hunger pangs? Why struggle in earthly prayer when it will come so easily in heaven? We may even be tempted to think (and this gets truly perilous) that since we already have salvation and we know we'll be forgiven, why not taste the sweets of a minor sin—just a taste, not a meal—and then quickly repent before we die?

On the other hand, many Christians want to grow, and their thirst for God increases as time goes by. We do not serve them by failing to answer when they ask, "Can I measure my advancement?" One of the primary needs today is a clear goal that Christians can look to as they seek to grow, a goal that will encourage people to think past salvation to a deeper, more meaningful walk with God. Some people who are touching the goal should be able to describe it, recount what they did to get there, and explain how others can follow along.

I am not convinced that all Christians should share the same goal. The activist and the intellectual will naturally choose different goals, and the contemplative will choose yet a third, but every Christian will benefit by having some goal.

Before I go on to suggest one of my own, think about what *your* goal might look like. Have you ever had one? Are you reaching for one now? What do you believe God would like you to become?

4

Hell Breaking Apart
at His Feet

As I sought to develop a goal, I wanted to particularly avoid falling into the exclusive "just God and me" mentality. We have seen that authentic spirituality leads us to seek the good of others. Unfortunately, we often ask, how can *I* become holy? How can *I* grow? How can *I* reach an advanced spiritual state? These questions may reveal that we are simply sugarcoating an unhealthy selfish preoccupation. Spiritual advancement is a good aim, but on its own it seems radically unlike the primary focus of Jesus, who told the story of the good Samaritan and said we should love our neighbors and make disciples of all nations.

This, of course, opens the door to a centuries-old argument about the way of action versus the way of contemplation. For hundreds of years, monks argued which was superior—to be devoted to prayer or to be involved in active work outside the monastery. Not surprisingly, most monks believed the superior life was a quiet life devoted to seclusion and contemplation. Thus grew the concept of forsaking the world to go into the desert or establish a monastery.

If we take Jesus as our model, we see that we don't have to choose one or the other. Jesus was active, though not prematurely so. He waited until He was 30 to begin His public ministry. And when He became active, He never lost His spiritual center. He regularly retreated into solitude and prayer.

Jesus's life, then, provided the first clue for my goal—contemplation (prayer, meditation, time alone with God) balanced with public ministry (teaching, healing, ministering to the poor). The two are not set against each other but joined together in a cooperative effort.

Christ's teaching provided the second clue. Jesus insisted that the love of God includes loving and serving others. When Jesus was asked about the greatest commandment, He answered by giving *two* commandments— loving God *and our neighbor* (Matthew 22:36-40)—as if to say the Christian life is not entirely or exclusively a one-on-one relationship with the Father.

When Jesus wanted Peter to renew his love for Him, He required two statements—a profession of love for Jesus and a willingness to tend Jesus's sheep (John 21:16).

Therefore, the only goal I could adopt had to direct me to serve others after it led me to focus on God. I would have to take into account Christ's pattern of prayer but also include His ministry that followed prayer. The Gospel of Mark pointed me to such a goal.

Hell Crashing Down

What must it have been like to actually watch Jesus in action? Imagine living in the first century and being trapped in illnesses, spiritual prisons, and deprivations. In the midst of these hopeless conditions, people witnessed a liberated man who did not seem to be subject to any of those prisons—One who even carried the keys to release others from them.

People were in awe when they saw Jesus move, but not because of a ring of light around His head or a spotlessly clean white robe. Rather, His presence and His power gave them hope that perhaps a new day and new existence lay ahead. Three elements marked Christ's ministry—He taught, He drove out demons, and He released the oppressed (or healed the sick)—and the first chapter of Mark describes all three.

Mark wrote that as Jesus began to preach, the people were amazed, struck with panic, or overwhelmed with astonishment, depending on how you choose to translate the Greek (verse 22).[1] All options reveal that Jesus's teaching had a power and authority that was previously unknown.

Jesus's teaching did more than stir up the crowds, however. It also stirred up the demons. After verse 22 describes Christ's teaching, verses 23-24 mention that a possessed man cried out and was then exorcised. Jesus didn't *schedule* an exorcism. The confrontation unfolded as Christ performed His ministry.

As soon as Jesus left the site of the teaching and exorcism, He went to Peter's home and healed Peter's mother-in-law. Again, this wasn't part of a carefully planned schedule. Jesus didn't have to script His day. His ministry was the natural outpouring of a tremendous individual step-by-step walk with the Father. He chased out ignorance, defeated the demonic, and released the ill and oppressed.

In other words, as Jesus walked, hell broke apart at His feet.

Jesus and hell could not occupy the same spot, so wherever Jesus went, hell was dismantled. Together, Jesus's life and teaching provide us with a clear goal—to walk with God in a way that makes hell break apart at our feet and allows the kingdom of God to appear.

Our calling is to develop a rich life of devotion, study, and prayer, manifesting itself in a spiritual strength and depth that results in active and often spontaneous ministry.

Someone once sent me a cartoon drawing that described a godly woman as someone of whom the devil says in a panic, "Oh, no! She's awake!" It pictures someone who is intimately in love with God as well as passionately determined to serve God. Hell gives way wherever she goes—the hell of ignorance, the hell of pride, the hell of gossip, the hell of greed, the hell of prejudice, and so on—because of God's presence within her.

This goal weds the contemplative life (which makes room for such a presence) and the necessary active life (which expresses such a presence). It requires going deep to reach wide, stressing the need to build a solid relationship with God so He can use us to touch others.

Devotionally Prepared for Service

During seminary I worked part-time at a public utility to pay some of my bills. One night as I was praying, the Lord kept bringing a specific coworker to mind. The next morning, I was making some copies in the copy room when this same coworker walked in. I asked her how she was doing. She responded with a quick "fine," but I felt impressed to ask a more direct question, so I mentioned her husband. Immediately, the woman broke into tears.

She and her husband were both Christians but were going through a very difficult time in their marriage. She didn't know if they would make it, and she just wanted her husband to make up his mind. Yes or no—was he going to stay?

It was early in the day, before many people had arrived, so we had about 15 minutes to talk. I knew this woman needed far more than I could give her, but I also knew God had called me the night before to function as a stop-gap measure. We talked and prayed, and the woman left—not completely healed, of course, but having been able to release her frustration and gain a new perspective. The conversation didn't change her life, but it did change her day, and one day matters to God just as one person matters to Him.

Another time I felt God calling me to write to the editor of a Christian publication and encourage her. I did so and then forgot about the letter until I received a reply. The editor told me she had been recently widowed. She and her husband had run the publication together for several years, but the issue I wrote about was the first one she had done by herself since her husband had died. After she had sent it out, she was plagued with doubts and confusion: Could she go on without her husband? Should she keep writing or let the publication die with her spouse?

As she read my letter, she knew God had heard her cries, and though she cried again, the tears were expressions of joy and relief, not sorrow and pain.

Satan is everywhere, discouraging and accusing Christians, especially after they step out into ministry. God wants to encourage and build up the body, and He'll often use us to do it—if we're available.

I've had other experiences of simply talking with friends or acquaintances when problems came to mind. Sometimes these problems are hidden attitudes or sins, slowly eating away at a person's spiritual life or marriage. Someone may be believing a lie or living a lie, and the presence of God exposes it.

We needn't be overly concerned with the miraculous. If it happens, it happens. More important is the ability to meet people one-on-one where they are and cooperate as God leads them out of their own private hell. I love the way Frank Buchman, the early twentieth-century founder and leader of a group called Moral Re-Armament (also known as the Oxford Group) put it: "Are people around you being changed?" If not, he questioned the person's spiritual passion. He believed a person pursuing God, growing in God, and living in the power of the Spirit will see a supernatural influence of God's power working through her or him. Obviously, we're not talking about everyone building a national ministry, and we're certainly not referring to pastoring a megachurch or starting a television program.

Rather, we can ask ourselves whether God is using us in the course of our daily lives to minister to family members and other individuals.

When our goals reach beyond making it into heaven and we focus instead on ministering and making an impact every day here on earth, maturity matters. I can be immature and reach heaven. I'm not sure, however, that I can remain immature and see hell break apart at my feet. Perhaps occasionally, but not consistently, and not often. If I am steeped in habitual sin, if I remain a spiritual adolescent, I cannot threaten hell, not while kissing its feet or lusting after its trinkets.

The goal I adopted—seeing hell break apart at my feet as a natural consequence of building and nurturing a life of devoted passion for God—encourages me to grow not only for my own sake but especially for the sake of others. It urges me to walk more closely with God so I can be His coworker and carry on the work of Christ as I commune with Him. Keeping first things first, instead of defining my life by how much ministry goes *out*, I want to focus on how much of Christ's presence comes *in*, confident that His presence cannot remain hidden.

We can't fake this kind of presence and maturity. We can't impress Satan with a mask. In fact, we are liable to be run over if we pretend.[2]

If we don't experience the dissolution of hell in our own lives, we would do well to ask ourselves why. Are we flirting with hell and thus unable to confront it? Have we refused to deal with our own needs, perhaps denying they exist, and therefore blinded ourselves to the needs and hurts of others? Or have we just become lazy, content to coast into heaven rather than run the race as faithful servants?

I found that I wasn't alone. Other Christians had adopted my goal too. They used slightly different terms, but the substance was the same. H.A. Walters wrote in the early twentieth century about changing others, and his words confirmed the direction of my goal.

> We of Christ's army need to remember our great task of the conservation of personality for the highest ends, as we seek to prevent the fearful human wastage taking place all about us through the ravages of sin. This task is not just the comparatively simple one of passing on a word of testimony that "Jesus saves." We are the human engineers by whom what is wrong with these intricate spiritual machines around us should be corrected.[3]

Walters argued that the terms *Christian* and *life-changer* ought to be interchangeable. The reason they are not, he said, includes spiritual laziness, cowardice, or sin that has paralyzed our energies. All of the blocks "point back to the lack of vital experience of the living Christ, out of which must flow the zeal, courage, tact, and consistent Christian living which make personal work possible and fruitful."[4]

Devotion, leading to spontaneous service—that's something I can understand, measure, and strive for.

Setting Your Own Goals

The goal I have adopted for my own life may not fit for you right now, or perhaps you believe you need something smaller or more concrete. That's fine. I have smaller goals that lead to my larger goal. At one point my goal focused on prayer; at another, I was determined to become wiser; and later, I was intent on displaying more of Christ's gentleness.

In case you want to explore this idea further, I'll mention some of the steps that helped me establish clear spiritual goals.

Review the Gospels. Spend some time rereading the Gospels and let Jesus's life inspire you. Does His courage confront your fear? Does His compassion for sinners call your accusing spirit into question? If you answered yes to either question, you immediately have a possible goal— to become courageous or compassionate like Christ.

Familiarize yourself with historical goals. Research the goals of Climacus, John of the Cross, John Wesley, Teresa of Avila, or others. Get a feel for what these authors were aiming at. As your reading becomes broader you'll be able to formulate goals that are less culturally conditioned and more in line with what God really wants to do in your life. You'll also be able to confirm your goals. H.A. Walters's writings refined my thoughts and helped to shape my conclusions.

Prayerfully review your goal. Spend some time in prayer and talk over your goal with God. Have you chosen one He's given you? Is this what God wants to do at this time in your life? Let Him redirect or affirm your goal.

Tell some significant others. Find a small group of people to whom you can explain your goal. Ask them to pray for you and seek their counsel about how you can let the Spirit amend your life. Be open to their correction. You may think you need to step out in a particular area of ministry, and they may say you need to reorder a few things in your own life first. Sin is powerfully deceptive, so we should formulate our goals in community, not in isolation.

Get more input. Use a Bible concordance to look up relevant verses once your goal begins to take shape. If you know of a good book that addresses your goal, buy it and *read it twice*. Spend some time on this one area rather than trying to improve everything at once.

Remember where you're going. The important thing is to have a sense of how you need to grow. Figure out some way to measure your progress (spiritual journals can be very helpful in this regard). If you set a goal and then forget it, you're no better off than those who never set one.

5

Training the Heart, Body, and Soul

When I was growing up, I was an avid tennis player, practically living at the local tennis club during the summer. One of the popular books at that time was called *Inner Tennis*. I don't remember much about the book except that it stressed imagining the successful completion of what you were about to do—serving that ace, hitting that crosscourt backhand passing shot, confounding your opponent at the net…

The only problem was, thinking all day couldn't make my backhand behave if I ignored drilling with the ball machine. You can meditate on tennis all day long, but who is going to improve more—the one who hits backhands for several hours or the one who sits and thinks?

It's a tempting notion, though—that if I could just think myself rich, athletic, or holy, I would be. (Some very successful books still teach precisely this.) Predictably, many versions of inner spirituality have come awfully close to imitating the message of *Inner Tennis* because the thought is so inviting. *Think and be, think and be, think and be…*

This contains an element of truth (the mind is a very powerful tool for good or evil), but it ignores the fact that in addition to sinful souls and minds, we also have bodies that are often unwilling. Our minds are very powerful elements of our persons, but they're not the only elements. If we don't address our bodies and our hearts, holiness will feel like a cheap, ill-fitting pair of shoes that pinch our feet when we walk. We can get lost in reverie all we want, but every time we take a step, our toes will scream their defiance.

The spiritual classics spend a good deal of time talking about *training* in the spiritual life. Setting challenging goals (the work of our minds) is not enough—we have to be willing to pay the price to make them come true.

Purposeful Spirituality

We might ask ourselves, "Why must I labor? Why is training even necessary?" The answer is that we live as fallen people in a fallen world. We don't realize how sick we are. Blaise Pascal opens our eyes to the depths of our depravity:

> The figure used in the Gospel for the state of the soul that is sick is that of sick bodies. But, because one body cannot be sick enough to express it properly, there had to be more than one. Thus we find the deaf man, the dumb man, the blind man, the paralytic, dead Lazarus, the man possessed of a devil. All these put together are in the sick soul.[1]

If we could witness the incarnate Jesus for just one day and then compare ourselves to *Him* instead of someone else, we would see how full of sin we really are. We would notice more of our attitudinal sins, such as pride, selfishness, and a sense of entitlement. We would be more aware of missed opportunities to love. In Jesus, we'd see a man fully alive to God, and that would help us see how little of God we actually express.

This kind of deep character transformation—in which Jesus Himself is the standard—is anything but quick and easy. It is a joyous pursuit, but it is often painful and agonizingly slow. Overcoming years of slothfulness, selfish ambition, greed, pride, and other attitudes and sins requires a life of training. If we let down our guard for just a second, sin is right there to claim us.[2] John Climacus warned, "We cannot afford to slip into carelessness even for an instant at any time up to the moment of death."[3]

The Christian classics teach us that spiritual growth doesn't happen by accident. It is a result of an intentional pursuit, a cooperation with God. He is the active agent, moving us forward in spite of our weaknesses and failures, but we must cooperate.

Two spiritual writers in particular saw the need for focused training in the spiritual life. Thomas à Kempis's classic work, *The Imitation of Christ*, emphasizes a purposeful Christianity that strives for continued growth.

He wrote, "Who hath a greater combat than he that laboreth to overcome himself? This ought to be our endeavor, to conquer ourselves, and daily to wax stronger and to make a further growth in holiness."[4]

According to à Kempis, there is little progress without purpose. "According to our purpose shall be the success of our spiritual progress; and much diligence is necessary to him that will show progress. And if he that firmly purposeth often faileth, what shall he do that seldom purposeth anything, or with little resolution?"[5]

In previous chapters we discussed the importance of goals; in this chapter we see that we can't achieve those goals without a strong commitment. If we look at our lives and can't see any measurable spiritual growth over the past several years, we might ask ourselves, "Have I applied myself to growth? Have I cooperated with God's sanctifying work in my life? Or have I relied on spiritual osmosis—hanging around spiritual people in hopes some of it will rub off?"

Please don't fall into the trap of picturing a goal and then assuming the goal is achieved. Pascal warned, "Men often take their imagination for their heart, and often believe they are converted as soon as they start thinking of becoming converted."[6] One of Satan's favorite traps is to let us acknowledge God's conviction and then mistakenly assume that just because we are convicted, we are changed.

A number of years ago a wise campus pastor, Brady Bobbink, challenged me on this issue. We were talking over one of my failures, and I casually mentioned that I saw my fault and the same situation wouldn't happen again.

"How do you know?" Brady asked me. "What are you going to do to ensure it won't?"

I learned from that encounter that sin's power needs more than an "I'm sorry" to be defeated. It often needs a plan.

I know this sounds awful. It sounds like a lot of work, but growth takes work. Salvation is free, but maturity comes with a price.

Awash in Superficiality

Thomas à Kempis's book inspired William Law to take the notion of purposeful spirituality one step further when he wrote *A Serious Call to a Devout and Holy Life* (with emphasis on the word *Serious!*). Law wrote, "Many will fail of their salvation, not because they took no pains or care about it, but because they did not take pains and care enough; they only sought, but did not strive to enter in."[7]

Is there a better description of so much of today's church? Do we not make occasional efforts instead of consistently striving to enter in? This is particularly so when people say striving is the problem, not the solution!

These would be the Christians who set goals and give them a good try—for a month or so. They quickly grow tired, however, and dismiss the goals as good ideas in principle but not really realistic. If we set goals but are unwilling to train toward them, we are worse off than we were when we ignored goals altogether, for we have simply added an element of insincerity to our lives.

William Law lived and wrote in a generation of superficiality. He saw what laissez-faire spirituality was doing to his countrymen. In eighteenth-century England (the era of the Enlightenment), faith was questioned, and compromised lifestyles were the norm. The pastorate was a profession for gentlemen and required nothing but a proper education. Unusual aspirations to devotion or holiness were considered un-English and fanatical, even for clergymen. Christianity was reduced to something that respectable people believed in.[8]

To this generation, William Law wrote his non-compromising treatise, *A Serious Call to a Devout and Holy Life*. Religion, William Law argued, is not the spice of the proper English life; it is the *essence* of a Christian's existence. Respectability and reformed manners are not enough. Our faith in Christ should be our primary concern, and that means we must invest the time and energy necessary to become better Christians.

> It is amazing to see how eagerly men employ their parts, their [intelligence], time, study, application, and exercise, how all helps are called to their assistance when anything is intended and desired in worldly matters, and how dull, negligent, and unimproved they are, how little they use their parts, [intelligence], and abilities to raise and increase their devotion![9]

We know we can't succeed in school, business, marriage, parenting, sports, or most other endeavors without purposefully applying ourselves to moving forward, yet many of us fail to realize the same is true of spiritual growth. Law went on to say, "The spirit of devotion [is] like any other sense or understanding that is only to be improved by study, care, application, and the use of such means and helps as are necessary to make a man proficient in any art or science."[10]

Pastor, have you spent more time trying to build your soul than you have trying to increase your church's membership? Parent, have you spent more time pursuing maturity in the faith than trying to improve your children's manners and education? Businessperson, have you applied the same energy and earnest effort to your character that you have to the success of your enterprise?

Law urges his readers, "You are to nourish your spirits with pious readings and holy meditations, with watchings, fastings, and prayers, that you may taste and relish and desire that eternal state which is to begin when this life ends."[11]

This type of spirituality requires more than five minutes of thought every day. It requires more than a one-hour tune up on Sunday morning or Saturday evening. Both Law and à Kempis teach us that our bodies and souls need *training* and our spirits need *nourishment*. Law gave his readers this warning:

> Unless holy fears animate our endeavors and keep our consciences strict and tender about every part of our duty, constantly examining how we live and how fit we are to die, we shall in all probability fall into a state of negligence and sit down in such a course of life as will never carry us to the rewards of Heaven.[12]

Foundational to spiritual training are the spiritual disciplines, and Law mentions "fastings and prayers" as two such elements. So much very good material has been written concerning the traditional spiritual disciplines that we don't need to repeat their teaching here. Other aspects of Christian training, however, have been lost or de-emphasized. Let's look at five of the forgotten or neglected methods of spiritual training:

pious readings

imitation of living examples

cultivation of virtues

early rising

a life of reflection

This is not an exhaustive list by any means. As I stated before, the spiritual disciplines are essential helps, as is the remembrance of death and the practice of holiness, which we'll address in later chapters. But these five practices will help root in our minds the necessity to train ourselves on the ancient journey toward godliness and maturity.

6

Pious Readings

I f we want to start a successful business, we should talk to successful business people. If we want advice on raising our kids, we should
find parents whose families we admire. The best way to improve in
golf, knitting, or fishing is to find experienced people who can share their
expertise. In the same way, if we want to grow in the Christian faith, who
better to turn to than those whose writings are so powerfully true that
their books continue to be studied and treasured centuries after they were
first written?

Law chastised his fellow Englishmen for neglecting the Christian classics that could train them in matters of the soul.

> Why then must the Bible lie alone in your study? Is not the
> spirit of the Saints, the piety of the holy followers of Jesus
> Christ, as good and necessary a means of entering into the
> spirit and taste of the gospel as the reading of the ancients is
> of entering into the spirit of antiquity?
>
> Is the spirit of poetry only to be got by much reading of poets
> and orators? And is not the spirit of devotion to be got in the
> same way, by frequent reading the holy thoughts and pious
> strains of devout men?...Is it not...reasonable for him who
> desires to improve in the divine life, that is, in the heavenly
> things, to search after every strain of devotion that may move,
> kindle, and inflame the holy ardor of his soul?[1]

Several engineers who met weekly for a barbecue entered into a friendly rivalry over who could be the fastest at lighting the coals and getting them white hot and ready for cooking. After several creative attempts, one engineer blew away the competition by having the coals ready in about three seconds. How? With a ten-foot pole, an ignition device, and carefully applied liquid oxygen!

The classics are like liquid oxygen to my soul. I don't agree theologically with everything that John of the Cross, John Climacus, or other saints have written. But their passion warms my cold heart. Their devotion fans into flame the sometimes smoldering embers of my faith.

Ralph Venning, a renowned Puritan preacher from the seventeenth century, actually urged his church members to read John Goodwin's *A Being Filled* even though Goodwin was a thoroughgoing Arminian (and thus at odds with Venning's Calvinism).

> Though I confess myself not to be of the same mind and opinion with the learned author in some other controverted points, yet I cannot but give my testimony concerning this piece, that I find an excellent spirit moving on the face, and acting in the heart of it, to promote the glory of God, the power of godliness, and consequently the good of men, especially of Christian men.[2]

Devotional reading differs from doctrinal reading in that we're looking not for answers to controversial theological questions but rather for insight into the ways of God with women and men. That's why Law urges us to find the classic writers who can "inflame the holy ardor" of our souls. Have you found such spiritual friends? My prayer is that this book will introduce you to many.

The practice of pious reading served William Law well. He was able to rise above the limitations of his outwardly respectable but inwardly decadent culture. He developed a taste for true and sincere faith by feeding at the table of Thomas à Kempis and others who sought the same God in a different century, and that's what is so helpful about reading the classics. It removes our generational blinders. Law could critique his fellow countrymen and arm himself against the prejudices of his day by reading outside his generation.

The practice of pious reading does even more than inflaming us with John of the Cross's passion for God, John Climacus's willingness to discipline himself for God, William Law's commitment to progress daily in God, Madame Guyon's submission to God, and Teresa of Avila's contemplative devotion for God. It also chips away at our personal prejudices. I rarely hear a contemporary sermon about pride that matches the seriousness we find in the classics. Our evangelical culture seems preoccupied with denouncing sexual sin and materialism, but Christian writers from centuries past usually talked about pride and the need to love others.

Might this be a reason why Christians today are so often self-righteous and proud? In some of our statements and preaching, we do seem to be full of ourselves. We have an answer, book, or sermon for every problem imaginable, and in our zeal to share the good news, we forget that repentance is the living room of the Christian life, not just the doorway. (We'll talk more about the classic view of humility and pride in a later chapter. This is simply an example of how I have been particularly challenged by rediscovering the wisdom of saints.)

A number of years ago, Dr. James Houston, a professor of spirituality at Regent College, encouraged us seminarians to read Teresa of Avila. Why? Because she was as different from most of us as anyone could possibly be. She was from another country, another century, and another tradition. She was female, and most of us were male. She wrote *The Interior Castle* near the end of her life, and most of us were at the beginning of ours. She could provide answers to questions we didn't even know to ask.

I found Teresa's commitment to prayerful intimacy with God very challenging. Prayer was often a battle cry for me—"Here I go, Lord; please come with me!"—until Teresa urged me to settle down and seek an intimacy far removed from works. Teresa naturally saw herself as part of the bride of Christ, but how could I, a male, have the same intimacy in a different way?

Teresa couldn't fully answer this question for me, though she pointed me in the right direction. I found some additional assistance in the works of Andrew Murray, a rather modern writer in comparison. Soon my prayer was not simply "Thy kingdom come—today!" but also "My precious Lord, I want to be often and long alone with You."

I realized how much I had changed when an Episcopalian priest asked me, "When do you feel like you can be yourself?"

"In the woods, when I'm alone with my Lord," I said. That wouldn't have been true earlier in my life.

Every Christian needs other Christians to point out new possibilities of faith and growth. None of us are self-sufficient spiritual machines who completely understand the Christian life. When I read the classics, I'm challenged by the fire and holy passion burning in the souls of men and women who ached to know God as intimately as He can be known.

And even though we need a spiritual diet that goes beyond our generation, pious readings can include modern writers. When we find someone writing today who speaks to our souls in a powerful way, we should eagerly but wisely consider the author's truth. Modern books are untested, but they can still be very valuable. Thomas à Kempis himself was once new.

Practicing a Lost Art

Reading pious works as part of our spiritual training is practically a lost art, so let's briefly consider some basic practices.

Read with your heart. The first thing to remember is that devotional reading is not solely an intellectual exercise. Its aim is the active transformation of the heart. James Houston has said that most damnation comes not through ignorance, but in keeping things in our heads instead of our hearts.

We read with our hearts by allowing God to challenge our attitudes, our reactions, and our emotions. Your mind may be tempted to dismiss a convicting truth because it is paired with a theological weakness or because the author is using an outdated method of biblical application. Don't fall into this trap. Devotional reading is meant to challenge the inner soul. I read systematic theology to find out how to think correctly, but I read the classics to measure the temperature of my heart.

We read with the heart by reading slowly, prayerfully considering each phrase and continually listening to God's Spirit. Perhaps He will emphasize a point or remind us of a Bible verse that underscores the point's importance. This may be the way He applies the truth we're reading to our souls.

Read repetitively. The second thing to remember is that reading a good book two or three times is usually more profitable than reading five mediocre books. I realize that all of us have different learning styles, but very few of us can "own" a book—in the sense that its truth becomes part of us—after one quick reading. We need to read and reread devotional books slowly so we can consider and ponder ideas and thoughts before moving on.

I've read Climacus's work at least five times, and most of the classics I'm quoting here I've read at least two or three times. I take that long to get at their heart. A worthy classic never fails to challenge me anew, regardless of how many times I've read it.

Note the writers' perspectives. The third thing to remember is that when we read the classics, we need to be aware of the writers' limited perspectives. William Law's later book, *The Spirit of Love*, has a considerably different emphasis from his *Serious Call.* The norm is that a writer will sound legalistic in the early years and then mature in the later years into a more grace-filled approach that stresses intimacy with God more than zealous works. Knowing where a writer is on his or her journey will help you maintain a biblical balance.

Find the kernel of truth. The fourth thing to remember is that God can play beautiful music through dented instruments. When we encounter spiritual writings, our tendency may be to completely reject a writer's particular emphasis rather than find the truth that he or she presents. We could easily read John Climacus's account of the monastic "prison" and painful acts of penance in a virtual torture chamber, become horrified by the self-abuse that was perpetrated in the name of Christianity, and dismiss his writings out of hand. Or we can be challenged by seeing what lengths other Christians have gone to in order to be rid of sin. We may disagree entirely with their methods, but we can learn a great deal from their motivation.

I have been occasionally criticized for quoting some writers (particularly the mystics and contemplatives) with whom others have theological differences. Apparently, unless a historical writers are in 100 percent compliance with contemporary evangelical thought, they are too dangerous to read or quote. This is absurd, unless we want to read only to confirm what we already believe and know.

Augustine wrote that all truth is God's truth, not meaning that every system is true, of course, but that every truth comes from God's system. Only Scripture has absolute authority. The spiritual classics don't, but they do contain much truth that we can filter and benefit from. Some people read books to find out what's wrong with them; I read books to find out what's right.

Another aspect of this is fascinating to me. When I read Johannes Tauler's sermons, I'm reading homilies that Martin Luther himself read, studied, and wrote marginal notes on (calling them "pure theology"). Just about everybody, of course, read and commented on Augustine. When I read Madame Guyon, I'm reading a book that John Wesley and Count Zinzendorf both found immensely fruitful. When I read *Spiritual Combat* by Lorenzo Scupoli, I'm reading a book that Francis de Sales carried with him daily for 18 years. François Fénelon mentions *The Imitation of Christ* by Thomas à Kempis as well as Francis de Sales by name. This means Scupoli taught de Sales, who taught Fénelon, who now teaches us. This kind of thing amazes me, connects me to the history of God's people, and creates an even greater understanding for the later classics.

You'll find an annotated reading list at the back of this book. My prayer is that you'll use it to make pious readings a staple of your spiritual training.

Imitation of Living Examples

The apostle Paul endorsed the idea of human examples as part of our spiritual training when he wrote, "Imitate me, just as I also imitate Christ."[1] Thomas à Kempis honored Paul's truth when he wrote, "Gather some profit to thy soul wheresoever thou art; so as if thou seest or hearest of any good examples, stir up thyself to the imitation thereof."[2]

No one follows Christ's example absolutely perfectly, but many human lives have elements of inspiration. You've probably noticed already that I often mention spiritual encounters from which I've learned something. I also regularly feed my soul from written biographies. This book, in fact, is dedicated to Dr. Klaus Bockmuehl, whose example moved me deeply before he died.

While working on *Pure Pleasure*, I traveled up to Regent College in Vancouver, BC, to meet with Dr. J.I. Packer, a seminary mentor of mine more than two decades prior. Dr. Packer, now 82, looked a little frailer, but he was still clearly focused on seeking first the kingdom of God.

On our way back to my car (I gave him a ride home), Dr. Packer confided that he was a little uncomfortable with the title *emeritus*. "I still feel like I have something left to say," he told me, "and plenty of work to do."

We talked more on the ride to his house. I assured him I'd send him a copy of my manuscript so he could approve his quotes, but Dr. Packer insisted that wasn't necessary. "If anything was helpful, put it in your own words."

He paused. "I just want you to write a *good* book."

The earnestness and sincerity of his plea floored me. Dr. Packer wasn't aware of a recent, comprehensive book dealing with spirituality and pleasure, and he thought I was onto something. His true desire was for his student to produce one. It clearly *mattered* to him.

Dr. Packer is now in his ninth decade. Who could fault him if he decided to take it easy, live off his royalties and reputation, and sleep his way to death's door? But Dr. Packer cares about the church, he's still an active warrior for God's kingdom, he wants to see God's rule advance on this earth, and he is pouring himself out as long as God gives him breath.

As I drove home, I was near tears. "Lord," I prayed, "I want to finish like that."

I remember walking around Second Baptist Church in Houston, Texas, for the first time, guided by Dr. Ed Young, who at the time was 71 years young (pun fully intended) and leading a church with a membership of more than 50,000. He displayed an infectious zeal for God's work and was so enthusiastic about continuing to reach his community for Christ, so committed to giving families and children the opportunity to encounter and grow in Christ, that once again I was moved to tears. Having seen so many men fail later in life, I was truly inspired to see a man growing increasingly zealous, increasingly dedicated to the work of the gospel.

Some time later, Second Baptist approached me about becoming a writer in residence, and one of the greatest draws for me was the chance to sit at Dr. Young's feet. I may be nearing 50, but I'll never outgrow my need to be inspired by others and learn from them.

Of course, I want to become someone from whom others can learn as well; that's part of my calling as a Christian maturing in the faith. But the process of maturation includes seeking out and learning from good, positive examples. When I see people who seem to have an unusual presence of Christ in their lives, I ask them questions. I want to know how they've become what they've become.

That's why I use Twitter and Facebook to find out what certain leaders are thinking and doing. (My links to Twitter and Facebook are included on my website, www.garythomas.com.) We can also read biographies of classical writers and feel as if we're sitting at their feet though they may have been dead for centuries.

My ultimate aim is to know God. But seeing how other men and women serve Him opens up new understandings about knowing Him today. The imitation of living examples by itself cannot provide the full spiritual training we need, but it's an extremely beneficial aspect.

Cultivation of Virtues

Just as body builders use weights to build a certain physique, so God's followers throughout the ages have used the virtues of Christ to build a certain character. The Bible emphasizes that character growth does not happen by accident.

> Make every effort to add to your faith goodness; and to goodness, knowledge; and to knowledge, self-control; and to self-control, perseverance, and to perseverance, godliness, and to godliness, brotherly kindness; and to brotherly kindness, love. For if you possess these qualities *in increasing measure*, they will keep you from being ineffective and unproductive in your knowledge of our Lord Jesus Christ (2 Peter 1:5-8).

Notice the admonition to possess these things "in increasing measure." We are thankful that our salvation is securely fixed in the finished work of Jesus Christ, but this assurance can also make us abominably complacent, and when we grow complacent we become, as Peter warns, "ineffective and unproductive."

Lorenzo Scupoli, a sixteenth-century priest of the Theatine order, wrote a book entitled *Spiritual Combat*. It was deemed so insightful that the Orthodox church soon adopted it as well. In it, Scupoli urges believers, "Imitate with all your might the virtues of the Savior."[1] The thinking went like this. We can identify certain traits in Jesus's life and character: courage, gentleness, kindness, self-control, and so on. With God's grace and empowering Holy Spirit, we can practice these traits and become more like Christ. One of the best ways to become gentler with others, for instance, is to consciously practice gentleness. One of the ways to become more humble is to conscientiously focus on putting others first in our actions. Scupoli puts it this way:

> This crucified Lord, beloved, is the book that I put into your hands, and by reading it, you may learn the true form of every virtue. It is the Book of Life, which not only by means of words enlightens the understanding, but also by its living example enkindles the will. The world is full of books, and yet, were they all put together, they could not teach so perfectly how to gain all virtues, as does the contemplation of a crucified God.[2]

I have seen far too many Christians use Jesus's admonition that we must be changed on the inside as license to neglect outer character transformation. Numerous Scriptures urge us to address outward behavior as well. And modern cognitive (brain) science has demonstrated that when we change our actions, we slowly change the way we think, behave, and even feel. Scupoli and other devotional writers understood this intuitively hundreds of years before science began researching neurochemicals.

> As habits of sin are produced by many and repeated acts of the higher will, yielding itself to the sensual appetite, so, on the other hand, habits of the virtues of the Gospel are acquired by the performance of frequent and repeated acts of conformity to the divine will, as it calls us to the practice of different virtues from time to time.[3]

Character Growth

All of this means that if we attend to prayer, Bible study, and evangelism but neglect our character growth, we fall far short of the biblical and classical admonitions toward maturity. Teresa of Avila gave her sisters this encouragement:

> It is necessary that your foundation consist of more than prayer and contemplation. If you do not strive for the virtues and practice them, you will always be small in the faith.

And, please God, it will be only a matter of not growing, for you already know that whoever does not increase decreases. I hold that love, where present, cannot possibly be content with remaining always the same.[4]

Many parents try to train their children to become patient, kind, honest, hardworking, and so on because they understand that virtues don't come by accident. They require a conscious effort on our part, even as adults. Why would we think that as soon as we are old enough to bear children, we've somehow arrived and can stop working on our own character?

Spiritual training assumes we can change—that in cooperation with the Spirit's work, the lazy can become more diligent, the selfish can learn to love, and the cruel can learn to be kind. We needn't see ourselves as slaves to the darker sides of our personalities. Progress isn't easy, but it's essential. "At the beginning of our religious life, we cultivate the virtues, and we do so with toil and difficulty."[5]

This is an *active, intentional* pursuit. It takes effort, focus, and much energy. The writers of the Christian classics weren't afraid of this and even ridiculed those who merely read about Christ's example but never put these traits into practice. Scupoli compares such believers to "soldiers, who, in their tents, before battle, are full of heroism, but when the fight really begins, cast away their arms and take to flight." To Scupoli and his contemporaries, everyday life presented battlefields on which character was won or lost. Sadly, fewer and fewer Christians even bother to fight this fight today. Listen to Scupoli's scathing comment about such neglect: "Can anything be sadder and more foolish than to contemplate as in a mirror the virtues of the Lord, to be enamored of them, and to admire them, and then, when an opportunity offers itself of exercising them, entirely to forget and neglect them?"[6]

Not everyone has the same obstacles to overcome in the cultivation of virtues. Some of us may have great discipline but struggle against selfish ambition. Others may be very gentle but avoid conflict at all costs—thus lacking in courage. Some of us have a natural temper while others tend toward greater sensuality. All these problems can be overcome. Just as a natural athlete can be defeated by a less gifted athlete who trains harder and smarter, so more naturally virtuous people can be surpassed by others who apply themselves more seriously to growth. Thomas à Kempis wrote, "All men have not equally much to overcome and mortify. Yet he that is diligent, though he have more passions, shall profit more in virtue, than another that is of a more temperate disposition, if he is less fervent in the pursuit of virtue."[7]

Cultivating virtues is a necessary part of the Christian life. "That's just the way I am" is a confession of sloth, not humility. It's admitting that we are too spiritually lazy to change, too selfishly indifferent to the way our weaknesses and lack of virtue hurt people. Whether we have a bad temper or an overly indulgent lifestyle, we injure others, weaken our witness, and grieve our Lord.

For more on this, see my book *The Glorious Pursuit*, which explores the historical discipline of practicing the virtues as a primary form of spiritual growth and character transformation. For now, let's allow the cultivation of virtue to become a passion in our lives. "Be vigilant, fervent, and careful, so as not to miss the least opportunity of exercising a virtue."[8]

Early Rising

Training in the spiritual life includes (to the despairing cry of many) benefiting from the sacred moments of the early morning. "Awakening the dawn" (Psalm 57:8) has become an important part of my life. Early rising has been a consistent part of Christian spiritual training throughout history. Consider William Law's comment:

> I take it for granted that every Christian that is in health is up early in the morning; for it is much more reasonable to suppose a person up early because he is a Christian than because he is a laborer, or a tradesman, or a servant, or has business that wants him.
>
> We naturally conceive some abhorrence of a man that is in bed when he should be at his labor or in his shop. We can't tell how to think anything fond of him who is such a slave to drowsiness as to neglect his business for it.
>
> Let this therefore teach us to conceive how odious we must appear in the sight of Heaven if we are in bed shut up in sleep and darkness, when we should be praising God, and are such slaves to drowsiness as to neglect our devotions for it.[1]

Training involves more than finding helpful teaching, more than setting realistic goals for steady results, more than listening to others and studying the life of Christ. It also involves *setting the right schedule*. One style of life is generally consistent with those who cultivate spiritual growth, and another style of life is generally consistent with those who wouldn't know a spiritual thought if it bit them.

I'm fully aware that all of us have different body clocks. Some people feel more alive at night than in the morning, and in fact, many earnest Christians have prayed during "night watches" while others slept. Even so, Jesus began an undeniable Christian tradition of meeting God first thing in the morning.

A biblical worldview considers each day a gift and an opportunity. The gift is to be enjoyed; the opportunity is to be used to serve God's kingdom. An early start sets these truths in our minds. Instead of letting the day waste away with a late start, how can we check in with God and go about using this day for His glory? We cannot get around the fact that sleep patterns do create certain mind-sets. Have we *ever* considered how our sleep schedule might affect our spiritual training in general and personal devotion in particular?

The Moral Side of the Morning

Rising early is about more than efficiency; it can have a major impact on our moral choices. A young man in our community got into a bit of trouble and was arrested. When he came out of his short stay in jail, he told my wife, "I know one thing; I'm never going out after one a.m. again."

"Why not?" my wife asked.

"From being in jail, I can tell you, that's when all the trouble starts. Just about everything everybody did happened after midnight."

As a sin-laden man living in a sinful world, I've found I'm much more vulnerable to particular types of sin after nine at night than I am when I arise at five in the morning, except perhaps for such attitudinal sins as the slavish pursuit of money or selfish ambition. I'm much less likely to gorge on a bag of potato chips in front of mindless television early in the day; that's a nighttime temptation. And don't those who drink heavily joke about trying not to start until after a certain time?

Therefore, as my schedule evolved into rising at five or even earlier, my opportunities and inclinations toward certain sins were not half as numerous as they were before. When I served as a college pastor with younger men, I noticed that many of their most troublesome difficulties occurred in the late evening. A disciplined schedule can actually reduce the opportunity to sin and thereby help break sinful habits in our hearts and lives.

Common sense tells us we do best to sleep when temptation is highest and arise when our spiritual faculties are sharpest.

Staying Sharp

Early rising does more than guard us from excessive temptation, however. It also guards us against overindulgence in sleep itself, which can have a slow but debilitating influence on the Christian life, as William Law noted:

> Now this is the case of those who waste their time in sleep; it does not disorder their lives or wound their consciences as notorious acts of intemperance do; but like any other more moderate course of indulgence, it silently and by smaller degrees wears away the spirit of religion and sinks the soul into a state of dullness and sensuality.[2]

This demonstrates what I love about the classics—they keep us sensitive to weaknesses no one in our generation even *talks* about. How many sermons have you ever heard about the danger of overindulging in sleep and succumbing to a "state of dullness and sensuality"? Law gives further warning:

> [This overindulgence] gives a softness and idleness to your soul, and is so contrary to that lively, zealous, watchful, self-denying spirit which was not only the Spirit of Christ and His Apostles, the spirit of all the Saints and martyrs which have ever been amongst men, but must be the spirit of all those who would not sink in the common corruption of the world.[3]

Law wasn't content with Christians who merely stayed out of trouble; he sought a spiritual training that prepared them to be zealous, active agents for God's kingdom. Are our schedules making us dull, forgetful, and passive? Are we sleeping away our zeal and napping away our sensitivity to the needs of the world and the call of God's Spirit on our lives?

Making the Most of Morning

In addition to empowering us to maintain a proper mind-set, fight temptation, and be vigilant, early rising can help us build worshipful hearts. Something about morning calls us to prayer. Seeing the sun appear lifts our spirits to God and calls us to give thanks. If your prayers have become rote recitations of intercession, you're probably praying two or three hours too late. Get up earlier and just try *not* to worship. It's a very difficult thing to do!

You may consider yourself a night owl; certain bodily predispositions are legitimate. If your habit of sleeping in isn't keeping you dull to kingdom service, feeding temptation, and making you insensitive to worship, perhaps this aspect of spiritual training isn't so crucial for you. But if you fight these symptoms on a regular basis, the classic devotional writings would challenge you to consider a change in lifestyle so your schedule serves your holiness instead of fighting it.

A Life of Reflection

S cripture's call to actively pursue training in godliness presupposes some times of reflection to determine how we have progressed or fallen short. Most weight rooms have large mirrors that allow athletes to examine their bodies and notice their progress. Of course, selfish preoccupation can kill a growing spirituality, but sensible reflection is an essential and healthy element of Christianity—a mirror held up to our spiritual progress. If we never take stock of where we are, years can fly by without us gaining any advantage from them.

Thomas à Kempis urged us to view life as a journey that leads to heaven. Each new season is another step in our travels, and we can use it to make sure we're headed in the right direction. "From festival to festival, we should make some good resolution, as though we were then to depart out of this world, and to come to the everlasting feast in heaven."[1]

You can choose New Year's day to do this or perhaps your birthday. Maybe you'd prefer to take stock during the season of Lent. The particular "festival" you choose doesn't matter as much as having some mechanism to honestly review your life. Have you grown in patience? Is last year's most common sin getting stronger or weaker in your life? How is your joy? Are you growing in your ability to love? Is any resentment taking root, any lack of forgiveness?

We are quick to remind God of His promises and ask Him to come through for us, but are we just as sensitive to our own faithfulness? Do we ever assess how we're doing?

The Puritans issued urgent calls to remain vigilant and reflective, particularly about the encroaching power of indwelling sin. Ralph Venning argues, "[True saints] maintain a continual war against the Devil, the world and the flesh because they would not sin. As much as they love peace they live in war. Indeed, they must live in war to preserve their peace, on which sin would make a breach."[2] Johannes Tauler uses the same metaphor:

> We must behave as people do in a besieged city: they watch
> where the attackers are strongest and the defenses weakest. If
> they fail to do this, the city is lost. In the same manner we should
> keep our eyes carefully on the point where the devil most often
> attacks us, where human nature is weakest, where our frailties
> lie, and here we should keep guard most vigilantly.[3]

How many of us have learned to accommodate our sin? If we have stopped fighting it, we can never even consider whether it is becoming stronger or weaker.

Such negligence comes at a high cost. When we forget how sin slowly and sometimes imperceptibly works its way into our attitudes, thoughts, words, relationships, and life habits, it can grow strong under the cover of ignorance and denial. Reflection opens us to God's grace as He reveals a sin when it is still weak and we are more likely to overcome it.

Stumbling Upward

Of course, we don't want to reflect exclusively or even primarily on where we might be falling short; reflecting on the *progress* we are making in every area of our souls is also helpful.

Through the years, Christians have used various means of reflection, including journaling, confession, or even a spiritual program (such as Teresa of Avila's seven dwelling places or John Climacus's 30 steps on the ladder of divine ascent) to track their progress. William Law practiced a time of reflection *every evening*, examining how he had progressed toward his spiritual goals. I have found birthdays to be an ideal time to reflect at length on my life's calling and spiritual growth. As I do this, I have been able to see particular weaknesses—such as an overly sensitive conscience—gradually transformed. That gives me hope that current weaknesses—a propensity toward people pleasing, for example—will also be transformed.

It's exciting to see God tear out a weakness or plant a strength during a moment of exhilarating prayer, but most often, God cultivates virtues in us the same way a plant grows. First a small stalk of green appears, then the separate leaves, and finally the flowers. Reflection reminds us that growth is a *process*, and that keeps us from getting lazy. It also keeps our hope alive when growth seems delayed. We all stumble in many ways (James 3:2), but reflection helps us to "stumble upward," to be more intentional about our imperfect progress as we become more like Jesus.

I also appreciate the urgency reflection provides. Regular reflection keeps the years from slipping by unappreciated; we can taste every one. A reflective person will not pass into eternity without having given this life much thought—what it means, how to live it, and what needs to be done. This too is a gift given to us through the wisdom of the communion of saints.

How can you build regular times of reflection into your own life? Consider daily or near-daily times that won't overburden you, weekly or monthly times that will give you more time to reflect, and perhaps a yearly reflection that can be more extensive and purposeful.

Learning to Live with Grace

Discussing training in the Christian life is potentially hazardous. For those who understand its context, training is a feast from Christians of centuries past. For those who tend toward legalism, it's a dangerous prescription that could be poisonous if taken in the wrong manner. Still, the concept of rigorous training in the spiritual life is so historically established that one can scarcely discuss Christian spirituality without mentioning it, even at the risk of leading some people to become legalists who respond to guilt.

Yet we must not lose touch with the fact that Christian spirituality is a spirituality of grace in which an awakened heart responds to God's mercy by giving all. We bring nothing to God; He gives us everything. God seeks us before we seek Him. Always, we must remember that our faith is rooted in His grace.

A righteous life and rigorous training without a heart full of grace is like an egg without a yolk—a fragile shell that will break under the slightest pressure. Pharisees are not only boring and bothersome but also prone to crack under the strain of impossible expectations.

That is only one side of the truth, however, for though Pharisees are eggs without yolks, those who try to exist solely on mercy without structure or discipline are like eggs without shells—sticky, gooey messes.

Legalism on the one hand and complacency on the other are twin enemies to true Christian spirituality. Paul spoke scathingly of anyone who added a milligram to grace, but he could scarcely mention the word without adding, in essence, "But we don't continue to live the way we used to."[1]

In all our efforts—setting the right schedule, obtaining the right teaching, cultivating the right virtue, and so on—we must never forget the covering of grace. Some of us will try to do too much too soon. Brother Lawrence warned of such a woman: "[She] wants to go faster than grace. One does not become holy all at once."[2] John Climacus cautioned his readers, "The fact is that no one can climb a ladder in a single stride," and "At the beginning of one's life as a monk one cannot suddenly become free of gluttony and vainglory."[3]

William Law, our champion of training in the spiritual life, stressed the importance of laboring with the *right spirit*. His strict writings, he said, were...

> not intended to possess people's minds with a scrupulous anxiety and discontent in the service of God, but to fill them with a just fear of living in sloth and idleness and in the neglect of such virtues as they will want at the day of judgment. It is to excite them to an earnest examination of their lives, to such zeal and care and concern after Christian perfection as they use in any matter that has gained their heart and affections.[4]

Responsibility and grace are the twin pillars that support the foundation of the Christian life. At times, we will be tempted to shirk responsibility. At other times, we may forget about grace. The latter is as much a temptation as the former.

Resting

Francis de Sales reminds us that "it is necessary sometimes to relax our minds, as well as our bodies, by some kind of recreation."[5] When I began running marathons, I trained hard but never truly rested. As a result, I struggled with various injuries. I had to learn from the wisdom of more experienced runners who warned, "You can't go too slowly on your recovery days." Recovery is an essential part of physical and spiritual training.

Thinking of Christians who feel as if they can't rest, who are suspicious of any kind of pleasure, I wrote *Pure Pleasure: Why Do Christians Feel So Bad About Feeling Good?* Never enjoying ourselves is often the road to spiritual breakdown, not maturity. Spiritual training doesn't mean we can't enjoy hobbies, good movies, fun conversation, great music, and good books. In fact, authentic spiritual training will make each one of these recreations *more* enjoyable, not less.

Sometimes we need to rest in God's grace and acceptance—and we can't go too slow in those moments—and sometimes we need to be challenged to step up to a more serious effort at spiritual training. God can open up ministry opportunities, but He can also hide us away from the press of the crowd. Even though we may not see anything happening in quiet seasons, we must remember that God, who is the source of life, can cause us to grow even while we sleep. Rest, spiritual and physical, is part of the growth process. One of the reasons the Ten Commandments call us to keep the Sabbath is so we can rest.

This is a good place to complete this discussion on spiritual training, for the Sabbath commandment contains the balance so necessary to a healthy Christian life. The Sabbath contains two elements: the call to work and the call to rest. "Six days you shall labor and do all your work, but the seventh day...you shall not do any work" (Exodus 20:9-10).

Some of us don't labor during the six days, and we don't rest during the seventh. We live in the gray wasteland of killing time, which is neither productive nor restful. Thus we feel unable to keep one day devoted to rest because we failed to fill the previous six days with work. Let's learn to work hard and rest well. As Law wrote, "We cannot offer to God the service of angels; we cannot obey Him as man in a state of perfection could; but fallen men can do their best, and this is the perfection required of us."[6]

Some of us are too complacent; others of us try to earn our righteousness and thus have little joy or rest in our hearts. As you approach the topic of spiritual training, one way to begin is with an honest assessment of where you feel weakest—is it pious reading, learning from a good example, cultivating virtue, waking up early, living a life of reflection? Maybe you're a complete stranger to the spiritual disciplines, which we haven't even mentioned yet. Or perhaps you need to dial it back a bit and rediscover God's joy and enabling power.

These first 11 chapters have reminded us that spiritual growth doesn't happen by accident and that unbroken passivity is tantamount to disobedience. Training is an active exercise, intentional and purposeful. That's the life both Scripture and the Christian classics lift up as most honoring to God. Let's embrace it today.

PART 2

Sin *and* Temptation

Holiness of the Heart:
Avoiding Sin and Facing Temptation

W hen I was in seminary, I often joined other students for study breaks at a nearby convenience store. One of the walls of the convenience store was full of magazines—some of them pornographic. One moment we were in class, hearing about an exciting development in church history or reveling in a high and holy thought from one of Dr. Packer's lectures on the book of Romans. The next moment we were buying snacks and drinks at the convenience store counter, cringing at the low and perverted baseness of the real world.

I experienced a curious sensation in that store. As a single man going to college, I had never even thought about pornography. I wasn't necessarily victorious over the temptation; it simply wasn't an issue for me. But now, a married man attending seminary, my heart began to flutter as I passed by those magazines. On the face of it, it didn't make sense.

One afternoon the temptation was acute. I was in a tense period in the school year, finances were so tight that I wasn't sure I'd even be able to continue going to school, and that convenience store seemed to be yelling out my name. Unwisely, I didn't address the temptation; I just put it off as an irritant. That did nothing to kill it or lessen it, however, and it stayed with me most of the day. Classes helped to keep my mind occupied, but when they were over and the day's structure was removed, I was amazed by how much the temptation seized me.

What was the turning point for me? I'm not sure—if I could bottle it for future use, I would—but somehow God broke through, and I said a loud and final *no*. I knew that even if that store was the last place on earth where I could get something to drink, I would not go in it, at least not that afternoon.

The temptation was over.

End of story, you might think—but not quite. Driving home, I felt pretty satisfied with myself. I had faced temptation, and I had won. I even began to think of ways I could work my victory into a sermon illustration. And then, as I was driving along, the Lord's voice swiftly cut through my thoughts. I almost had to pull over.

God tore away the veil of my heart and showed me the evil within it. I had avoided one sin only to fall into another—self-righteous pride. As I recounted the experience to a fellow seminarian, I remarked that instead of going from strength to strength (Psalm 84:7), I was living from sin to sin.

This was a frustrating recognition. If I faced a temptation, I could give in and sin, or I could resist, become proud, and still end up sinning. How could I win?

I had to learn that in one sense, I couldn't win. My problem was that I was making myself, my actions, my thoughts, and my attitudes the measurement of my faith. The holiness God desires in us is rooted in Christ's death and resurrection, a holiness that changes our hearts, not just our actions. In the words of Francis de Sales, I had to learn that "obedience must rather be loved than disobedience feared."

I also learned, however, that even when I gain mastery over bodily sins—something that will never be complete this side of heaven—God is still concerned about my internal world, my heart and attitudes. Paul urges us to "purify ourselves from everything that contaminates body and spirit, perfecting holiness out of reverence for God" (2 Corinthians 7:1).

As I read the classics and consider the lives of their authors, I am encouraged by the honest approach to sin, holiness, and temptation. I'll be quoting several authors in the next few chapters, but you'll notice in particular the work of two who focus on building a holiness of the heart—François de Salignac de La Mothe Fénelon (who, with your pardon, I'll refer to simply as Fénelon) and Francis de Sales. Two others focus on a very practical and disciplined approach—William Law and the Puritan Ralph Venning. These authors can lead the way toward a very practical and heartfelt Christian holiness.

The Teachers of Holiness

Fénelon, a seventeenth-century mystic, was well known as a skilled spiritual counselor.[1] He soon found himself charged with educating and reforming Louis XIV's grandson, the duke of Burgundy. This was a great honor and a great challenge. A contemporary of the young duke described him this way: "[He was] born terrible, and in his early youth he made everyone tremble. Hard and irascible to the utmost passion, incapable of bearing the slightest resistance without flying into a rage…obstinate… passionately fond of every kind of pleasure."[2]

Modern wisdom might tell us to send such a youth to military training and let strict discipline bring his life into order. Fénelon, however, pursued a different approach. "[A teacher must] mingle teaching and play; let wisdom show herself to the child only at intervals, and with a smiling face. If he forms a sad and gloomy conception of virtue, all is lost."[3] Fénelon's method must have worked, for the same person who gave us the earlier description of the duke described the transformation this way:

> The marvel is that in a very short space of time, devotion and grace made quite another being of him, and changed his many and dreadful faults into the entirely opposite virtues. From this abyss a Prince was seen to issue, at once affable, gentle, humane, generous, patient, modest, humble, and severe toward himself.[4]

In the midst of his call to reform others, Fénelon remained very much aware of his own failings. The man who offered so much spiritual advice to others wrote of himself, "I am to myself…the whole of a great diocese, more burdensome than the outside one, and a diocese which I am incapable of reforming."[5]

I appreciate Fénelon's attitude that his first student was *himself.* To teach virtue, he had to walk in virtue, and being sensitive to his own imperfections instead of denying them gave him increased understanding and wisdom with which he could help others. None of us can be a perfect teacher, and the world is all too eager to discount everything we say if we fall but *once.* People may charge us with hypocrisy, but we're not hypocrites if we begin by making a confession like Fénelon's. This is not an excuse to take sin lightly; it is rather a call to live in honest authenticity and let others see our progress. They can't see progress if we pretend we're already perfect.

A Passionate Man

Francis de Sales was also a noted spiritual adviser in his day. Though he lived a fairly pious life, de Sales admitted that the two most difficult passions for him were love and anger. He once said to his friend Jeanne Chantal, "There is not a soul in the world, I think, who loves more cordially, tenderly, and so to say more amorously than I."[6]

Yet de Sales was still able to have appropriately real, deep, and meaningful relationships with others—including women—without falling into sin because he learned the art of diversion, transforming a worldly passion into love of God.

Because de Sales was aware of his own temptations, he was able to be gentle (rather than afraid) when addressing others' temptations. He wrote, "I have never allowed myself to give way to anger or reproach without repenting of it; if I have had the happiness of reclaiming heretics, it has been by gentleness. Love is a stronger power over souls."[7]

Are you catching the spirit behind all these words? Fénelon and de Sales called people to great holiness, but they did so from the platform of encouragement, not condemnation; humility, not arrogance; love, not hatred; confidence in Christ, not fear.

When Fénelon and de Sales speak to us, we know they are men who worked with real people in real-life situations. They were aware of the sin in their own hearts, yet they found a way to live lives worthy of emulation. Oh, how we need teachers of their sort in this day and age, women and men who are honest about their own struggles, chastened before God, urging others toward holiness in a spirit of compassion with wisdom borne from Scripture and life experience in their own active battle against sin.

Let's see what they, and others, have discovered.

The Absurdity of Sin

The desire to live a holy life is an ancient one; indeed, the writers of the Christian classics were all but obsessed with walking in purity. Their first lesson to contemporary Christians who perhaps desire it with less intensity would focus on the reasons why holiness is worth the effort. They would want us to understand the absurdity of sin.

Julian of Norwich describes sin this way: "The sharpest scourge that any chosen soul can be struck with, it is a scourge which lashes men and women so hard, and batters them and destroys them."[1] Fénelon pointed out that sin is self-defeating. "We refuse ourselves to God, who only wants to save us. We give ourselves up to the world, which only wants to tyrannize over us and destroy us."[2] Venning agrees: "Sin promises like a God but pays like a Devil."[3]

What do these testimonies mean? Away with the self-serving testimonies that sound as if we do God a favor by repenting of our sin! God does *us* a favor by making us hate the sin that destroys us, by giving us the will to fight it, and by offering His grace to forgive it.

Quotes like these also remind us that if sin is a rat, we should start treating it like a rat. If you didn't want rats to break into your house, you wouldn't leave out food for them, and you would plug up any holes through which they might enter. If you were unable to keep them out on your own, you'd ask for advice or get some help. If you truly hated rats, you'd go to great lengths to get rid of them.

But how often do we accommodate sin, feed its desires, and treat it in the aftermath as a casual or minor mistake? We don't take sin as seriously as did the devotional writers of centuries ago.

Sin creates massive disturbances in our lives; holiness brings peace. When we look honestly at what each brings, we have to ask ourselves why sin is even tempting to us. William Law wrote, "These passions are the causes of all the disquiets and vexations of human life. They are the dropsies and fevers of our minds, vexing them with false appetites and restless cravings after such things as we do not want, and spoiling our taste for those things which are our proper good."[4]

Don't you find this to be true? When does lying ever bring peace of mind? When does lust ever create soul satisfaction? When does gossip ever serve community? When does gluttony ever promote health? Doesn't each sin eventually bring more problems with it than any solution?

Ralph Venning devotes an entire book to discussing the sinfulness of sin. The first several chapters of his volume point out how destructive sin is, leading Venning to conclude, "They speak best who speak the worst of sin."[5]

We live in a world that wants to sin, that treasures sin, that resents Christ's call to repent from sin. People will hate us for even suggesting something is shameful about sin. In fact, in their self-defeating logic, they will all but argue that it's a sin for us to oppose sin! Even so, God's people are to remind everyone that sin is, in Venning's words, "most immeasurably spiteful, poisonous and pernicious, because it kills men."[6]

Julian of Norwich is just as strong, saying there is "no harder hell than sin, because for a well-natured soul there is no hell but sin."[7]

When we see sin as it really is—offensive to the God who created and saved us, and a personal slow suicide—the moral calling of Christianity takes on a whole new light. William Law put it best when he wrote, "Surely it can be no uncomfortable state of life to be rescued by religion from such self-murder and to be rendered capable of eternal happiness."[8]

Any other way of living is "living wholly against ourselves and will end in our own shame and confusion of face."[9] Sin in this sense is nothing but self-abuse.

Christian, we must arm ourselves with the understanding that sin may sometimes seem inviting and pleasurable, but it is always ruinous. God will not withhold anything that serves our greater good, and in the same way, He will not sit idly by while His children walk in a path that will destroy them. We must trust His judgment over our own because sin lies even as it tempts.

Prisoners of Passions

Some people say they are free of the restraints of Christianity, but Law saw it another way. "They may live a while free from the restraints and directions of religion, but instead thereof they must be under the absurd government of their passions."[10] And our passions, as any thoughtful Christian knows, are merciless taskmasters compared to our God of mercy and grace.

Have you ever met truly happy drug addicts or alcoholics? They may occasionally laugh and party, but are their souls satisfied? Have you ever seen materialistic people actually enjoy what they have and experience true contentment? Does gambling and prejudice ever serve the people they overcome, or do they just lead to personal destruction and alienation?

God's will and judgment aside (which should be deciding factors in their own right, of course), sin simply doesn't make much sense. A life dedicated to holiness, in this sense, is actually self-serving—but it's self-serving as it first affirms God's order and purpose of creation. In this it's pleasing to God and ultimately pleasing to ourselves. That's why the Christian classics view sin as so absurd. Law explained, "By these rules we change the childish satisfactions of our vain and sickly passions for the solid enjoyments and real happiness of a sound mind."[11]

An Attack on God

So we take a step toward holiness when we see sin for what it is. But lest we get lost in the human-centered element of the previous paragraphs, let's consider what Venning considers the real issue: Sin "goes about to ungod God, and is by some of the ancients called *Deicidium*, God-murder or God-killing."[12] Imagine hearing your preacher ringing out with Venning's strong, forceful charge:

> Will you love that which hates God, and which God hates? God forbid! Will you join yourself to that which is nothing but contrariety to God, and all that is good?...Oh, say to this devil...Away! Away! Shall I be seduced by you to grieve the God of all my joy, to displease the God of all my comfort, to

vex the God of all my contentment, to do evil against a good
God, by whom I live, move, and have my being? Oh no![13]

Venning believed God-centeredness is the primary motivation to conquer temptation. "The main thing which keeps them from committing sin,
or for which they repent when they have committed it, is that it is against
God." He adds, "[Sin] is not to be committed for any reason because it is
contrary to God, against his will and glory. This reason overbalances and
outweighs any reason that can be given for sinning."[14]

This God-centeredness is based not on fear but on love. Nearing the
age of 50, I'm at a place in my life where I don't want to be a part of anything that God can't be a part of. Jeanne Guyon expresses this so well: "If
you seek the Lord and yet are not willing to stop your sinning, you shall
not find Him. Why? Because you are seeking Him in a place where He
is not."[15]

Don't we want to go where God is? If we do, we must leave the land
of sin.

No more false reasoning or accommodation or searching for exceptions. The spiritual truth is this: Sin is absurd. It's a bad choice, the *wrong*
choice, always, in every circumstance. It is destructive to us and hateful
toward God. In the enduring words of Julian of Norwich, our passion for
God demands that "we must feel naked hatred for sin and unending love
for the soul, as God loves it."[16]

God hates sin because it is bad for us. We must hate sin because God
hates it and loves us.

Counterfeit Holiness

We must beware of the many "false fronts" that can distract us from a holy life. If Satan can't keep us away from pursuing God, he will do his level best to keep us away from true holiness by distracting us with a counterfeit faith. Let's look at some of these traps.

The Passion Behind Pure Piety

Pascal warns, "experience shows us an enormous difference between piety and goodness."[1] Perhaps you've noticed this difference in your interaction with other Christians. We feel God's redeeming love and grace when we get together with some believers. Their holiness is a warm hearth, a shelter that invites us to come in from the cold. Even though we sense an underlying strength that tells us sin and manipulation are not acceptable in their presence—and this can be somewhat fearful—we still find ourselves drawn to them.

Other people's holiness seems to be a prison. It is forced, uncomfortable, and ragged at the edges. The biting edge of accusation and judgment pushes us away from them. When they talk about sin, their voices seem marked by fear and not by understanding or wisdom.

The spiritual fathers taught that true holiness has at its root an overwhelming passion for the one true and holy God, not for rules, principles, or standards. This holiness is relational.

> It is not by fussiness that we become faithful and exact in the smallest things. It is by a feeling of love, which is free from the

reflections and fears of the anxious and scrupulous. We are as
though carried away by the love of God. We only want to do
what we are doing, and we do not want to do anything at all
which we are not doing."[2]

Teresa of Avila joined Fénelon in this understanding of a relational
holiness that results from drawing near to God and having our appetites
transformed: "[The soul] has already experienced spiritual delight from
God, it sees that worldly delights are like filth. It finds itself withdrawing
from them little by little, and it is more master of itself for so doing. In
sum, there is an improvement in all the virtues."[3]

Most of us want to be rid of our longstanding sins in a day. We think
that by praying, "I'll never do it again!" we can somehow shout ourselves
out of years of habitual failure. True holiness focuses on drawing near to
God. As the love of God fills our hearts, the desire for sin is cut off and
withers. But this is a process, not an overnight experience. Stress, confusion, weariness...any number of things can resurrect old sinful habits.
That is why we must continually apply ourselves anew to loving God.

When we yearn for our Creator "as the deer pants for the water" (Psalm
42:1), when we learn to love the Lord our God with all our heart, soul,
mind, and strength (Mark 12:30), holiness will be the by-product of our
passion. We cease from sin not simply because we are disciplined, but
because we have found something better.

Principles can serve us, but they can't save us. Our outward actions, at
their best, are imperfect pictures of the state of our hearts; it is possible to
do everything right and still be 99 percent hypocrite.

Using Sin to Fight Sin

"We do not keep ourselves virtuous by our own power," Pascal warned,
"but by the counterbalance of two opposing vices, just as we stay upright
between two contrary winds. Take one of these vices away and we fall into
the other."[4]

What did Pascal mean by this? A man or woman who works very hard
may simply be avoiding the sin of laziness by being filled with selfish ambition or greed. Remove the hunger for more money, and this person is likely
to become as lazy as any of us.

Others might be very disciplined around food. They would be the last persons on earth you would label as gluttons. Yet they are disciplined around food because they want to have a body that will draw attention to themselves, not because they don't want food to have a hold on their hearts and steal their affection for God. They may be free from gluttony only because they are slaves to vanity.

Do you see how we play vice against vice—using vanity to destroy gluttony, for instance—and are upheld by the struggle of two sins? This holiness is very different from the biblical and classic Christian view of a transforming passion that gives birth to pure virtue. That's why Jesus constantly pointed us to the heart, the one battlefield that really matters. The state of our heart is the true state of our virtue.

Spared Only by Opportunity

A famous athlete walked up to my book table at a private conference. He had been in the newspapers for all the wrong reasons, yet as we talked, he spoke of his desire to grow in his faith and asked for some guidance. Before, I had been only a fan; now, as a Christian brother and witnessing his earnest sincerity, I saw his struggles in a new light.

Later, I was challenged even more as I prayerfully considered what my life would have been like if I had been rich, famous, single, and without the Lord in my early twenties. No wife to be held accountable to; no children to be responsible for; no Holy Spirit within to convict, confront, or counsel me; no Christian brothers to ask probing questions; no church to teach me; no active conscience to unsettle me...It was a horrifying thought, and it challenged forever any notion I might have of so casually judging the rich and famous who fall.

Ralph Venning reminds us that not doing something doesn't mean we wouldn't do it if we had the chance. "Some men are kept back from sin for lack of opportunity; if they had it they would sin. They do not lack the heart but the occasion, not the inclination but the opportunity. If tempted to sin they would sin."[5]

This calls us to humility when judging others. How do we know that we wouldn't do the same things if we had the same opportunities? I'm not just talking about the wealthy—what if your marriage was racked by loneliness, and then you were cleverly, stealthily, and consistently pursued by an attractive suitor? What if you had to live with financial pressure that was intense, grating on you day after day after day—might your temper might be a little more active?

Many of us are kept from sin only because God graciously removes the occasion to sin. If not for His governing hand, we'd fall along with everyone else. This isn't true holiness; it's simply the lack of opportunity.

Pleasing People, Not God

Our holiness is also counterfeit if we merely refrain from acts that society will ridicule us for doing. People who do this, Venning warns, "avoid sins that would bring disgrace, but they can easily embrace pleasant, fashionable and profitable sins."[6] In other words, such people would never utter a racist comment, as that would cost them socially, but they might well gossip about a renowned Christian leader if doing so will win them favor with their social group. These people aren't motivated by what's right; their sole motivation is social acceptance. They don't reject gossip *per se*; they just reject gossip that would make them look bad to others.

The truly holy person takes his or her standard from God Himself. God hates gossip and prejudice of all kinds against anyone. I remember having this conversation with a young Emergent pastor. He talked about his ability to speak with gays, but in the same conversation personally attacked fundamentalists. I responded, "It's no credit to you when you love gays but not fundamentalists. You've simply focused your prejudice instead of getting rid of it."

Truly holy people will hate what God hates, even if the world loves it. They will love what God loves, even if the world hates it. Holiness is nothing less and nothing more than being radically God centered.

Unfortunately, even radically God-centered people will face intense times of temptation. Fortunately, the Christian classics have much wisdom to share about this as well. We'll look at this in the next chapter.

When Temptation Strikes

As our growing holiness reduces certain temptations, sin will find more subtle ways to attack us. This side of heaven, none of us will become so mature that we never have to look temptation in the face. How did the devotional masters say we should respond when that happens?

Again, a holy passion for God is the primary antidote. We are consistently told to run like little children into the Father's arms. Fénelon taught that we should act like a small child who is shown something horrible. "[He] only recoils from it and buries himself in his mother's breast, so that he will see nothing. The practice of the presence of God is the supreme remedy. It sustains. It comforts. It calms."[1] Francis de Sales gave similar advice:

> As soon as you perceive yourself tempted, follow the example of children when they see a wolf or a bear in the country; for they immediately run into the arms of their father or mother, or at least they call out to them for help or assistance. It is the remedy which our Lord has taught: "Pray, that ye enter not into temptation."
>
> If you find that the temptation, nevertheless, still continues, or even increases, run in spirit to embrace the holy cross, as if you saw our Savior Jesus Christ crucified before you. Protest that you never will consent to the temptation, implore his assistance against it, and still refuse your consent as long as the temptation shall continue.

But, in making these protestations and refusals of consent, look not the temptation in the face, but look only on our Lord...Divert your thoughts to some good and pious reflections, for, when good thoughts occupy your heart, they will drive away every temptation and suggestion.[2]

John Climacus warns us that we should not arrogantly try to fight a stronger foe.

Do not imagine that you will overwhelm the demon of fornication by entering into an argument with him. Nature is on his side and he has the best of the argument. So the man who decides to struggle against his flesh and to overcome it by his own efforts is fighting in vain...Offer up to the Lord the weakness of your nature. Admit your incapacity and, without your knowing it, you will win for yourself the gift of chastity.[3]

I love this approach because we are not to see temptation as a chance to somehow prove our piety to God. Rather, each of us can humbly admit, "Lord, without You, I don't have a chance of successfully fighting this temptation. Please help me." Instead of the temptation setting me up against God ("I want to do this, but He'll be really angry at me if I do") it draws me *to* Him.

Here's what I've found: We should never stop talking to God, even (especially!) in the face of temptation. Don't shut Him out. Run to Him, find refuge in Him, and bury your face in His shoulder. Once you stop the conversation or act as if you can face the temptation on your own, the battle is lost.

Focusing on sin, either by committing it or by being consumed with fighting it, keeps us from practicing God's presence. God forbid that we should ever define ourselves or our days solely by what we *didn't* do. Instead, let's be people who define ourselves by practicing God's presence. Let's use temptation to remind us to think of Him, our soul's true delight.

Temptation's Training

We all seek the ideal of perfect obedience, but in reality, sin is something we are going to have to learn to live with. That doesn't mean we should be complacent about it, but rather that our nature is steeped in sin. As soon as we find victory over one sin, another will rise up to take its place.

The classic writers were practical in this regard. Sin is something all of us do, so they urged us to learn even from our failings. To suggest that we should sin so we can grow would be heresy. Sin is always the wrong choice. However, when we do sin, we might as well cooperate with God and learn a lesson from our fall so we don't repeat it.

A fall can lead to the soul-renewing experience of genuine repentance, which places us in a posture of learning. Fénelon highlights the value of this:

> The sin seems hideous, but the humiliation which comes from it, and for which God has permitted it, seems good. As the reflections of pride about our own faults are bitter, worried and chagrined, so the return of the soul to God after its faults is recollected, peaceful, and sustained by confidence.[4]

At some stages of the Christian life, we may actually feel closest to God right after we've blown it and met Him in repentance. This is because our pride, which is so repugnant to God but which we tend to ignore, is finally broken by sin and even at times by temptation.

> Thou allowest a mixture of good and evil even in the hearts of those who are most devoted to thee. These imperfections which remain in good souls serve to humble them, to detach them from themselves, to make them feel their own weakness, to make them run more eagerly to thee.[5]

In this, Fénelon calls us to let sin lead us into repentance, which in turn will lead us into the Father's loving care. When people struggle with persistent sin, the deceiver often tricks them by being soft on the consequence of their sin before they commit it ("You can always be forgiven") but harsh and unyielding once the deed is done ("Now you're really going to get it!"). This is a ruse to pull us away from our heart's desire, to see God as our enemy instead of our truest friend. When you sin, accept the lesson in humility and go to God in weakness. I've found I am rarely stronger than when I am newly repentant and receiving God's consoling forgiveness.

Thomas à Kempis also found great potential for growth in temptation. "Temptations are often very profitable to us, though they be troublesome and grievous; for in them a man is humbled, purified, and instructed."[6] He added later, "Wherefore to many it is more profitable not to be altogether free from temptations, but to be often assaulted, lest they should be too secure, and so perhaps be puffed up with pride; or else too freely give themselves to worldly comforts."[7]

When a persistent weakness keeps us close to God, when it makes us more careful in tempting situations and more thoughtful in seeking God's face, we can see how God can use even a potential weakness for His good purpose. If you know you are particularly susceptible to people pleasing or gossip, for instance, you'll learn to be especially mindful of God when you enter into conversation. You would certainly agree that you would be a better person without this sin, but would you be a better person without this temptation? Wouldn't you be more likely to enter conversation without seeking God's assistance?

When ongoing temptation reminds us to clothe ourselves with humility and seek God's face, God is able to use even that which wars against us. He is taking our enemy's own sword and stabbing him in the heart.

After the Fall

After we sin, rather than make promises to God that we are almost certain to break ("I promise I'll tell the truth next time, God—I really will!"), we should respond by humbly asking the right questions. What led to this sin? Why was I so susceptible to a fall? What were my motivations? What was the appeal? How did I forget to practice God's presence? Francis de Sales wrote, "Content not yourself with confessing your…sins, merely as to the fact, but accuse yourself also of the motive that induced you to commit them."[8]

I have had to ask myself, "Why is it hard for me to sometimes speak the truth to someone when I know that truth will be hurtful?" That question led me to see that I want to be liked. The next question to ask was obvious—why do I value being liked more than being honest? I'm still answering that one, but the point is that even though I hate the sin, it has opened the door to my heart so I can confront some long-neglected motivations. Every time I fail, if I ask the right questions, I learn something new. God can use my strengths to help me grow, but He can also use my weaknesses. God's ability to use even rebellion for His benefit is one of the more profound realities of His sovereignty and lordship.

Our failing might be an intellectual one. Maybe we were deceived by God's enemy. We got into a discussion with the devil about our sin and found ourselves duped into rationalizing that maybe, just this once, it might be somewhat okay…And on that flimsy rationalization, we jumped headfirst. Venning is typically clear: "Sin says, 'It is one sin only, and this only once.' But if sin is good, why only once, and if evil, why once?"[9]

The best course of action is to avoid rationalizations altogether and instead to find refuge in clear and untwisted truth. We can say, "I got lost in rationalizing that sin last time, but no more. In the future, I'll consider what Scripture says instead of looking for the exceptions clause."

In this regard, discussing with someone else the motives of our sins can be particularly helpful. Francis de Sales offered this counsel:

> But the sovereign remedy against all temptations, whether great or small, is to lay open your heart, and communicate its suggestions, feelings, and affections to your director; for you must observe, that the first condition that the enemy of salvation makes with a soul which he desires to seduce is to keep silence…whereas God, on the other hand, by his inspirations, requires that we should make them known to our superiors and directors.[10]

Living by grace does not mean living by spiritual laziness. We don't continually berate ourselves about committing the sin, but we do try, in a spirit of repentance, to discern the cause of the sin and the reason for its power to motivate us. One of the best ways to take this seriously is to discuss our sin with another believer who can provide an objective voice.

In the end we must never forget that God's grace covers all our battles and assures us of a glorious end. Julian of Norwich once lamented that her longing for God seemed vandalized by her constant battles with sin. God gave her a comforting assurance, one we would do well to receive: "Sin is befitting, but all shall be well, and all shall be well, and all manner of things shall be well."[11]

We fight sin, give in to sin, and repent of our sin under the providence of God and in a relationship of His grace. Though fighting sin and facing down temptation can be vexing and even exhausting at times, we can take courage and hope and continue to persevere, knowing that because of Christ, all shall be well, and all shall be well, and all manner of things shall be well.

Consistent Climbing

Talk about holiness can be dangerous. Some of the more zealous among us will overdo it, wanting to progress from being the young and lusty Augustine to the mature bishop of Hippo in the course of a year or even a week. Perhaps you've heard about the asceticism and harsh measures of the desert fathers. You would do well to also recognize the strong tradition of gentle and consistent progress in holiness. Fénelon gave a warning worth heeding:

> Most people, when they wish to be converted or reformed, expect to fill their lives with especially difficult and unusual acts, far more than to purify their intentions, and to mortify their natural inclinations in the most usual acts of their condition. In this they often badly deceive themselves. It would be much more valuable for them to change their actions less, and to change more rather the disposition which makes them act. When one is already leading an honest and regulated life, it is far more important, in order to become a true Christian, to change the within rather than the without.[1]

We are far better off keeping a constant and steady vigilance in the small things rather than trying to prove heroic in the big things. Holiness is not something obtained between Tuesday and Wednesday, but rather the fruit of a life lived consistently and thoughtfully over the course of years and decades. "A continual and moderate sobriety is preferable to violent abstinences, practiced occasionally, and mingled with great relaxations. A moderate use of discipline awakens the appetite of devotion,"[2] Francis de Sales wrote.

A heroic approach to holiness often tries to pour in the holiness as quickly as possible, but it ignores the millions of tiny holes that drain us dry. De Sales explains how this works:

> Wolves and bears are certainly more dangerous than fleas; yet the former neither give us so much trouble, nor exercise our patience so much, as the latter. It is easy to abstain from murder, but it is extremely difficult to restrain all the little sallies of passion, the occasions of which present themselves every moment. It is very easy for a man or a woman to refrain from adultery, but it is not as easy to refrain from glances of the eyes, from giving or receiving marks of love, or from uttering or listening to flattery…Wherefore I say, that being ever ready to fight courageously against great temptations, we must in the meantime diligently defend ourselves against those that seem small and inconsiderable.[3]

Here's a convicting example: You don't think of yourself as a hateful person, but would somebody know that from the way you drive? Are you often at silent war with other drivers? You'd probably *never* get into a fistfight walking down the sidewalk, but do you argue with nameless, faceless drivers when you're behind the wheel?

See how this works? It's these "little" things, the not-so-obvious sins and ugly attitudes, that shape our character. Working in a soup kitchen once a week can't overcome hateful feelings cultivated by driving like a demon *seven* days a week.

We would eagerly live like an ascetic for a day or two if only we could grant ourselves the privilege of then forgetting about religion and living the rest of the week is if it had no serious claim on our lives. Yet we have an enemy who is willing to surrender the yards he loses during our heroic measures in order to gain the miles he wins when we return to soft living.

Thus the call for "consistent climbing"—a steady progress of faith in all areas of our lives. William Law warned that this includes the most common areas, such as casual conversation and even what we eat and drink.

> A person that eats and drinks too much does not feel such effects from it as those do who live in notorious instances of

gluttony and intemperance; but yet his course of indulgence, though it be not scandalous in the eyes of the world nor such as torments his own conscience, is a great and constant hindrance to his improvement in virtue; it gives him eyes that see not and ears that hear not; it creates a sensuality in the soul, increases the power of bodily passions, and makes him incapable of entering into the true spirit of religion.[4]

I am one of the world's worst at fasting. A prolonged fast inevitably humiliates me as I collapse in failure in a ridiculously short period of time. But I have tried to live in the spirit of fasting—addressing food's hold on me throughout the day, every day—and this has been helpful. I used to be notorious for snacking in the evening. Now I routinely fast after dinner, immediately brushing my teeth and saying that's it until breakfast. You may rightly laugh at such a small fast, but this seemingly insignificant act has addressed a real weakness in my life and has begun to build in me a more disciplined attitude toward food in general. This new outlook stays with me throughout the entire day in a way that trying (and often failing) longer fasts failed to do. Attempts at heroic holiness have overwhelmed me, but consistent climbing has strengthened me greatly.

Slowly Overcoming Vice with Virtue

Consistent climbing sees character as something that is planted and watered and that develops over time. One of the great lessons of the classics is that we need to focus on what we are to *become* more than we focus on what we are to *avoid.* Francis de Sales reminds us that we will never be fully free of temptations, and therefore we should avoid the trap of wasting our energy by becoming preoccupied with them.

> As to these smaller temptations...as it is impossible to be altogether freed from them, the best defense that we can make is not to give ourselves much trouble about them; for although they may tease us, yet they can never hurt us, so long as we continue firmly resolved to dedicate ourselves in earnest to the service of God...Content yourself with quietly removing them, not by contending or disputing with them, but by performing some actions of a contrary nature to the temptation, especially acts of the love of God...This grand remedy

is so terrible to the enemy of our souls, that as soon as he per-
ceives that his temptation incites us to form acts of divine love
he ceases to tempt us...He who would wish to contend with
them in particular would give himself much trouble to little
or no purpose.[5]

Treating the vice with the opposite virtue is a favorite tactic of de Sales.
"Consider...what passions are most predominant in your soul; and, having discovered them, adopt such a method of thinking, speaking, and acting, as may contradict them."[6]

Replacing a vice with a virtue can even be used to change our social
environments. I once worked in a grocery store to supplement the salary I
earned as a college pastor, and the backbiting and slander there were abominable. After praying about the situation, I came up with a plan. When
I was alone with one worker, I solicited a positive reply about another
worker by asking a leading question. "Don't you think Mary is good with
customers?"

The coworker answered, "Yes, I do. She really knows what she's talking about."

I waited until the next shift when I was alone with Mary. "Susan talked
to me today about how helpful you are with the customers. She said it's
obvious you know your stuff."

"Oh really?" Mary said. "Susan's a sweet gal; she's a great person to
work with."

Of course, the next time I worked with Susan, I recounted what Mary
had said. I repeated the same plan with as many coworkers as possible,
spreading as much positive "gossip" as I could. The atmosphere of our
department changed as the virtues of encouragement and appreciation
took root. Giving my coworkers a sermon about the evil of gossip would
certainly not have had the same effect.

De Sales also urged us to use this practice before temptation strikes—
thus being proactive instead of reactive. "In time of peace, that is, when
temptations to the sin to which you are most inclined do not molest you,
make several acts of the contrary virtue."[7] Are you wallowing in negativity?
Find things to be thankful for when your critical spirit is absent. Go out of
your way to be grateful and appreciative, complimenting others and ver-
bally mentioning their strengths. Is lust a constant failing? Ask God to help

you look at people as your brothers and sisters in Christ. If you're tempted to look lustfully at people, try praying for their souls and families.

Just as failing in one area can slowly eat away at our spiritual lives, so improving in one area, even a small one, nourishes our spiritual lives. Law wrote, "A man of business that has brought one part of his affairs under certain rules is in a fair way to take the same care of the rest. So he that has brought any one part of his life under the rules of religion may thence be taught to extend the same order and regularity into other parts of his life."[8]

In order to grow consistently, however, we must learn to avoid the trap of soul sadness. Let's look at this phenomenon in the next chapter.

Soul Sadness

A Pharisee who does nothing but focus on avoiding sin is still concentrating on sin, which makes him or her just as obsessed with sin as the person who voraciously lives in it. Both are consumed by sin—one to avoid it, the other to live in it. Both lack the joy, peace, and freedom of life in Christ.

Undue fretting leads to "soul sadness," or despondency, or, as Francis de Sales put it, "inquietude." Soul sadness is the result of a performance-based holiness, and it often plagues those who most want to serve God.

De Sales wrote that true holiness is cultivated with "patience, meekness, humility, and tranquility, expecting it more from the providence of God than from [our] own industry or diligence." If, however, we seek deliverance from sin out of performance (which is merely a form of self-love and self-exaltation), we will fatigue ourselves and fall into a soul sadness that, "instead of removing, aggravates the evil, and involves [the soul] in such anguish and distress, with so great loss of courage and strength," that we imagine ourselves incurable.[1]

Thus de Sales asserted that soul sadness, resulting from self-love and self-effort, "is the greatest evil that can befall the soul, sin only excepted." Soul sadness saps our strength, which is needed to resist the temptation. This is how it keeps us in the maze of performance.

We can desire holiness for the wrong reasons. Perhaps we simply want to use holiness for notoriety, as others might use a beautiful voice or eloquent speech. Or perhaps we are steeped in pride and simply unwilling to count ourselves among the truly sinful. This unholy desire for holiness produces a soul sadness that Satan exploits to further defeat us, with the intent of driving us off the cliff of despair.

Soul sadness "proceeds from an inordinate desire of being delivered from the evil which we feel, or of acquiring the good which we desire: and yet there is nothing which tends more to increase evil, and to prevent the enjoyment of good, than an unquiet mind."[2]

The essence of the Christian life is a love relationship with God. Our standing in the Christian life rests with Christ. When acquiring virtues and avoiding sin become the primary focus of our walk, we have elevated the (admittedly important) secondary over the primary. Another way of putting it is that we have made an idol out of our own piety.

True holiness results from a tranquil reliance on God for the care of our souls. It depends on grace, not self-effort, and it cooperates with God instead of trying to replace God. True holiness recognizes that apart from God, we can't help but sin, and it is willing to live with this truth, for true holiness is humble holiness.

When we want to be freed from sin or to do something good for the kingdom of God, we must be careful to "settle our mind in repose and tranquility" and *gently* seek what we desire. De Sales explained, "When I say gently, I do not mean negligently, but without hurry, trouble or inquietude; otherwise, instead of obtaining the effect of your desire, you will mar all, and embarrass yourself the more."[3] Elsewhere, De Sales used this engaging illustration:

> As the mild and affectionate reproofs of a father have far greater power to reclaim his child than rage and passion; so when we have committed any fault, if we reprehend our heart with mild and calm remonstrances, having more compassion for it than passion against it, sweetly encouraging it to amendment, the repentance it shall conceive by this means will sink much deeper, and penetrate it more effectually, than a fretful, injurious, and stormy repentance.[4]

Can you do this? When you fall, can you speak to yourself as you would to a child, with gentleness and encouragement, not with harsh accusations? If you can, you'll be exercising humility as you confront the reality of your sin, and humility is the surest foundation on which to build a life of holiness. If you arrogantly berate yourself ("How could you? You're better than that!"), you're displaying *and feeding* the very pride that got you into this situation.

Fénelon brings this idea to a firm conclusion. "Go forward always with confidence, without letting yourself be touched by the grief of a sensitive pride, which cannot bear to see itself imperfect. Your fault will serve, by this inner confusion, to make you die to yourself."[5]

The Hope of All Hope

When we pursue holiness humbly, we stop depending so much on ourselves, fully admit our weakness, and fervently embrace all that God provides for our defense.

One of the great spiritual tragedies of our time (that's not hyperbole—this is truly sad) is that so many believers fight daily sin and temptation in an *individual* war. The greatest strength is actually found within God's church. When pastors or leaders feel that they must hide their struggle or risk losing their jobs; when parents think they must maintain the lie of perfection to maintain their authority; when teachers think they alone do not, as James 3:2 insists, "stumble in many ways," these people will be engulfed in individual struggles that will include more defeats than victories. And of course this will cast the people into pervasive soul sadness.

God intends for us to fight sin as an army, not as a soldier. We may seek to be Davids fighting the Goliaths, but this is our arrogance exalting our courage, not God inspiring our resistance. God is glorified just as much when we are one of many fighting side by side.

As an evangelical, I was struck by the way Johannes Tauler, who lived in an order of preachers during the fourteenth century, emphasized finding our hope in what God provides *through His church*. Saying that a man giving in to the devil "can be compared to a well-armed soldier running away from a fly," Tauler offers this reminder: "We possess much stronger weapons than he: our holy Faith, the Blessed Sacrament, the Word of God, the examples of the saints, the prayers of Holy Church, and much besides. Compared to all this, the devil is weaker than a fly."[6]

What if we evangelicals preached the necessity of the church as much as our Roman Catholic and Eastern Orthodox brothers and sisters do? What if we said we need to take Communion more seriously, to remind ourselves of the power in the Last Supper? Yes, we see it as symbol and remembrance, not a renewed Passion, but it is not and never has been a *powerless* remembrance. What if we reminded each other of the need to study God's Word together, that though there is great benefit in personal study, we can learn volumes from those particularly gifted to study and explain God's truths? What if we respected the classics and relied on the examples of previous saints, not praying to or through them, but remembering their examples and keeping fresh their wise words of counsel? What if we found refuge in well-written prayers of confession and forgiveness and intercession, instead of always relying on our own? What if we asked each other to pray for our temptations instead of hiding them? *What if we made the journey toward holiness a corporate pursuit instead of a solitary one?* Isn't this one of the primary ways God makes Himself known to us and His power available to us? Then, like Tauler, we might find that the battle against Satan could be likened to a well-armed soldier taking on a fly.

The Presence in the Passion

Everything we've been saying leads to this: True holiness is a relational holiness—it is God's overwhelming presence in our lives, causing us to want to do what He wills as He gives us the strength to do it, however imperfectly we may live it out. The essence of true holiness, then, is loving God. As Fénelon explains, the more we love God, the more we will want to live according to His will.

> Let us plunge into [the love of God]. The more we love him, the more we love also all that which he makes us do. It is this love which consoles us in our losses, which softens our crosses for us, which detaches us from all which it is dangerous to love, which preserves us from a thousand poisons, which shows us a benevolent compassion through all the ills which we suffer, which even in death opens for us an eternal glory and happiness. It is this love which changes all our evils to good.[7]

With such a faith, such a passion, such a love, we can face our failures without despair and welcome any victories without pride as we slowly, consistently, and humbly grow because of the God who is redeeming our souls.

PART 3

Absolute Surrender

18

Joyful Surrender:
Christian Submission

I n 1654 Blaise Pascal faced his life's greatest test. His friendship with a duke had thrust him into the upper class, but the attractions and amusements of high society threatened his burgeoning spirituality. We know about his inner crisis because of a letter he wrote to his sister at the time.

On the night of November 23, Pascal had an ecstatic experience that affected him for the rest of his life. In fact, he wrote down the insights he gained that night and sewed them into his jacket, transferring them from garment to garment as each one wore out. He maintained some of his former relationships after the experience, but he no longer felt any ambivalence about his call to surrender to God's will for his life and work.

About two years later, Pascal began making notes for what he hoped would become a full-scale apology of the Christian religion. He wanted to use the brilliant mathematical mind God had given him to defend the faith.

Pascal's notes now fill up several hundred pages in the book we call *Pensées.* The scope of what Pascal intended must have been enormous because he stated that it would take ten years of good health to bring the book to completion—this from a man who had already accomplished more in his first 35 years than most people accomplish in a lifetime.

The notes were made in 1657 and 1658, but in 1659 Pascal entered a period of serious illness from which he never fully recovered. In the midst of his illness he wrote a prayer and titled it *"Priere pour demander a Dieu le bon usage des maladies"* ("Prayer asking God for the right use of illnesses") in which he tried to find a Christian meaning for his suffering so he could discern God's will and submit to it wholly and trustfully. In the prayer, Pascal asked God to dispose of his health and his sickness, his life and his death, first for the glory of God and then for his salvation and the good of the church.[1]

Pascal could have been bitter. He could have argued that God was treating him unfairly. He could have prayed, "God, I gave up everything to serve You in this, and now I'm too sick to complete it. How can You allow this to happen?" Rather than complain, Pascal devoted his final years to ministering to the poor. He couldn't summon the strength for a serious intellectual enterprise, but he could hand out blankets and pour out soup. Instead of retreating back to the world, he simply found a new way to continue serving God.

During his life, Pascal argued against the theology of the Roman Catholic Jesuits and the Protestant Calvinists, so there are, no doubt, plenty of traditions that could find fault with him. But when I read his biography, I am moved by the heart of this man who was so surrendered to God. He surrendered not only the temptations of the world— this I can understand—but also the glory of a particular service to God, and this is what humbles me. He placed *everything* on the altar, and he expressed no bitterness at all when God decided to keep it. Pascal just kept serving Him.

This is a mark of a truly classic spirituality. Many modern-day church-goers, undoubtedly well meaning but sadly misinformed, earnestly pray to a vending-machine God who supposedly cranks out what we ask for as long as we push the right buttons. Christians of centuries past saw faith as a struggle of a different sort—not to get God to do our will, but to die to ourselves so we can accept God's will. Scupoli, Fénelon, and John of the Cross each express this eloquently:

> [During prayer,] your attention should be to unite your will to God's, not to bend His to yours. And the reason for this is that your own will, being tainted and corrupted by self-love, very often errs and knows not what it asks. But the divine will, always united to ineffable goodness, can never err.[2]

> What [God] asks is a will which will no longer be divided between him and any creature, a will pliant in his hands, which

neither desires anything nor refuses anything, which wants without reservation everything which he wants, and which never, under any pretext, wants anything which he does not want.[3]

I should like to persuade spiritual persons that the road leading to God does not entail a multiplicity of considerations, methods, manners, and experiences…but demands only the one thing necessary: true self-denial, exterior and interior, through surrender of self both to suffering for Christ and to annihilation in all things.[4]

Such surrender doesn't come easily to me. By disposition and perhaps by birth order, I am something of a striver. Call me to sacrifice for Jesus, and I'll quickly raise my hand. Tell me to take a risk for the Lord, and I'm willing. But ask me to surrender? No thanks.

I am slowly learning that the real test of true faith is not how successful I am, but how surrendered I am. In the Christian faith, we are called to die daily (see, for example, Luke 9:23). A Christian with his or her own agenda is like a horse with a head on both ends. This person will always be in a "push me–pull you" struggle with God.

Johannes Tauler, the fourteenth-century theologian who fed Martin Luther's mind with "pure theology," put surrender above miracle-working power, intellect, and even virtue: "I would prefer a man who was utterly surrendered, with fewer works and accomplishments, to one of dazzling works of virtue whose surrender was imperfect."[5]

The most Christian prayer we can ever pray is the prayer Jesus prayed in Gethsemane—"Not my will, but thine, be done" (Luke 22:42 kjv). So we should not be surprised that when Jesus taught His disciples to pray, He first blessed God ("Hallowed be thy name") and then expressed His surrender ("Thy kingdom come. Thy will be done in earth, as it is in heaven" [Matthew 6:9-10 kjv]).

All our prayers, all our lives, should echo these prayers.

Thy Will

I try not to have favorites among the classics, but if I did, Henry Drummond would be among the finalists. His work contains such depth and boldness couched in compelling language. This example is particularly rich: Drummond speaks of "the eternal calm of an invulnerable faith; the repose of a heart set deep in God."[6]

Unpack that sentence and you get this: We should seek a supernatural calm, the kind that exists in a faith that can't be defeated because the heart is resting secure, "set deep" in God and His will. God can't be defeated, so if our will is aligned with His, we can rest peacefully, securely, and without fear.

With compelling logic, Drummond makes the Christian life sound so simple and so clear: "The end of life is to do God's will...That is the object of your life and mine—to do God's will. It is not to be happy or to be successful, or famous, or to do the best we can...It is something far higher than this—to do God's will."[7]

Christ modeled this submission to God's will at Lazarus's tomb. Jesus's delay in coming to Lazarus's aid provoked Mary and Martha to feel cheated and disappointed. Drummond paraphrases Christ's response: "I came down from Heaven not to do what I liked, or what Lazarus liked, or Mary liked or Martha liked, but to do the Will of Him that sent Me."[8] He adds, "The principle on which Jesus stayed when everyone thought it the right thing that He should be in Bethany was simply this—that the end of life is not to look after one's sick friends but to do the Will of God."[9]

Such surrendering to God's will helps us to overcome the common ambitious thinking that assumes faithfulness should lead to fame, to notoriety, or even to work that seems more important than what we're doing. On the contrary, a submissive spirit leads us to accept whatever God brings our way, even if it's far more humble work. Drummond again:

> Suppose we are beginning to feel the splendid conviction that, after all, our obscure life is not to be wasted; that having this ideal principle within it, it may yet be as great in its homely surroundings as the greatest human life—seeing that no man can do more with his life than the will of God, that though we may never be famous or powerful, or called to heroic suffering or acts of self-denial which will vibrate through history; that though we are neither intended to be apostles nor missionaries nor martyrs, but to be common people living in common houses, spending the day in common offices or common kitchens, yet doing the will of God there, we shall do as much as apostle or missionary or martyr—seeing that they can do

no more than do God's will where they are, even as we can do as much where we are—and answer the end of our life as truly, faithfully and triumphantly as they.[10]

Whether I am sick or healthy, my aim is to do God's will. Whether I am wealthy or poor, famous or anonymous, happy in my marriage or greatly frustrated, single or widowed or divorced, multitalented or barely able to function with a drastically reduced IQ, my call is the same—to do exactly what God wants me to do.

Christian health is not defined by how happy we are, by how prosperous or healthy we are, or even by how many people we have led to the Lord in the last year. Christian health is ultimately defined by how sincerely we wave our flag of surrender, how earnestly we want to do and be exactly what God wants us to do and be.

The questions leading to spiritual growth and health, then, are these: What is God's will for me in this hour and day? Where is God leading me? How can I surrender to Him? Law provided a clue.

> He therefore is the devout man who lives no longer to his own will, or the way and spirit of the world, but to the sole will of God, who considers God in everything, who serves God in everything, who makes all the parts of his common life parts of piety by doing everything in the name of God and under such rules as are conformable to His glory.[11]

We want to baptize our old nature rather than trade it in. We're not told to wash the old nature, however, but to kill it. True Christianity includes an utter, absolute, and complete surrender to God.

19

The Two Essential Questions

Our journey toward complete surrender to God leads us to grapple with two fundamental questions. The first is this: Is God good? Only if we truly believe in God's goodness can we entrust ourselves so completely to His care.

The second question is this: Is God the Lord? That is, does God actually rule over the affairs of His world?

Both the goodness and providence of God are well established in Scripture, but both are questioned today. If God is so good, why does He allow evil things to happen? If God is in control, why is the world such a mess? Until we resolve these two questions in our own minds, we will find ourselves at odds with God.

I am not suggesting that wrestling with the questions is inappropriate. They are fair questions, and we need to be honest about our doubts if we are to enter into a new intimacy with the Father. However, maturity will eventually require that we come to this conclusion: Yes, God is good, and yes, God is the Lord. Until we have done that, the intimacy of surrender simply will not be possible.

How can we ask ourselves to surrender to a God of whom we're suspicious? And even if we convince ourselves He's good, how can we surrender to Him if we think He's powerless to make a difference?

Scripture provides a clear witness of God's goodness:

- "Good and upright is the Lord...All the ways of the Lord are loving and faithful" (Psalm 25:8,10).

- "For the LORD is good and his love endures forever; his faithfulness continues through all generations" (Psalm 100:5).

- "I am the good shepherd" (John 10:11).

- "We know that in all things God works for the good of those who love him" (Romans 8:28).

- "If God is for us, who can be against us?" (Romans 8:31).

- "Every good and perfect gift is from above, coming down from the Father of the heavenly lights" (James 1:17).

- "You have tasted that the Lord is good" (1 Peter 2:3).

Scripture also proclaims God's lordship and providence:

- "You intended to harm me, but God intended it for good to accomplish what is now being done, the saving of many lives" (Genesis 50:20).

- "He does as he pleases with the powers of heaven and the peoples of the earth. No one can hold back his hand or say to him: 'What have you done?'" (Daniel 4:35).

- "Do not worry...Look at the birds of the air; they do not sow or reap or store away in barns, and yet your heavenly Father feeds them. Are you not much more valuable than they?" (Matthew 6:25-26).

- "This man was handed over to you by God's set purpose and foreknowledge" (Acts 2:23).

I have purposefully avoided some of the more contentious verses used by Calvinists and Arminians in their never-ending battle to promote certain systems because I want to appeal to God's greater truth: The Bible clearly declares that God is *always* good and in control. How that speaks to the issue of human will and the mechanics of salvation has been debated, but that God is intimately involved in this world as a truly benevolent force is an indisputable biblical truth in which we must find refuge if we are ever to enter the land of Christian surrender.

There is no getting around the fact that the men and women who wrote the classics of Christian devotion believed in God's goodness and

His lordship. Thomas à Kempis had this to say about the goodness of God (notice how this was the foundation for his call to surrender):

> "Do with me whatever it shall please thee. For it cannot be anything but good, whatever thou shalt do with me. If it be thy will I should be in darkness, be thou blessed; and if it be thy will I should be in light, be thou again blessed. If thou grant me comfort, be thou blessed; and if thou will have me afflicted, be thou still equally blessed." My son, such as this ought to be thy state, if thou desire to walk with Me. Thou must be as ready to suffer as to rejoice. Thou must cheerfully be as destitute and poor, as full and rich.[1]

William Law wrote this about God's providence:

> Every man is to consider himself as a particular object of God's providence, under the same care and protection of God as if the world had been made for him alone. It is not by chance that any man is born at such a time, of such parents, and in such place and condition…Every soul comes into the body at such a time and in such circumstances by the express design of God, according to some purposes of His will and for some particular ends.[2]

Moving forward in surrender will be impossible if we do not agree with Thomas à Kempis regarding God's goodness and William Law regarding God's providence. Many of us carry wounds that require healing before we can embrace these two truths. Surrender is fundamental to the Christian faith, so we need to do the soul work that is necessary to arrive at an understanding of God's goodness and God's providence. Others of us may have some intellectual mountains to climb before we can wave our white flags of surrender. Whatever the case, we should do what we must do so we can resolve these two fundamental questions without delay.

20

The Death of Complaining

When my son was three years old, he fell on a fireplace hearth and cut himself just above his left eye. I rushed him to the hospital and stayed with him as the nurses immobilized his arms. As the doctor began putting stitches in Graham's head, I held his hand and almost lost my composure when Graham whimpered, "Please, Daddy, he's hurting me. Make him stop. Please, Daddy, don't let him do this, *please*."

It broke my heart. Graham felt betrayed. As a toddler, he ran to me when he was scared. He climbed into my arms when he needed comfort. He depended on me, and he couldn't understand why the father he had grown to trust was letting a strange man stick a needle in his head. The sense of betrayal in his words—"How could you?"—tore me up.

Because of his limited understanding, however, there was nothing I could say. Explanations would have done little good. "Hey, Bud, I know you think girls have cooties now, but the time is coming when you're going to want to ask one out on a date, and it's not really going to help you if you have a flap of skin hanging over your eye." Or "Graham, if we don't treat it properly, you might get an infection. It's near your brain. You could die. You need to endure this pain to be spared an even greater injury later on."

Graham was only three years old. He couldn't imagine caring what a girl thought about his looks. He didn't understand the biology of infection. He just wanted me, his protector, to protect him, and he felt deeply betrayed because he thought I wasn't.

I *was* protecting him, of course. But this time, I was protecting him from himself. In the long run, he needed the stitches. I had to let him go through the pain.

Now, imagine if another man was on the other side of Graham during the stitching, whispering in his ear, "See, Graham, your dad doesn't really love you; otherwise, he wouldn't make you go through all this pain. If you were my son—if you followed me   I wouldn't make you go through this."

That's an accurate picture of what often happens when we go through difficulties. God knows what is best for us, but our spiritual adversary often tempts us with thoughts that if God *really* loved us, He would spare us the ordeal.

This is shortsighted thinking, and paying attention to that lie can be spiritually crippling. This is where a life of surrender is so crucial—it preserves a heart of worship.

Sometimes, I have to remind myself daily, *God knows best.* And when I accept the fact that God knows best, my life has no room for complaining. William Law makes this clear.

> Resignation to the divine will signifies a cheerful approbation and thankful acceptance of everything that comes from God. It is not enough patiently to submit, but we must thankfully receive and fully approve of everything that by the order of God's providence happens to us...
>
> It is very common for people to allow themselves great liberty in finding fault with such things as have only God for their cause...It sounds indeed much better to murmur at the course of the world or the state of things than to murmur at providence, to complain of the seasons and weather, than to complain of God, but if these have no other cause but God and His providence it is a poor distinction to say that you are only angry at the things but not at the cause and director of them.[1]

I see some doing this theologically when they complain about hell. They think they are particularly enlightened if they say, "I wish there wasn't a hell. *I* certainly wouldn't send anyone there."

But most of what we know about hell comes directly from the mouth of Christ Himself, so this arrogant Christian is actually saying, "God should have tried just a little harder to create a world that didn't require a hell. I could have created a better universe of reality than God, because if I was Creator, everyone would go to heaven, and wouldn't that be nice? Yes, I suppose this does mean I'm more compassionate than God, because I wouldn't do what He does—send people to hell."

What utterly arrogant blasphemy!

We must humbly surrender not only to God's will for our lives but also to the world He has created and the truth He presents in the Scriptures. We may never understand why God does everything He does, but to question Him? To suggest He should have tried just a little bit harder to make things more to our liking? God have mercy on us!

Finding Fault with God

Many of us will struggle to admit we are complaining about God, but honesty is essential if we are to be delivered from this sin. We can't gripe about every decision a coach or a politician makes and then pretend we support him or her. God designed our individual bodies, He designed a world with various climates and seasons, and He created us in His image with a free will that allows us and others to do some horrendously awful things. We must be very careful to check our complaining, for we'll often find that our ultimate complaint is with God.

At a particularly frustrating time in my life, when it felt as if God had kept me in a hole for eight long years, I found myself going through the motions of worship but continually asking, "God, why are You doing this to me?"

The problem with such a statement is that we can't worship someone we don't trust. I couldn't learn my lesson until I was broken enough to surrender, for my questioning came very close to crossing the line from honest pain into prideful blasphemy.

I learned that faith isn't tested by how often God answers my prayers the way I like, but by my willingness to continue serving Him and *thanking* Him even when I don't have a clue as to what He is doing. This required a radical shift in my thinking; I had to become convinced of God's oversight in my life. When I looked back on the difficulty of those eight long years, I saw their necessity in a new light.

> Had you been anything else than what you are, you had, all
> things considered, been less wisely provided for than you are

now; you had wanted some circumstances and conditions
that are best fitted to make you happy yourself and service-
able to the glory of God.

Could you see all that which God sees, all that happy chain
of causes and motives which are to move and invite you to
a right course of life, you would see something to make you
like that state you are in as fitter for you than any other. But as
you cannot see this, so it is here that your Christian faith and
trust in God is to exercise itself and render you as grateful and
thankful for the happiness of your state as if you saw everything that contributes to it with your own eyes.[2]

So I had no more room for complaining. I could finally *rest* in God's
providence rather than fight it.

Today, for the good of your own soul, put to death all complaining.
If even one small detail of your life had been changed, you might have
become a very different person from who you are now (and don't assume
that would be better). If one detail of any major issue were different, a
much more difficult situation could have resulted.

In the next chapter, we'll discover one of the most powerful weapons
to defeat a complaining heart: the discipline of giving thanks.

21

The Birth of Thanksgiving

The classical writers offer a tremendously powerful tool that can transform a complaining heart into one that joyfully worships God and surrenders to His will: thanksgiving.

Not surprisingly, replacing my sin of complaining with the opposing virtue—thanksgiving—was initially a struggle. Fortunately, over time, God in His mercy placed gratitude in my heart, and like a snowball rolling down a hill, that gift of gratitude grew, and the complaining began to fade.

I eventually reached a milestone and was able to thank God even for my eight-year desert. I saw so much of my inner sin, and I saw that the desert was the perfect tool for God to use to heal me. If God had answered my prayers for an earlier reprieve, He wouldn't have been acting out of love; He would have left me in immaturity, as surely as I would have left Graham with an open wound in the hospital if I had forced the doctor to stop stitching him up. I would have continued to make a mess out of my life. Law wrote this about our need to thank God in all circumstances:

> For if [a Christian] cannot thank and praise God as well in calamities and sufferings as in prosperity and happiness, he is as far from the piety of a Christian as he that only loves them that love him is from the charity of a Christian. For to thank God only for such things as you like is no more a proper act of piety than to believe only what you see is an act of faith.
>
> Resignation and thanksgiving to God are only acts of piety

when they are acts of faith, trust, and confidence in the divine goodness.[1]

My only hope of salvation was for God to pull me away from the steering wheel of my life. The difficult period I endured was God's way of doing that, and as I realized the effectiveness of it, I even became *thankful* for it. This is when I learned that thanksgiving is a discipline, and like all the disciplines, it requires practice. Law taught me to begin by practicing thanksgiving in the small things.

> Don't…please yourself with thinking how piously you would act and submit to God in a plague, a famine, or persecution, but be intent upon the perfection of the present day, and be assured that the best way of showing a true zeal is to make little things the occasions of great piety.

> Begin, therefore, in the smallest matters and most ordinary occasions, and accustom your mind to the daily exercise of this pious temper in the lowest occurrences of life. And when a contempt, an affront, a little injury, loss, or disappointment, or the smallest events of every day continually raise your mind to God in proper acts of resignation, then you may justly hope that you shall be numbered amongst those that are resigned and thankful to God in the greatest trials and afflictions.[2]

That traffic light you had to stop for? Such tiny inconveniences can become points of spiritual discipline if we embrace them as such. Sitting at the red light, we can regather ourselves, confront our hurried spirits, and seek God's peace.

Prayers of thanksgiving can be mixed with prayers of surrender for even greater effect. Thomas à Kempis provided us with this model:

> My son, say thou thus in everything: "Lord, if this be pleasing unto thee, let it be so. Lord, if it be to thy honor, in thy name let this be done. Lord, if thou seest it good, and allowest it to be profitable for me, then grant unto me that I may use this to thine honor. But if thou knowest it will be harmful unto me, and no profit to the health of my soul, take away any such desire from me."[3]

God Defines What's Good

If our hearts are going to truly surrender to God, we must allow God to define good and evil and shape us according to His will. We must not only be willing to do what is right but also let God define what is right. Whatever God desires is good; whatever God prohibits is evil.

At first, conforming to God's will may simply be an act of the will. We may obey God not necessarily because we want to, but because we know we should. However, if we are faithful to surrender our will to God, we will soon want to obey and eventually be thankful for what God wills. Law wrote, "When you love that which God loves, you act with Him, you join yourself to Him, and when you love what He dislikes, then you oppose Him and separate yourself from Him."[4]

This is why willful rebellion against God is so spiritually debilitating. Obedience and disobedience are both habitual. Our appetites and passions are like our taste buds—we crave what we grow used to. To experience true surrender, we must die to our own desires so God can give us new desires. Thankfulness thus *feeds* the attitude of surrender just as surely as complaining *attacks* it.

When God birthed thanksgiving in my heart, my purest cry was simply, "God, I want to be on Your side." My only request was to be wherever God was. If God was in riches or poverty, sickness or health, at home or far away, I wanted to be there. Whatever God was doing, that's what I wanted to be doing. Nothing else mattered.

The Joy and Peace of Surrender

Just as complaining leads to bitterness, resentment, and a smoldering anger, so thanksgiving leads to tremendous joy and peace. Fénelon wrote, "O bridegroom of souls, thou lettest the souls which do not resist thee experience in this life an advance taste of felicity."[5]

The glory of the Christian life is found in the fact that God doesn't ask us to surrender only to difficult things. At first, that may seem to be the case, but eventually, if we don't hold back, we'll find that God wants us to surrender to many very wonderful things. This too depends on our trusting in His goodness. When we surrender to a good God, we shouldn't be surprised that we must surrender to good things. Sin tastes sweet but turns bitter in our stomachs. Holiness often tastes bitter initially but later turns sweet, like fine wine, which seasons over time.

One of the joys of surrender is a deep peace. Rebellion means war, so surrender logically brings peace. This peace gives us a new freedom in our relationships. As always, true Christian spirituality has implications for community living in families and churches. Thomas à Kempis warned that if we are not surrendered to God, we will also be at war with others.

> He that is well in peace, is not suspicious of any man. But he that is discontented and troubled, is tossed with divers suspicions: he is neither at rest himself nor suffereth others to be at rest…He considereth what others are bound to do, and neglecteth that which is bound to himself.[6]

I suspect that a thousand years from now we'll all have a pretty good understanding of why our lives have gone the way they have. But for now, we must be content in trusting that God knows what He is doing. Our model in this is Christ. À Kempis imagined Him saying this:

> Of My own will did I offer up Myself unto God the Father for thy sins, My hands being stretched forth on the cross, and My body laid bare, so that nothing remained in Me that was not wholly turned into a sacrifice for the appeasing of the divine Majesty. In like manner oughtest thou also to offer thyself willingly unto Me every day…with all thy strength and affections, and to the utmost stretch of thine inward faculties. What do I require of thee more, than that thou study to resign thyself entirely unto Me?[7]

God will not lay down His arms. He has declared war on all who stand in rebellion. The vanquished receive eternal life; the obstinate are condemned by their own foolishness. But there will be no peace until we surrender. Surrender to God is the essence—and the greatest blessing—of the Christian life.

A Prayer of Surrender

If you would seek to grow in the grace of surrender, try copying this prayer, written by Francis de Sales, and begin praying it on a regular basis until it shapes your heart.

> Turning myself towards my most gracious and merciful God, I desire, purpose, and am irrevocably resolved to serve and

love him now and forever; and to this end, I give and conse-
crate to him my soul with all its powers, my heart with all its
affections, and my body with all its sense, protesting that I will
never more abuse any part of my being against his divine will
and sovereign majesty, to whom I offer up and sacrifice myself
in spirit, to be forever his loyal, obedient, and faithful creature,
without ever revoking or repenting of this my act and deed.

But if, alas! I should chance, through the suggestion of the
enemy, or through human frailty, to transgress in any point,
or fail in adhering to this my resolution and dedication, I protest from this moment and am determined, with the assistance of the Holy Ghost, to rise as soon as I shall perceive my
fall, and return again to the divine mercy, without any delay
whatsoever. This is my inviolable and irrevocable will, intention, and resolution, which I declare and confirm without reservation or exception, in the sacred presence of God.[8]

If you can, in good conscience, sign the paper on which you've cop-
ied this prayer, claiming it as the prayer of your heart, do so and mark the
date. Then carry this prayer with you. When God's Spirit prompts your
heart to surrender and you feel yourself resisting, take the prayer out of
your purse or wallet and read it, reminding yourself of the pledge you have
made by the grace of God.

PART 4

A Quiet *and* Humble Life

Cultivating the Quiet: Simplicity

G od," I prayed as a ten-year-old, "I'm staying in here until I see You. You showed yourself to Moses; You can show Yourself to me."

Silence. The linoleum floor pushed back against my knees. I started to get hungry.

"Okay," I said out loud. "I'm going to close my eyes. When I open them again, I want You to show Yourself to me. *Please.*"

I closed my eyes and bristled with anticipation. When I opened my eyes, I saw a sink and a bathtub but no God incarnate.

Suddenly, there was a loud knock on the door.

"What's this?" I asked myself. My heart leapt.

"Gary," my mother's familiar voice rang out, bringing my heart back to normal, "are you okay? You've been in there a long time."

"Sheesh," I said to myself, "it's not easy being Moses when you have parents."

God never did show up in bodily form, much to my preadolescent dismay. At the time, giving God 30 minutes to do so seemed to me to be quite generous on my part, but years later, I read through the book of Exodus and changed my mind.

In chapter 24, we're told that Moses went up on a mountain to meet God, and a cloud immediately covered the mount. "For six days the cloud covered the mountain, and on the seventh day the LORD called to Moses" (verse 16).

Moses sat and waited on that mountain for six days before God started to speak to him. Six days! When I sit down to pray with God and wait for six *minutes*, I get proud of myself. All too often, I'm thinking, "All right, God, let's get going. I'm a busy man. I have things to do."

Moses was willing to sit silently for six days!

And what about the people of Israel? "When the people saw that Moses was so long in coming down from the mountain, they gathered around Aaron and said, 'Come, make us gods who will go before us'" (32:1).

Sadly, the Israelites were swept into idolatry by mere *boredom*. They were bored! And that was enough to turn them to false gods. They simply got tired of waiting.

The same is true for many of us today. Ask us to give money, and we'll write a check. Ask us to show up for a demonstration or special church service, and we're there. Ask us to give up something, and we'll sacrifice. But ask us to face boredom, and we turn on the TV, tune in the radio, log on to the Internet, or plug in our iPods.

Please, don't ask us to be bored.

This aversion makes us a culture ripe for idolatry.

To the devotional masters, a loud, overcrowded and hurried life was a secular life. These classic Christian writers urge us to give God room, time, and quiet. But we moderns and postmoderns have developed ingenuous ways to keep God at arm's length. One of the most insidious is our spiritual game of hide-and-seek.

Our Game of Hide-and-Seek

Few of us Christians fall into the sin of shaking our fists at God and defying Him to His face. That is more common among unbelievers. Our sin is that we passively rebel against God, filling our lives with so much noise and busyness that God's voice cannot (or will not) penetrate.

When my children were young and playing outside, I could whisper, "Ice cream," and they would hear me from across the field. On the other hand, if they were two feet away from me and I screamed out, "Dinner!" their hearing suddenly became amazingly poor.

They knew better than to shake their fists at me and say, "Forget you, Dad, we're playing." (They had tasted the fruit of such behavior and found it wanting.) So instead, they adopted a stealthier approach. "Oh, were you calling us, Dad? Sorry, we didn't hear you."

This isn't blatant rebellion, but it's rebellion all the same, and it serves the same purpose. Their busyness kept them from following their father's voice to a new place. The same thing happens with us, as Fénelon explains:

God does not cease speaking, but the noise of the creatures without, and of our passions within, deafens us, and stops our hearing. We must silence every creature, we must silence ourselves, to hear in the deep hush of the whole soul, the ineffable voice of the spouse. We must bend the ear, because it is a gentle and delicate voice, only heard by those who no longer hear anything else.[1]

Cultivating the quiet is a painful experience when we are addicted to noise, excitement, and occupation. Opening the door to spiritual quiet can also open the door to spiritual fear and loneliness. Facing God requires a great amount of courage.

According to Pascal, we're often afraid that if we start to slow down, the truth of our deeply felt misery will assail us. We lack the courage to confront this misery, so we live at breakneck speed with maximum noise, too numb or too busy to notice the pain.

Pascal believed that many young people live a fundamentally dishonest existence, pretending they are having a good time while they are actually in constant terror of the truth of their hearts.

[Their] lives are all noise, diversions, and thoughts for the future. But take away their diversion and you will see them bored to extinction. Then they feel their nullity without recognizing it, for nothing could be more wretched than to be intolerably depressed as soon as one is reduced to introspection with no means of diversion.[2]

Augustine wrote that adults frequently criticize this youthful addiction to diversions but are often guilty of the same thing. He confesses being the target of such criticism: "[My] sole delight was play; and for this [I was] punished by those who yet themselves were doing the like. But elder folks' idleness is called 'business'; that of boys, being really the same, is punished by those elders."[3]

Pascal agreed with Augustine, writing that even a king without diversion is a very wretched man.[4] Young or old, rich or poor, powerful or weak, influential or anonymous…the thing we fear most is quiet. Yet inner peace is conceived in the quiet. Without this quiet, we grow restless. Our lust for diversion proves our unhappiness, for if we were truly happy, Pascal noted, "we should not need to divert ourselves from thinking about it."[5]

Our chaos of the soul and busyness of the spirit robs us of our God-given destiny to find fulfillment in a relationship with Him. A voice deep within our souls tells us something is wrong, but we are too afraid to slow down and find out how life could be different. Pascal described people struggling with this dilemma.

> They have a secret instinct driving them to seek external diversion and occupation, and this is the result of their constant sense of wretchedness. They have another secret instinct, left over from the greatness of our original nature, telling them that the only true happiness lies in rest and not in excitement. These two contrary instincts give rise to a confused plan buried out of sight in the depths of their soul, which leads them to seek rest by way of activity and always to imagine that the satisfaction they miss will come to them once they overcome certain obvious difficulties and cap open the door to welcome rest. All our life passes in this way: we seek rest by struggling against certain obstacles, and once they are overcome, rest proves intolerable because of the boredom it produces. We must get away from it and crave excitement.[6]

Pascal said the boredom that drives us to diversion could be the catalyst that calls us to change—if only we were not afraid to face it head-on. But Satan offers us his narcotics as alternatives, and they bring us "imperceptibly to our death." Much of our television watching and Internet dabbling is a quiet, sleepless death in which we kill our souls by letting time race by. We can spend several hours in front of the television or computer screens, and what have we gained? We haven't actually talked to anyone, we haven't accomplished anything, and we usually haven't gained any insight or inspiration. Yet time has slipped by, and it will never return again. In essence, we have willingly forfeited a precious slice of the time God has given us on this earth.

The difficulty of simplicity is that it will sometimes (especially in the early stages as we break our addiction to diversion) lead us into soul boredom, gloom, maybe even a mild sense of depression. These are facts of the spiritual life that we must confront. I would be less than honest if I suggested that one day our lives are filled with diversions and the next day we walk hand-in-hand with God in glorious rapture. A drug addict cannot expect to give up drugs without paying the price of withdrawal. We who have been drugged by diversions cannot expect to enter the quiet without a struggle. Our souls will roar for diversion, the fix that saves us from God's presence.

Confronting these demons of boredom and fear requires great courage. They merely show their faces, and we dutifully lapse into unceasing activity to escape them. But we *must* confront them. If we allow fear and boredom to push us back into these diversions, we will never know the blessing of simplicity.

In the midst of all this noise, God calls us into the quiet (Isaiah 30:15) to draw us into a deeper communion with Him. If we are to quit hiding from God, however, we need to know the reasons why we hide.

The Reasons We Hide from God

As we draw closer to God, the supernatural agitation in our hearts reminds us that we are dealing with Aslan, the fierce and regal lion who, as Lucy found out in C.S. Lewis's *Chronicles of Narnia: The Lion, the Witch and the Wardrobe*, is anything but a tame lion. We cannot control God, and what we can't control, we often fear and therefore avoid.

Yes, entering the quiet and letting go of all distractions will require great courage for several reasons. First, we are spiritually fearful people, and alone before God, we stand naked and vulnerable. We won't be able to pretend anymore. Before God, we will have the choice to obey or to disobey, but pretending and rationalizing will no longer be options. If we are miserable, we will have to face our misery. If we are sad, we will have to face our sadness. When we dwell in God's presence, we must dwell in truth. We cannot control the outcome or even the conversation.

Second, we may hide because we fear the test of faith. We suspect that when we get down on our knees, instead of being met by an overwhelming sense of God's presence, we'll face a seemingly eternal void, a loud nothingness that chills our faith and tempts us to doubt. We don't want our faith to be proven false, so we never prove it at all.

Third, we may be unconvinced that God is able to satisfy the hunger in our souls, so we never give Him the chance. We might believe in the gospel intellectually but be unwilling to bet our emotional fulfillment on it.

And finally, we may hide from God because we are living in disobedience. Like Jonah, we may be running from a duty we know God wants us
to carry out. Or like Adam and Eve, we may be hiding because we've committed a sin and fear God's presence. We'd be happy to follow God as long
as He allowed us to nurse that grudge, hold on to that inappropriate relationship, or continue in that questionable business practice.

Confronting these tests calls for courage—sometimes more courage
than we possess. So rather than face them, we pretend they're not tests at
all, and we simply avoid God by staying busy. Just as someone who is aller-
gic to cats recognizes the early symptoms of a reaction and makes haste
to get away, so we often unknowingly begin to recognize the sensation of
God breaking into our hearts, and we rush into some activity or diversion
to avoid His presence.

If we would live and love the way that Christians throughout history
have, we must learn to value what they valued, beginning with silence. Listen to Scupoli: "Silence, beloved, is a safe stronghold in the spiritual battle, and a sure pledge of victory. Silence is the friend of him who distrusts
self and trusts in God; it is the guardian of the spirit of prayer and a wonderful help in the attainment of virtues."[7]

In a loud and busy world, will we allow Scupoli and others to lead us
forward on this silent path? This is such a blessed journey, we'll spend one
more chapter exploring its riches.

23

Entering the Quiet

P reparing for a cross-country move, we called a moving company and learned that they charged by the pound. We felt as if paying that money would be like buying back our own possessions. We opted instead to sift through all our stuff, deciding whether each item was worth the cost of moving it. Unless we really liked something, it was gone.

When we told our friends about this, we were consistently met with a yearning sigh that said, "That sounds so wonderful...I wish we could get rid of everything and start over."

This outward expression of simplicity and freedom is a picture of inner simplicity. Inner simplicity sets our souls free in a refreshing and liberating way. Christians throughout history have highlighted four themes that are particularly helpful for Christians who want to live in the quiet. They are the disciplines of a captivated heart, a bridled tongue, a limited curiosity, and a slow reentry into daily life after a time of prayer.

A Captivated Heart

Just as we have a limit to our physical strength, so we have a limit to our emotional and spiritual strength. John of the Cross said, "The more people rejoice over something outside God, the less intense will be their joy in God; and the more their hope goes out toward something else, the less there is for God."[1]

A basketball player who showed up for a game exhausted because he just ran a marathon would get a justified and stern rebuke from his coach.

A woman who showed up at work exhausted because she had been watching television all night wouldn't have an acceptable excuse for her boss. Coaches and bosses expect us to conserve our energy for what really matters. God expects no less.

A defining moment in my spiritual life occurred when I realized that if I was consumed by every major sporting event, every political race, every move of the stock market, every parenting concern...if I let these things seize my heart, I simply could not enter into a true celebration of the Sabbath, a baptism, the Lord's Supper, Christmas, Easter, or any other significant celebration. I have learned the necessity of guarding my heart (Proverbs 4:23) because my heart does not have an infinite capacity to rejoice or be alarmed. When we become preoccupied with passing things, we exhaust our hearts' ability to care about the things that really do matter. We become like the young Augustine, who said, "Thus with the baggage of this present world was I held down pleasantly, as in sleep." [2]

The deeper Christian life consists of finding ways to bring the remembrance of God into our daily existence. Fénelon urged this upon his readers:

> Let us become accustomed to recollect ourselves, during the day and in the course of our duties, by a single look toward God. Let us thus quiet all the movement of our hearts, as soon as we see them agitated. Let us separate ourselves from all pleasure which does not come from God. Let us cut off futile thoughts and dreams. Let us not speak empty words. Let us seek God...and we shall find him without fail. [3]

This focus on God is absolutely essential to keep simplicity from becoming a prison, as Fénelon explains:

> A continual effort to push away the thoughts, which occupy us with ourselves and our own interests, would be in itself a continual occupation with ourselves, which would distract us from the presence of God and the tasks which He wants us to accomplish. The important thing is sincerely to have surrendered into the hands of God all our interests in pleasure, convenience and reputation. [4]

We want to have simple and quiet hearts because we want to hear from

God. If we want to be captivated by Him, we must be willing to give up everything else in order to truly *know* and walk with Him. Some of what we give up may be given back, but we will accept back only those elements that allow our God-focus to remain.

A Bridled Tongue

One of the most practical ways to enter into the quiet is to *be* quiet. A constantly moving tongue is proof of an overly busy mind. Ignatius wrote, "Idle words are not to be spoken, by which I mean whatever does not profit me or anyone else, or whatever is not ordained to the end."[5] John Climacus saw talkativeness as the great enemy of spiritual depth and maturity.

> Talkativeness is the throne of vainglory on which it loves to preen itself and show off. Talkativeness is a sign of ignorance, a doorway to slander, a leader of jesting, a servant of lies, the ruin of compunction, a summoner of despondency, a messenger of sleep, a dissipation of recollection, the end of vigilance, the cooling of zeal, the darkening of prayer. Intelligent silence is the mother of prayer, freedom from bondage, custodian of zeal, a guard on our thoughts.[6]

Climacus urged monks, "Once outside your cell, watch your tongue, for the fruits of many labors can be scattered in a moment." When we are burning with the desire to speak, we should pause and check the source of that fire. "A man should know that a devil's sickness is on him if he is seized by the urge in conversation to assert his opinion, however correct it may be."[7]

Oddly, those who talk the most often pray the least, frequently giving the excuse that they simply have no time. To these persons, Thomas à Kempis counseled, "If thou wilt withdraw thyself from speaking vainly, and from gadding idly, as also from listening to novelties and rumors, thou shalt find leisure enough...for meditation on good things."[8]

The mark of a spiritual man or woman is a listening heart, not a lecturing tongue.[9] A simple Christian wants to hear from God and has little enjoyment hearing his or her own voice.

Simplicity also qualifies our listening, of course. Thomas à Kempis urges, "Withdraw thyself...from listening to novelties and rumors," which calls us to the next act of simplicity, a limited curiosity.

A Limited Curiosity

Simplicity frees us from being tabloid Christians. Whenever we smell a scandal, local or national, we usually want all the messy details. In this we're spiritual Peeping Toms. We may try to cover our curiosity with prayerful concern or feigned love, but often we just want to satisfy our own spiritual lusts.

Early Christian writers were almost shockingly strict in this regard. Scupoli writes, "You must become as one dead to all earthly things that do not concern you, even though they may be harmless in themselves."[10]

I recently conversed on the phone with a man who started explaining his personal disagreement with another Christian leader. "Do I really need to hear this?" I asked. "I don't think I do."

This isn't easy for me to say because it can sound so sanctimonious, but in such instances, we must fear God more than we fear our friends' judgment. The Christian classics remind us that receiving gossip is as sinful as giving it.

Brother Giles, a famous early Franciscan friar, had a sanctity that drew people from all around, including people who wanted to pass on "prayer requests," hoping that Brother Giles might do something about them. His response was curt: "I do not want to know about another's sin."

Quite simply, if someone is not accountable to us, we don't need to know the details. Our responsibility is not to pronounce judgment on everything and everyone, but to keep ourselves at peace. Besides, I've found that I have so much to work on myself that I really don't have the time to listen to the faults of others. Thomas à Kempis believed God would have him feel the same way.

> In every matter attend to thyself, what thou doest, and what thou sayest; and direct thy whole attention unto this, that thou mayest please me alone, and neither desire nor seek anything beside me. But as for the words or deeds of others judge nothing rashly; neither do thou entangle thyself with things not committed unto thee; and doing thus thou mayest be little or seldom disturbed.[11]

When we dive unnecessarily and uninvited into the lives of others, we lose our own inner grounding. "Stay away from what does not concern you," Climacus urged, "for curiosity can defile stillness as nothing else can."[12]

The day before a marathon, I feel full of energy. But just 24 hours later, after the marathon is over, I am barely able to walk a step. I've overused my muscles and am virtually incapacitated, whereas just 24 hours prior, I felt like I had all the energy in the world.

Living a busy life is like running a marathon—we tax our ability to care, our ability to focus, our strength to manage disappointment, our sense of peace and rest. Consequently, we live on the edge of exhaustion, irritation, and anger. We have to regather ourselves, guard our peace, and focus so we will be free to care about the things that really matter and fully give ourselves to the tasks God calls us to address.

During the Vietnam War, the infantry often formed groups of circles that prevented each group of soldiers from being overrun, flanked, or ambushed by the enemy. Each soldier's job was to protect his portion of the circle; if everyone focused on his specific task, everyone was protected. If someone wandered off, the circle would be broken, and disaster would erupt.

In the same way, as Christian soldiers we each have a specific place in the circle to tend. God might call you into politics (as an office holder or advocate), business (as an owner or employee), education, the arts…any number of possibilities. The key is for us to recognize the boundaries of our circles and cut off undue curiosity outside of them. This doesn't mean we work *less*; it simply means we concentrate our effort where God directs us, and we trust Him, as our general, to fill in any gaps that open up.

We don't have enough money to respond to every financial appeal that crosses our desks or every desire that crosses our hearts. Our minds are more valuable than our bank accounts and every bit as finite, so let's conserve our thoughts no less than our dollars. Let's refuse to allow some news editor in New York to dictate our topics of conversation on a day-to-day basis. Instead, let's earnestly seek to hear what God is teaching His people. Let's surrender our thoughts to be governed by eternal principles, not the latest opinion poll that nobody will care about six months from now.

Thomas à Kempis still blesses me with these words:

> My son, in many things it is thy duty to be ignorant, and to esteem thyself as dead upon earth, and as one to whom the whole world is crucified. It is thy duty also to pass by many things with a deaf ear, and rather to think of those which

belong unto thy peace. It is more useful to turn away one's eyes from unpleasant things, and to leave everyone to his own opinion, than to be a slave to contentious discourses.[13]

A captivated heart, a bridled tongue, a limited curiosity, and a slow reentry after prayer are necessary disciplines of simplicity.

A Slow Reentry After Prayer

The goal of simplicity is communion with God, which Thomas à Kempis referred to as "spiritual contemplation." Since spiritual contemplation is largely a lost art in today's busy culture, we need to be reminded that spiritual truths, when first birthed, are fragile. A busy mind will choke them out as surely as weeds choke flowers. Francis de Sales prescribed quiet as a preventative measure.

> After prayer, be careful not to agitate your heart, lest you spill the precious balm it has received. My meaning is, that you must, for some time, if possible, remain in silence, and gently remove your heart from prayer to your other employments; retaining, as long as you can, a feeling of the affections which you have conceived.[14]

We have talked a great deal about the tyranny of the television set, but we also need to mention the tyranny of the telephone or text messages. When I am talking to God, why should I let a $200 machine break my thoughts? Who has more to reveal to me than the Creator of the universe? Rarely are calls or texts so urgent that they can't be put off for 30 minutes or so, but our inner spirit acts as if ignoring a diversion for a while is a felony.

When we charge from prayer into the blare of diversion, we crush the small blossom God has given us for the day. The precious truths, entrusted to us by God Himself, are carelessly discarded and soon resemble dirty roses lying crushed in the middle of the street.

Rise slowly, with reverence, and keep your eye trained on God's face. This is where I find a spiritual journal so helpful. Profound insights can have a shorter shelf life than milk if I don't write them down, a practice that further implants them in my mind. These thoughts are some of my most precious possessions, entrusted to me by God, and I will be held accountable for them.

We must occasionally focus on external cares and perhaps even be consumed with them. But we don't have to remain diverted. When necessary interruptions break in, we should strive to return as quickly as we can. God is always with us, waiting for us to practice His presence. De Sales offered this encouragement:

> Remember…to retire occasionally into the solitude of your heart while you are outwardly engaged in business or conversation…Withdraw, then, your thoughts, from time to time, into your heart, where, separated from all men, you may familiarly treat with God on the affairs of your soul.[15]

Some of my best times of prayer occur in large crowds or at festive social gatherings. I like to slip out of the party, find a quiet and solitary place outside, and check in with God. It's as if the noise and the chatter make me hunger to hear God's voice. Like a husband or wife who reaches out for the spouse's hand to reconnect, so I reach out to touch God's hand to be reminded that I'm not alone, that someone is experiencing the night with me.

Simplicity, then, is both silence in solitude and detachment in diversion. It ties life together. Simplicity brings eternity into our time and helps us use time for eternity. It gives us strength to do what we must do as citizens of earth but liberates us to live as citizens of heaven.

Quiet's Reward

Of all the spiritual insights I have gained from reading the classics of the Christian faith, the teaching of simplicity is one of the most precious because of its power to usher me into God's presence. The spiritual life is impossible in a heart full of noise and occupation.

Simplicity has its own rewards, but at best, it is a means to an end. It is a filter, not an idol. We seek simplicity because God is so great, we want to strip away the clutter that keeps us from Him. We want absolutely nothing to stand between us and God because when we are faced with such beauty, we would be fools to settle for anything less. De Sales exhorted himself, "Since, O my soul! thou art capable of God, woe be to thee if thou content thyself with anything less than God."[16]

If simplicity is the true prayer of your heart, copy this prayer by Thomas à Kempis on a piece of paper:

O Lord, it is the work of a perfect man, never to relax his mind from attentive thought of heavenly things, and so to pass amid many cares, as it were, without care…I beseech thee, my most gracious God, preserve me from the cares of this life, lest I should be too much entangled by them; also from the many necessities of the body, lest I should be captivated by pleasure; and from whatever is an obstacle to the soul.[17]

Begin each day with this prayer until it becomes your unconscious yearning. Whenever your heart grows distracted, pull out this prayer and read it again. Practice using this prayer to turn your heart toward God, and let God lead you into the joy of simplicity.

The High and the Low:
A Double-Sided Truth

Augustine was a talented, ambitious, and gifted young man. But after his conversion to Christianity and the death of his mother, he felt ready to retire. He moved to his birthplace, Tagaste, seeking a life of contemplation and reflection. Such a personality isn't easily missed, however, and Augustine's quiet life was broken shortly thereafter when, during a visit to Hippo (in modern-day Algeria), he was ordained a priest. Just five years later he was consecrated bishop of Hippo. He came to wear authority like a perfectly tailored coat.

Such a meteoric rise up the fourth-century ecclesiastical ladder doesn't happen by accident, and Augustine's career verified his calling and the speed of its recognition. His writings have left a permanent imprint on the life of the church. You'd be hard-pressed to find a Christian classic that *doesn't* quote Augustine.

Augustine could have allowed the church to remember him only as a powerful saint, bishop, and church father. The unflattering details of his early life were quickly forgotten as his career and influence swelled to great heights. If Augustine had remained silent about his past, he could have been remembered as a figure without spot or blemish, leaving only his influence and theological system to be passed down for future generations.

But Augustine became concerned about the growing gulf between his reputation and the truth of his beginnings. The crowds saw his powerful personality, his expert training in rhetoric and philosophy, and his leadership. Augustine, however, could still remember a young, willful, and proud man caught in idleness and immorality, a heretic with an ambitious thirst for fame, and then, finally, a mother's earnest and lifelong prayers answered in the conversion of her son.

This human side could have been lost, but Augustine decided to write his confessions and tell the whole story. Ironically, it was this move of humility that helped further launch his fame and establish his place in history. *The Confessions of Saint Augustine* remains one of the most widely read Christian books of all time.

Augustine realized what all the saints have understood: Humility and honesty are essential ingredients of an authentic and mature Christian life. Augustine wanted people to see God's greatness, and he realized this is often best revealed through human weakness. To suppress his whole story would have been to rob God of the glory due Him for the remarkable work of transformation He accomplished in Augustine's life.

The Twin Pillars of Humility:
Our Lowliness and God's Greatness

According to the great Reformed theologian John Owen, the twin pillars of a truly Christian spirituality are rooted in humility: "Two things are needed to humble us. First, let us consider God in His greatness, glory, holiness, power, majesty, and authority. Then, let us consider ourselves in our mean, abject, and sinful condition."[1] The spiritual writers speak with virtual unanimity on the need to be shaken in the depths of our being by God's grandeur and our poverty. These twin pillars can be combined into one word: *humility.*

Fénelon wrote, "All the saints are convinced that sincere humility is the foundation of all virtues. This is because humility is the daughter of pure charity, and humility is nothing else but truth. There are only two truths in the world, that God is all, and the creature is nothing."[2]

Thomas à Kempis believed humility is the common element of the most mature Christians. "The greatest saints before God are the least in their own judgments; and the more glorious they are, so much the humbler within themselves."[3] He was joined in this belief by Teresa of Avila, who saw humility as the foundation of our entire spirituality, without which we cannot grow.

> This whole building...has humility as its foundation. If humility is not genuinely present, for your own sake the Lord will

not construct a high building lest that building fall to the ground. Thus...that you might build on good foundations, strive to be the least and the slaves of all, looking at how or where you can please and serve them. What you do in this matter you do more for yourself than for them and lay stones so firmly that the castle will not fall.[4]

It is possible for ambitious young men and women to try to use Christianity just as they might use athletics, the arts, or politics—to make a name for themselves—but in this instance they want to be known as extraordinary Christians. They may thus go to great lengths to "improve" their faith, but their pursuit is odious if it is rooted in pride.

John Climacus, who lived in the high-striving monastic world among many who sought to be renowned Christians, realized that humility, not sacrifice, is at the heart of a true faith. "And there are men who wear out their bodies to no purpose in the pursuit of total dispassion, heavenly treasures, miracle working, and prophetic ability, and the poor fools do not realize that humility, not hard work, is the mother of such things."[5]

Even William Law, who, like Climacus, is known for his strict discipline, writes, "[Humility] is so essential to the right state of our souls that there is no pretending to a reasonable or pious life without it. We may as well think to see without eyes or live without breath as to live in the spirit of religion without the spirit of humility."[6]

Scripture breathes humility throughout, reminding us on three separate occasions that God opposes the proud but gives grace to the humble. And consider Romans 12:3, where Paul urges us, "Do not think of yourself more highly than you ought, but rather think of yourself with sober judgment." Verse 16 has *two* admonitions: "Do not be proud...Do not be conceited." One chapter, three calls to grow in humility!

Here's what makes humility the most powerful of virtues: True, God-breathed humility makes sin impossible. If I am humble, I can't sin sexually against another person, because the thought of abusing someone for my own pleasure would be abhorrent. I couldn't steal from them, because I would rather be wronged or even go hungry than take what rightfully belongs to someone else. I couldn't use gossip as a way to be accepted in the crowd, because I would be more concerned about someone else's reputation than my own. I couldn't be materialistic, because I would be moved by compassion for others more than I would by my own perceived wants and needs.

Humility undercuts virtually every temptation. To grow in humility is to pull up sin by its roots.

Humility is gloriously present in the person of Christ, exalted in the teaching of Scripture, and cherished in the witness of the saints, so let's take a closer look at the foundation of humility and its place in the Christian life.

Christian, Know Yourself!

S piritual sickness sets in when we fail to recognize that the source of many of our problems is our pride. We thus try to treat the symptoms rather than the disease, but that's like using moisturizer to treat leprosy.

Proud women and men relate everything back to themselves. They are all but incapable of seeing any situation except for how it affects them. Empathy is something they may read about but will never truly experience. Scupoli says that "we may gather from their lives and conversation" a clear picture of arrogance.

> For in everything, whether great or small, they seek their own advantage and like to be preferred before others. They are self-willed and opinionated, blind to their own faults, sharp-sighted when it comes to the faults of others, and they severely condemn the sayings and doings of others.[1]

The thing to notice here is how painfully unaware pride makes us. Pride hides itself *behind* itself! It not only makes us spiritually sick but also blinds us to the fact that we are growing even sicker. It's an ingenious, diabolical vice that is as hidden to the proud as it is obvious to the spiritually well.

Thus Scupoli and others urge us toward self-knowledge—not as a form of self-love, but as a protection against this stealthy, soul-emptying vice.

Know Yourself

Some of us hide our true selves behind a glittering image (we'll talk about "spiritual cosmetology" in a moment), but others of us simply don't know who we really are, as Climacus pointed out: "It happens...that most of the proud never really discover their true selves. They think they have conquered their passions and they find out how poor they really are only after they die."[2]

Thomas à Kempis believed that an accurate self-knowledge always leads to humility. "Whoso knoweth himself well, is lowly in his own sight and delighteth not in the praises of men."[3] It follows that if we *aren't* lowly in our own sight and *are* dependent on the praise of others, we don't know ourselves very well.

Teresa of Avila drew this out. Like Thomas à Kempis, Teresa equated accurate knowledge with humility. "Knowing ourselves is something so important that I wouldn't want any relaxation ever in this regard...While we are on this earth nothing is more important to us than humility."[4]

This points to a danger hidden in our desire for spiritual growth. We can become so enamored by the people we want to become that we lose touch with the people we now are. This trap held me back for several years. I once feared sin so much that I focused almost exclusively on not sinning. Of course, sin is a very disturbing thing, and you might well ask what could be wrong with fearing it. The answer is that my fear was so separated from God's grace that I was afraid to take an honest look into my own heart. I thus lost touch with my weaknesses, and the result was pride. I lived in an illusory and self-deceiving imitation of holiness that was based on discipline and works. All the while, my heart was full of evil attitudes and judgments. God used a period of dryness to reveal the true state of my heart. You can imagine how I was struck by these words of John of the Cross:

> In the dryness and emptiness of this night of the appetite, a person also procures spiritual humility, that virtue opposed to the first capital vice, spiritual pride. Through this humility acquired by means of self-knowledge, individuals are purged of all those imperfections of the vice of pride into which they fell in the time of their prosperity. Aware of their own dryness and wretchedness, the thought of their being more advanced than others does not even occur in its first movements, as it did before; on the contrary, they realize that others are better.

From this humility stems love of neighbor, for they will esteem them and not judge them as they did before when they were aware that they enjoyed an intense fervor while others did not. These persons will know only their own misery and keep it so much in sight that they will have no opportunity to watch anyone else's conduct.[5]

Notice that John of the Cross said that humility is "acquired by means of self-knowledge." This is why the anonymous author of *The Cloud of Unknowing* urged us, "Labor and sweat, therefore, in every way that you can, seeking to obtain for yourself a true knowledge and feeling of yourself as you are." This is *not* a search for a secular and autonomous self-understanding. Rather, it is based in the awareness that "lack of knowledge," as the author puts it, "is the cause of a great deal of pride."[6]

Growing in Self-Awareness

So how do we get there? If knowing ourselves is so important, what path do we take to arrive at that understanding? Let's consider five helpful measures we can employ.

Value Humility More than Reputation

The beginning point is to value humility more than our reputation. Another way to put this is that we must value *authenticity* over *appearance*. If we want to become like Christ more than anything else, we will welcome insights about our shortcomings. If we supremely value our reputation—that is, if we are motivated by pride—we will resent any implication that we are weak or any revelation that shows our failings. We would rather *appear* righteous than truly *become* righteous. Such an attitude kills any future growth.

Self-awareness begins by valuing humility the way God does. As we become self-aware, we will accept, as Paul did, that we are the chief of sinners and that therefore we must be on guard against the way sin affects so much of what we do, think, and say. To be ignorant of our sinful tendencies is to give sin freedom to work its destruction under cover of darkness. I love the way Scupoli puts it: "Distrust of yourself is so necessary in the spiritual combat that, without it, you may be assured that you will neither gain the desired victory, nor be able to overcome even the weakest of your passions."[7]

We should *assume* that pride is operating in all our actions, our words, our emotions, our motivation, and even often in our prayers. *Not* to distrust myself is to cast aspersion on Scripture, which says that the heart is deceitful above all things, and to grant pride the chance to advance in stealth.

On the positive side, this is thrillingly freeing! Instead of fearing that I'll be found out, I am eager to be called out so I can grow. Humility leads us to a place of restful reliance on God, in whose authority alone we live and minister. Rather than consistently (and arrogantly) promising God that we'll never, ever fall again, we can adopt the prayerful approach of Jeanne Guyon:

> As you come to Him, come as a weak child, one who is all soiled and badly bruised—a child that has been hurt from falling again and again. Come to the Lord as one who has no strength of his own; come to Him as one who has no power to cleanse himself. Humbly lay your pitiful condition before your Father's gaze.[8]

Compare Yourself to Christ

Many of us Christians compare ourselves to unbelievers, younger believers, or less mature believers. "Compared to them," we think (but would never say out loud, lest we sound arrogant), "I'm pretty holy. Sure, I could grow in some areas, but at least I'm not like that."

We need the perspective of James, the apostle who grew up as Christ's brother. Of course, Jesus and James didn't share the same earthly father because Jesus was conceived miraculously, but they did share the same mother and the same childhood home. And from this perspective—having lived with a brother who was perfect in every way and having witnessed every day His attitude, His actions, His tone, and His eagerness to take advantage of opportunities to love—James lived with a keen sense of his own sin: "We all stumble in many ways" (James 3:2). In context, James is talking about *mature teachers*.

If you would know yourself, compare yourself to Christ. How courageous are you, compared to Him? How compassionate? How wise? How gentle? How loving?

Glory in Your Nothingness

In every sense, we are divinely created children of God and deeply loved. We should revel in this, embrace this, and be encouraged in this.

But in earlier centuries, Christians were far more willing than we are to explore another theological truth: Apart from God, we are nothing. Here's how Scupoli describes it:

> Place yourself on the safe and level ground of a true and deep conviction that you are nothing, that you know nothing, that you can do nothing, that you have nothing of your own but misery and imperfection, and that you deserve nothing but eternal damnation...
>
> If you consider the time before you were created, you will see that, through all that abyss of eternity, you were absolutely nothing, and that you did nothing and could in no way minister to your own creation. And now, through the goodness of God only, having been created, if you leave to Him that which is His—His continual governance, whereby He sustains you at every moment—what are you of yourself now but still equally nothing?[9]

With the wrong spirit and attitude, and without the corresponding truth of our adoption as God's children, the attitude of nothingness can create a sick personality—but at root, isn't it true? Without God, we wouldn't even exist. Without God, we wouldn't have been able to even imagine a God as wonderful as Him, much less actually get to know Him. Without God, we couldn't have turned from our sins and come to Him. We owe everything to Him. From that understanding, where is a foothold for pride?

I love Jeanne Guyon's honesty, which I find tremendously liberating: "You and I are very weak. At our best we are *very* weak."[10]

Ask Others

My wife and I discovered, quite by accident, that the best way to truly get to know your friends is to invite their eight- or nine-year-old child to spend the night. When our kids were young and asked their friends to our house for sleepovers, it was comical how much slipped through a young child's mouth. We'd gently steer the conversation to safer places.

But since kids know what's going on in our hearts, why not ask them how we're doing: "What is your mommy or daddy's greatest passion?" "What do I do that you wish I wouldn't do?" "Where do you see me growing?"

Of course this needs to be an age-appropriate exercise, commensurate with the relationship you have with your child. But it can be eye-opening if we have the guts to ask. It has the added benefit of *modeling* humility, demonstrating that we are works in progress, just as they are.

In the workplace, if you know coworkers who are believers, be bold enough to take one out to lunch and ask, "How do I treat people? Do I treat administrative assistants the same way I treat vice presidents? Do you think I'm a hard worker? Am I too self-absorbed, or do I show genuine interest in others? Am I quick to admire and praise other people's good work and accomplishments, or do I appear jealous and resentful of their success?" Assume you have room to improve, listen carefully, and begin building a humble heart.

Ask Your God

Finally, let me ask you, how humble are your prayers? A proud Christian prays as if she is scolding or trying to manipulate God: "God, You said You'd do this, so I'm expecting You to deliver!" "Lord, please don't let that happen to me." "Lord, my life would be so much easier if You would just change so and so, and I've been asking You for a long time to do this, so how about getting on it today?"

A humble Christian spends more time listening: "Lord, where is my heart growing cold? Where do I need to grow? What service would You call me to today?"

A humble Christian doesn't pray to God as if He is an errand boy; a humble Christian treats God like the Lord and Master that He is. If we spent more time questioning ourselves in prayer and less time questioning God, we'd see much more humility in the church.

The Encouragement of Humility

Ironically, if our self-understanding is truly born in heaven, our familiarity with our faults will actually encourage us rather than discourage us. This might sound bizarre, but it's true. God's revelation comes with His comfort. His gentle corrections arrive with His affirmation, and the experience feels like a bath rather than a scolding. Fénelon commented on this:

> As the inner light increases, you will see the imperfections
> which you have heretofore as basically much greater and more

harmful than you had seen them up to the present...But this experience, far from discouraging you, will help to uproot all your self-confidence, and to raze to the ground the whole edifice of pride. Nothing marks so much the solid advancement of a soul, as this view of his wretchedness without anxiety and without discouragement. [11]

Once our self-view is no longer tied to our own worth but to the worth ascribed to us in God, we can readily admit our shortcomings and begin working on them. We become like a ballplayer who welcomes constructive criticism from his coach; he wants to improve, and if the coach sees a little thing that will help him do so, he welcomes it with eagerness rather than collapsing into despair. The coach isn't cutting him from the team or even taking him out of the lineup—he's simply trying to help his player improve.

Some of us may lack an accurate understanding of our true selves, but others know their true selves so well that they spend all their energy trying to put up a false front, thinking some people wouldn't accept them if they knew the truth. This false piety is devastating to true spiritual growth. Another phrase for it is *spiritual cosmetology*. It deserves a chapter all its own.

26

Spiritual Cosmetology

When we are ashamed about our spiritual condition, we have two choices: We can create a false front and a glittering image (the spiritual-cosmetology approach), or we can be honest before God, ourselves, and others about our weakness and allow transformation to occur. We do not have the energy or resources to do both. We must choose one or the other.

Pascal wrote, "We are not satisfied with the life we have in ourselves and our own being. We want to lead an imaginary life in the eyes of others, and so we try to make an impression. We strive constantly to embellish and preserve our imaginary being, and neglect the real one."[1]

In Galatians 1:10, Paul warns that if our motivation is the approval of others, we cannot at the same time be growing in Christ and dedicated to His service. William Law added, "He that acts upon the desire of praise and applause must part with every other principle; he must say black is white, put bitter for sweet, and sweet for bitter, and do the meanest, basest things in order to be applauded."[2] Jonathan Edwards warns us of a very subtle, judgment-based temptation that Christians are particularly susceptible to:

> There is a false boldness for Christ that only comes from pride. A man may rashly expose himself to the world's dislike and even deliberately provoke its displeasure, and yet do so out of pride. It is the nature of spiritual pride to prompt men to seek distinction. Many times they will be militant with those they

call carnal in order to be more highly exalted among their own party. True boldness for Christ transcends all, it is indifferent to the displeasure of either friends or foes.[3]

We often think of "people pleasing" in terms of pleasing those in the world, but the apostle Paul and Jonathan Edwards warn us that we can also be people pleasers in the church. We want fellow Christians to think more highly of us, so we'll speak to unbelievers in a caustic manner, deliberately provoking a harsh response, because we think that by doing so we'll be all the more distinguished as believers. But it's all a show; it's not born out of a true hatred of sin and desire for bringing others to repentance. We just want fellow believers to admire our so-called boldness. Such an arrogant display uses the motivation of one sin (pride) to condemn another.

Exposed!

When we live a lie long enough, we eventually lose touch with reality. Our lives become sideshows, and we fail to become whole and integrated people. That's why spiritual cosmetology is a circus act that has no place in the Christian life.

It is also an act that God will eventually expose if we ever find our way to a healthy community. We conceal, but God wants to heal, and to do that, He must first expose. The light of God's presence naturally exposes things. Those who walk closely with God can often see through pretense. Consider just a few of the scriptural gifts of the Spirit that expose things: prophetic utterance, words of knowledge, the discernment of spirits, and interpretation of tongues. God is in the business of making the unknown known.

When Ananias and Sapphira gave a large gift to the Christian community and pretended it was all they had, they were exposed and found guilty of trying to mislead the community regarding the extent of their sacrifice. God found this pretense worthy of death (Acts 5). God hates all lies; His enemy, the devil, is the father of lies (John 8:44). Jesus described Himself as the way, the *truth*, and the life (John 14:6). So it is no surprise that in the model Christian community Paul describes, unbelievers will sense God's presence when the secrets of their hearts are revealed (1 Corinthians 14:25). God exposes our secrets because concealed sin is a cancer eating away the spiritual life within us. Without humility, we cannot see the face of God.

Humble people welcome this exposure because they are more concerned with actually growing in righteousness than appearing righteous. Every step toward the truth is therefore a welcome step.

This is the plea of the Christian classics (and Scripture): Let's find refuge in the *truth*. We are what we are—sinners in desperate need of grace, living to call attention to the God who provides such grace…and more.

An Idol of Humility

We must address one more equally subtle temptation. Because humility is so valuable, Satan will attempt to counterfeit it and use it against us. Spiritual cosmetology becomes particularly dangerous when humility becomes part of our makeup.

De Sales comically warns us, "We often confess ourselves to be nothing, nay, misery itself, and the refuse of the world; but would be very sorry that any one should believe us, or tell others that we are really so miserable wretches."[4]

It comes down to this: Do we truly want to be humble? Or do we just want to be known as humble? When I'm in a community that I know values humility, *in my pride* I will attempt to mimic humility, and I'll talk as if I'm humble, but my motivation is to impress!

So in the name of humility, we must not even try to appear humble. Rather, we must seek to actually *be* humble. We must focus our efforts on growing in humility and stop caring about what others think. The only judge who matters to a holy woman or man is a holy God.

People who constantly disparage themselves, calling attention to their weaknesses and stating the obvious (that we are not worthy and not capable on our own) may have fallen into this trap. Admittedly, leaders may need to speak such words occasionally to model humility, but if they are speaking words to impress, they are abusing the spirit of humility to appear humble—one of the worst forms of spiritual cosmetology imaginable.

The goal is for humility to become such a growing part of who we are that we don't even recognize it in ourselves.

Fighting Against God

God supremely values humility and opposes the proud, so those of us who practice spiritual cosmetology are fighting against God. Lest you have any doubt, God will win this battle, so the fight is ridiculously futile.

And why would we want to fight it when we can rest in the truth and peace of grace? Let's admit it—we all struggle with sin, just as James, Jesus's brother, reminded us. Jeanne Guyon talks about "defects which God deliberately leaves even in His greatest saints, to keep them from pride and to keep them from the praise of men who judge only from outward appearance."[5]

Can we finally reject the game of "gotcha spirituality"? Every pastor, every father, every mother, every child, every college student, every athlete, every businessman…every person *sins*. Let's be honest and appropriately vulnerable so we can help each other grow away from sin and toward Christ. If we pridefully try to catch each other, we'll be too afraid to confess our own sins, and we'll cover them up, pretending to be something we're not. We'll waste energy and time putting on spiritual makeup instead of truly being transformed from glory to glory.

Covering sin is like feeding a cancer. It will kill us sooner rather than later. Spiritual cosmetology is a deadly game that has no business in the Christian church. It is ugly, vicious, and even demonic. Have nothing to do with it.

Christian, Know Your God

W e have seen that humility embraces two truths—the lowliness of humanity and the greatness of God. According to the classic devotional writers, the way to build humility isn't to obsess and fixate on how lowly we are, however, but to spend time reflecting on the surpassing glory of God. This is a long-term plan and process that nurtures the spirit of humility. Consider these lines from *The Cloud of Unknowing*:

> [We] should choose rather to be humbled under the wonder-
> ful height and worthiness of God who is perfect than under
> [our] own wretchedness which is imperfect. That is to say,
> take care that your particular attention is directed more to the
> worthiness of God than to your own sinfulness.[1]

Such an understanding of God's greatness is born in revelation. John of the Cross wrote, "God will give illumination by bestowing on the soul not only knowledge of its own misery and lowliness but also knowledge of His grandeur and majesty."[2] Edwards put it this way:

> The greater the view and sense that one has of the infinite
> excellence and glory of God in Christ, and of how bound-
> less is the length and breadth, depth and height of the love
> of Christ to sinners, the greater will be the astonishment one
> feels as he realizes how little he knows of such love to such a
> God, and to such a glorious Redeemer.[3]

Distorted Reference

Fénelon explained that without a direct experience of God, humility is impossible because our frame of reference is distorted.

> A peasant shut up in his village only partially knows his wretchedness, but let him see rich palaces, a superb court, and he will realize all the poverty of his village. He cannot endure its hovels after a sight of so much magnificence. It is thus that we see our ugliness and worthlessness in the beauty and infinite grandeur of God.[4]

Have you ever been invited to a home just after the family had done some remodeling? Let's say they fixed up their kitchen by increasing the floor space, adding new cupboards, doubling their counter space, and maybe even putting an island in the middle of the kitchen. Imagine that they really did it right—their choice in color, the style...everything is perfect. When you go home, you walk into your own kitchen...and sigh. Three hours ago, your kitchen seemed fine. The kitchen didn't change at all in those three hours, but your *perception* of what a kitchen can be certainly did.

In the same way, we can easily be proud of our holiness or character until we catch a glimpse of God's holiness. Once we see what could be, humility is as natural a reaction as is squinting our eyes to block out the glare of the sun. The light is so brilliant, we can't take it at full force.

Fénelon said we can use any human measurement we want to reveal our humble state, but such reasoning "only skims the heart. It does not sink in." Only a direct encounter with God shakes the depths of our being. "If the ray of the divine light shines within, he sees the abyss of nothingness and evil which is the corrupted creature."[5]

This work of humility can and should be an ongoing reality in our lives. And yes, it requires a supernatural touch and even a mystic's pursuit—merely reading *about* God won't cut it. We must actually *encounter* God to have our hearts transformed in this way.

Keeping the Train on the Tracks

An additional challenge in all this is that the spirit of humility is like the tide—it can come in and out. It is rarely static and never something we possess. If we become lax in pursuing God or take shortcuts and fail to consider His grandeur, pride will gleefully jump in unannounced.

That's why John Owen labeled the second step in the stages of moral decline and decay as losing reverence for God.[6] For all things in life—holiness, relationships, identity, purpose, ministry—we need to maintain an appropriate awe and fear of God. That's what keeps the train on the tracks. If we ever become too familiar with God, if we ever lose that profound reverence that leaves us standing silent in fascination and wonder at who He is, pride and sin will be waiting to claim our souls. All they want is a *little* opening, a *gradual* cooling, a mind that is content with concepts and a stranger to reality, and they will pounce.

If we ever start comparing ourselves to other believers (or even nonbelievers) instead of God, our humility will crumble like an overbaked cookie. Teresa of Avila wrote, "We shall never completely know ourselves if we don't strive to know God. By gazing at His grandeur, we get in touch with our own lowliness; by looking at His purity, we shall see our own filth; by pondering His humility, we shall see how far we are from being humble."[7]

Consider who is talking. Traveling back in history and meeting Teresa of Avila might be similar to meeting Mother Teresa. We might think we had found the picture of purity! Why would such a woman need to repent? The answer is simple: Women like this learn to embrace humility not by looking left or right, but by looking up.

Keeping sight of God, then, is vital to humility, just as keeping in touch with humility is vital to seeing God. We cannot maintain one without the other. "Christianity is strange," Pascal wrote. "It bids man to recognize that he is vile, and even abominable, and bids him want to be like God. Without such a counterweight his exaltation would make him horribly vain or his abasement horribly abject."[8]

I've seen the consequences of this when people value humility alone rather than letting a focus on God create humility as a by-product. Their focus on their vileness and "abominable" nature may undercut the counterbalancing truth of God's provision, work, and glory. True worship—spending time in God's presence—is essential if we are to walk in a balanced, biblical humility. Jonathan Edwards referred to this as an evangelical humility.

Evangelical Humility

Jonathan Edwards distinguished between what he called legal humiliation and evangelical humiliation.

In legal humiliation, "men are made aware that they are small, indeed nothing, before the great and terrible God. They feel undone, and wholly insufficient to help themselves. But they do not have a responsive frame of heart in true self-abasement nor do they feel the need to exult in God alone."[9]

These are people who feel naturally humbled but not supernaturally informed. They are impressed with God, but their souls aren't awakened to the extent that they begin living for God's glory. In other words, they may admire God, but as Edwards explains, they aren't willing to serve Him as Lord.

> This attitude comes only in evangelical humiliation, when the heart is overwhelmed by the realization of God's holy beauty. In a legal humiliation, the conscience is convicted, but there is still no spiritual understanding, nor is the will broken, nor is the inclination of the heart altered.

Only when people experience evangelical humiliation do they become truly free. When you live for God's glory, which never changes, your joy has no end. Your sin or circumstances do not touch the glory of God; your health, marital status, and personal trifles and troubles do not mar God's overwhelming beauty. When you live to enjoy, rest in, and proclaim *that* glory, you are truly free.

Scupoli shows that this affects even our attitude toward our own sin. "If, after a fall, you give way to despondency and vexation, and despairingly complain that you can make no progress, such feelings evidently show that you have been trusting in yourself and not in God."[10]

Think of this from God's perspective. How silly must we look to Him when, immediately after we fall, we promise God we won't fall again! A humble Christian, trusting in God, is more likely to pray, "Oh, that's me again, and without Your touch, Lord, I'll do it again and again and again. But I'm trusting in You, in Your redemption, and in Your power to pull me out of this sin."

Evangelical humiliation not only affects our failures but also sharpens our ministries. Jonah's problem was that he was more concerned about his reputation as a true prophet than he was about God's reputation as a compassionate forgiver. Pride and ministry simply don't mix. The same is true of parenting, business decisions, or any human endeavor: In all these endeavors, we seek God's glory and truth. *We* stop being the center of what matters. Our focus is fixed only on how we can help others see the glory of God's goodness, reign, and power. Once we get a glimpse of God's glory, worrying about our own glory is pathetic. We become more enthralled with God than with anything that pertains to us.

Humility, then, is both developed and maintained by becoming radically God-focused, which is why classic Christian writers valued it to such a high degree. Jonathan Edwards said, "We must view humility as one of the most essential things that characterizes true Christianity."[11] Calvin, in his *Institutes*, is even stronger: "If you shall ask me concerning the precepts of the Christian religion, first, second, third, and always I would answer, 'Humility.'"[12]

Thus far we have considered humility primarily as it relates to ourselves. Let's now look at the way humility affects our relationships with others.

28

Humility in Community

Four-year-old Nolan was delighted when he got his first fishing tackle box (which he unknowingly began calling his "taco box"), particularly when he compared it to his older brother's box. Standing by his older brother, he deliberately placed his tackle box right next to Michael's.

A big smile spread across Nolan's face. Michael didn't understand what was going on, so Nolan made it very clear. In a voice rife with challenge, Nolan said, "My taco box is bigger."

Such preening among kids is common, but often adults do the very same thing. The only difference is that our posturing has a spiritual veneer. Instead of saying, "My car costs more than yours," our tendency is to think words of judgment and accusation, indirectly elevating our character: "I'd never treat my spouse that way." "Look at that—I'm a much better parent than she is." "I may have my weaknesses, but at least I'm not addicted to *that*."

Such preening, spoken or not, has a devastating effect on true Christian fellowship. Christian communities, including Christian families and churches, break down when their members lose humility. John Owen noted this hundreds of years ago:

> The person who understands the evil in his own heart is the only person who is useful, fruitful, and solid in his beliefs and obedience. Others only delude themselves and thus upset families, churches, and all other relationships. In their self-pride and judgment of others, they show great inconsistency.[1]

Anyone who has been in authority has suffered the assault of blind and arrogant self-righteousness. I know a pastor who grieved over having to lay off some staff members during a difficult economic time. Members of the congregation actually asked him if he had considered using less paper instead! He and the elders had agonized over *every* expense, trying to find any solution other than letting some beloved staff members go, and these church members were acting as if the layoffs were a simple decision made in five minutes without an ounce of reflection.

Every boss, every head coach, and every parent has seen how overly confident people can be when they're not accountable for the consequences. Second-guessing assumes we know all the facts, but most of us who aren't in leadership *don't* know all the facts, and when we act and speak arrogantly, we can do great damage.

Accusation is a very dangerous thing—and one of Satan's favorite tools. According to Fénelon, humility is the only antidote for this spiritual poison. "Can we with justice feel contempt for others and dwell on their faults, when we are full of them ourselves?"[2]

What if the church members who questioned the layoffs had asked themselves, "Have we given all that we should? Have we been as productive as possible?" It may well be *their* lack of responsibility that placed the leadership team in an awkward spot. But we rarely think that way; instead, we jump to the conclusion that leaders simply don't know what they're doing.

Our "strong feelings about the faults of others" is itself a "great fault," Fénelon added later.[3]

Forbearance

We desperately need forbearance rooted in a biblically informed theology of sin. Why do we act surprised when sinners sin against us? What else do we expect them to do?

When we resent the fact that others mistreat us, we have clearly forgotten that only God's mercy and grace cleanses us and encourages us to act with love. (We've also forgotten that our own ongoing sin also occasionally hurts others.) When somebody outside of grace treats us as enemies because we speak the truth of the gospel, we must remember that we would be doing the same if not for God's presence in our lives.

Think about this the next time you're tempted to judge a sinner for acting like a sinner: Both Jesus and Stephen, as they were being murdered, prayed that God would not hold their murderers' sin against them. This is an understanding of grace, a level of humility, a walking in mercy that most of us can only dream about.

The way we treat others is a better test of our humility than the way we speak about ourselves. Fénelon emphasizes this relational aspect of humility:

> If you were in this happy [humbled] state, far from impatiently enduring those who are not, the immense stretch of your heart would make you indulgent and compassionate toward all the weaknesses which shrink selfish hearts. The more perfect we are, the more we get along with imperfection. The Pharisees could not bear the publicans and the women sinners, whom Jesus Christ treated with such gentleness and kindness.[4]

In his blunt style, Thomas à Kempis said, "Do not think that thou hast made any progress, unless thou feel thyself inferior to all." He believed that humility, especially in relation to others, has a very practical and positive effect. "It is not harmful unto thee to debase thyself under all men; but is very injurious to thee to prefer thyself before any one man."[5]

This is where many of us fail miserably. We are quick to excuse our own sins but vicious in holding other Christians to the standard of perfection. Francis de Sales said we are "like the partridges in Paphlagonia, which have two hearts; for we have one heart, mild, favorable, and courteous towards ourselves, and another hard, severe, and rigorous towards our neighbor."[6]

When we sin, we explain that we have been under extra stress, that we have been tired, that Satan has been unceasing in his enticements, or that other people's actions were so egregious that they practically forced us into a sinful response. But when other people sin, these excuses do not come to mind. Rather, we base our judgment of others on the bottom line. "You sinned; therefore you're guilty."

This tendency to excuse ourselves and quickly judge others is proof that pride has gripped our hearts. William Law's words call us to a severe honesty in this regard:

The fuller of pride anyone is himself, the more impatient will he be at the smallest instances of it in other people. And the less humility anyone has in his own mind, the more will he demand and be delighted with it in other people...You must therefore act by a quite contrary measure and reckon yourself only so far humble as you impose every instance of humility upon yourself and never call for it in other people.[7]

When we harshly judge others, we elevate ourselves to a position that rightfully belongs to God. We do not know a person's full story, and even if we did, we would lack the perfect objectivity and unpolluted sense of justice to render an accurate opinion. Pastors and appointed leaders must make decisions, but we are arrogant when we judge the concerns of people who are not accountable to us.

William Law deserves to be quoted at length in this regard. Remember that his book, *A Serious Call to a Devout and Holy Life*, is one of the most demanding spiritual treatises ever written, yet notice the way Law treats sinners:

No one is of the Spirit of Christ but he that has the utmost compassion for sinners. Nor is there any greater sign of your own perfection than you find yourself all love and compassion toward them that are very weak and defective. And on the other hand, you have never less reason to be pleased with yourself than when you find yourself most angry and offended at the behavior of others. All sin is certainly to be hated and abhorred wherever it is, but then we must set ourselves against sin as we do against sickness and diseases, by showing ourselves tender and compassionate to the sick and diseased. All other hatred of sin which does not fill the heart with the softest, tenderest affections toward persons miserable in it is the servant of sin at the same time that it seems to be hating it.[8]

In fact, if we want to take this seriously, we must learn to develop a holy double standard.

A Holy Double Standard

Have you ever noticed that when Jesus faced self-righteous hypocrisy,

He was brutal and unyielding in His confrontation, but when He faced those caught in the misery of sin, He often showed a softer face, refusing to break a bruised reed or blow out a smoldering wick (Isaiah 42:3)? Law says those who are most like Christ will have a ministry like Christ.

> This, therefore, we may take for a certain rule, that the more we partake of the divine nature, the more improved we are ourselves, and the higher our sense of virtue is, the more we shall pity and compassionate those that want it. The sight of such people will then, instead of raising in us a haughty contempt or peevish indignation toward them, fill us with such bowels of compassion as when we see the miseries of a hospital.[9]

The spiritually mature hold themselves to a high standard while being gracious toward others—they have a double standard *in others' favor*. Edwards commented, "False zeal is against the sins of others while having no zeal against [our] own sins. He who has true zeal exercises it chiefly against his own sins."[10]

When we know we have been forgiven and when we're not cherishing sin in our hearts, we can more easily offer a word of healing and grace to others who are struggling. In fact, because we have received healing and grace, we will naturally call others out of their sin with the same attitude that Christ used to call us out of our sin.

I remember a conversation many years ago with a fellow believer who was railing about the need to loudly confront and proclaim God's judgment against various evils in some individuals' lives. I'm all for calling people to holiness, but my friend's delivery troubled me "Tell me," I asked him, "when God won you over, was it through judgment or grace?"

"Grace," he replied. "Why do you ask?"

"If grace won you over, maybe that would be most effective way for you to win others."

Galatians 6:1 (NKJV) exhorts us, "Brethren, if a man is overtaken in any trespass, you who are spiritual restore such a one in a spirit of gentleness." William Law challenged us to consider where we would be if God treated us the way we treat other sinners:

> A man naturally fancies that it is his own exceeding love of virtue that makes him not able to bear with those that want

it. And when he abhors one man, despises another, and can't
bear the name of a third, he supposes it all to be a proof of his
own high sense of virtue and just hatred of sin...If this had
been the Spirit of the Son of God, if He had hated sin in this
manner, there [would have been] no redemption of the world;
[if] God had hated sinners in this manner day and night, the
world itself [would have] ceased long ago.[11]

When we are humble, we may see ourselves as the greatest sinners
of all.

The Greatest Sinner

The spiritual truth is this: We treat others harshly because we don't recognize the depth of our own sin. This is not because of our maturity—
after all, the apostle Paul confessed himself to be the chief of sinners. But
in an age of widely publicized serial killers, child abusers, drug pushers,
and white-collar criminals, many of us might find Paul's sentiments difficult to adopt as our own. We know we have our problems, but Adolf Hit-
ler we're not.

William Law has some helpful words for us in this regard. We may
justly condemn ourselves as the greatest sinners we know, he wrote, because we "know more of the folly of [our] own heart than [we] do of other
people's," and "the greatness of our guilt arises chiefly from the greatness
of God's goodness toward us." Therefore, "every sinner knows more of
the aggravations of his own guilt than he does of other people's, and consequently may justly look upon himself to be the greatest sinner that he
knows." Law continued his explanation:

> How good God has been to other sinners, what light and
> instruction he has vouchsafed to them, what blessings and
> graces they have received from him, how often he has touched
> their hearts with holy inspirations, you cannot tell. But all
> this you know of yourself, therefore you know greater aggra-
> vations of your own guilt and are able to charge yourself with
> greater ingratitude than you can charge upon other people.[12]

Law teaches us that the best way to develop humility is not to compare our lives with others':

You must consider your own particular circumstances, your health, your sickness, your youth or age, your particular calling, the happiness of your education, the degrees of light and instruction that you have received, the good men that you have conversed with, the admonitions that you have had, the good books that you have read, the numberless multitude of divine blessings, graces, and favors that you have received, the good motions of grace that you have resisted, the resolutions of amendment that you have often broken, and the checks of conscience that you have disregarded.

For it is from these circumstances that everyone is to state the measure and greatness of his own guilt. And as you know only these circumstances of your own sins, so you must necessarily know how to charge yourself with higher degrees of guilt than you can charge upon other people.

God Almighty knows greater sinners, it may be, than you are, because he sees and knows the circumstances of all men's sins. But your own heart, if it is faithful to you, can discover no guilt so great as your own, because it can only see in you those circumstances on which great part of the guilt of sin is founded.[13]

If others had our advantages, they might have been much more faithful than we have been. If we had their disadvantages, we might have done much worse. We simply don't know, and therefore we are incapable of accurately judging anyone.

The other side of this is that if we truly understood the depth of sin in our own hearts, we wouldn't have time to judge others. Brother Giles's take on this is classic: "If a man were to live a thousand years and not have anything to do outside himself, he would have enough to do within, in his own heart, nor would he be able to bring the work to perfect completion—he would have so much to do only within, in his own heart!"[14]

When I truly understand how much sin affects so much of what I do, when I drink deeply of God's grace and mercy, when I look on the holy and perfect Son of God and see what true glory and character excellence really is, what ledge can I stand on to judge? There is none.

Let's end this chapter with a marvelous comment from a Franciscan monk who earlier in his life had been a renowned soldier. After he became a Friar Minor, he was asked why he hadn't joined the Templars or a similar order that would have allowed him to pursue a religious life and still fight. The former soldier replied, "So far I have been strong in fighting others— from now on I want to be strong in fighting myself!"[15]

How Do Humble People Lead?

I f you are a leader in any capacity (and almost everyone is), nothing will bring more rest to your soul than a life of humility. I daresay that without humility, ministry will eventually make you miserable. With humility, ministry will grow sweeter by the day.

Carefully consider this important statement as well: Living in the truth of humility means more than no longer lying about our weaknesses or trying to cover up our faults. It also means we shouldn't lie about our strengths.

That statement flows from the foundation of humility—acknowledging and then accepting the truth—as Law points out:

> Humility does not consist in having a worse opinion of ourselves than we deserve, or in abasing ourselves lower than we really are. But as all virtue is founded in truth, so humility is founded in a true and just sense of our weakness, misery, and sin. He that rightly feels and lives in this sense of his condition lives in humility.[1]

Edwards has a similar take: "I do not want to be understood to say that the more saints on earth experience God's grace, the lower will be the opinion of themselves. In many ways it is quite otherwise, for when grace is most exercised, there is proportionate freedom from the corruption of sin."[2]

Gifted businesspeople are *not* being humble when they say, "It was all luck; I really had nothing to do with my success." Lying is not the same as being humble. A successful and humble businessperson might say, "God has certainly given me the ability to motivate people and manage a budget. At times, I wish I was a little more patient and a little less self-absorbed, because I know I've hurt some people along the way."

People who can't admit their strengths are also unlikely to admit their weaknesses. Sometimes confessing false weaknesses ("I'm not really a good manager") is easier than confessing true ones ("I can be brusque and a bit harsh when I'm angry").

Lying about your strengths robs God of the glory He deserves for giving you those strengths.

Don't Let Pride Determine Your Ministry

Without humility, you may never find God's preferred place for you to minister. You'll leave or stay where you are for all the wrong reasons.

This is because an arrogant man or woman runs toward applause as surely as water runs downhill. Humble leaders are so focused on serving others, they don't gauge success by their followers' response. Like Paul, their minds are preoccupied with their followers' spiritual health: "My dear children, for whom I am again in the pains of childbirth until Christ is formed in you..." (Galatians 4:19).

When followers grumble, humble leaders don't assume it's time to move on. Rather, they take advantage of the opportunity to grow in humility as they confront and perhaps endure the grumbling. Amazingly, the classic Christian writers actually *welcomed* rejection, ridicule, and insults.

Francis of Assisi was the master practitioner of this. The monks' clothes he designed for his early followers purposefully resembled children's clothes. In the early days of the order, before people became familiar with the Franciscan habit, the monks' appearance evoked ridicule, as if a contemporary speaker showed up at a formal church service dressed in one-piece pajamas, complete with the little plastic feet covering his toes and Winnie the Pooh embroidered on his chest. People would think he had lost his mind, just as they thought the Franciscans had lost theirs.

And that was precisely the point.

In the early Franciscan classic *The Little Flowers of Saint Francis*, Brother Ugolino describes the early Franciscans as "crucified men...[who had] a greater desire to receive shame and insults for the love of Christ than the vain honors or respect or praise of the world. On the contrary, they rejoiced in being insulted, and they were made sad by being honored."[3]

Bernard, Francis's first official follower, once walked into a town and peacefully endured much ridicule and abuse by children and townspeople. Finally, a wealthy businessman stopped the abuse by pointing out how Bernard was displaying commendable Christian maturity in the face of never-ending scorn and mockery. In fact, the rich townsman suggested, Bernard might even be a saint. Overnight, the Franciscan friar became a celebrity, and people began sitting at his feet, asking for his opinions, and bringing him choice food, at which point Bernard *left* that town, explaining to Francis that he needed to find another village where he could be ridiculed instead of praised. "Because of the great honor that is shown me, I am afraid of losing more than I would gain there."[4]

We mentioned earlier that Augustine wrote his *Confessions* so people who knew him only as a bishop wouldn't have an overly exalted view of him. When Paul was forced to recite his credentials to the Corinthians, he made sure he ended with a humiliating weakness (2 Corinthians 11:22–3:10). We live in a day in which Christian leaders value, proclaim, and guard their résumés and lists of accomplishments. Doing so too earnestly denies the very spirit of Christlikeness all of us should seek to emulate.

Every time I speak, I am humbled by the example of Teresa of Avila, the great leader of the Discalced Carmelites: "I'm saying that we should walk in truth before God and people in as many ways as possible. Especially, there should be no desire that others consider us better than we are."[5]

When to Defend

So we affirm that, as Augustine warned, we must avoid the "lust" of vindicating ourselves.[6] And I also admit that we might even want to adopt the approach of Brother Giles, an early Franciscan friar, who advised, "If someone says something bad to you, you ought to help him by saying something worse about yourself."[7] Yet for holy reasons, we may occasionally need to speak up in our own defense. Humility allows us to present a defense when doing so is vital to preserving a work that God has called us to do. De Sales wrote about preserving a good name:

> Humility would despise a good name if charity did not need it; but, because it is one of the foundations of human society, and that without it we are not only unprofitable, but prejudicial

to the public, by reason of the scandal it would receive, charity requires, and humility consents, that we should desire [a
good name] and carefully preserve it…

[However,] we must not be over-nice in regard to the preserva-
tion of our good name…Persons, by endeavoring to maintain
their reputation so delicately, entirely lose it…An excessive fear
of losing our good name betrays a great distrust of its foundation, which is the truth of a good life.[8]

In such instances, we are defending God's work more than we are
defending ourselves. To make no defense because of a misguided view
of humility would be to put our piety over our service, which isn't a wise
thing to do.

The Anchor of Our Calling

Humility thus serves as the anchor of our calling and vocation. One
of the worst tricks of pride is that it can turn us against our own purpose
in life by filling us with ambitious yearnings that cause us to neglect our
true call for today.

Tomorrow's dreams are poor substitutes for today's obedience. Without humility we can fall prey to deceitful desires that hinder our present
effectiveness. Teresa of Avila wrote, "Sometimes the devil gives us great
desires so that we will avoid setting ourselves to the task at hand, serving
our Lord in possible things, and instead be content with having desired
the impossible."[9]

Francis de Sales's words are strikingly similar. "The enemy often sug-
gests a great desire of things that are absent, and which shall never occur,
so that he may divert our mind from present objects, from which, however
trivial they may be, we might obtain considerable profit to ourselves."[10]

Desiring to do great things for God is noble, but when our desire for
future ministry blocks us from our present tasks, we should prayerfully
(and with the assistance of spiritual counsel) consider whether the desire
is God's inspiration to move or Satan's distraction to keep us from living
fruitful lives right where we are.

If I could say one thing to twenty- and thirtysomething Christians, I'd
urge them to let humility drive their decisions and their schedules while
they are still actively raising children. Let those who do not have such

heavy responsibilities at home serve as elders and leaders. The parenting season may seem as if it will never end, but it will pass more quickly than you can believe. Give yourself fully to the task at hand, for those who have proven themselves faithful in home life are most qualified to then lead church life (1 Timothy 3:5). Home life *prepares* you for church life; it doesn't compete with it. If you skip this God-ordained preparation and cheat your family so you can "build" God's church, you're giving that church an incomplete and immature servant.

Men and women who neglect their young families in a misguided attempt to serve God will in fact also be unfaithful with the later calling. If you don't think your ministry to your family is important enough for you right now, getting a little humility will save you from much regret.

Dreams born out of our own ambitions can be demonic messengers disguised as angels of light. Dreams born in the heart of God can be precious motivators. Humility reminds us that our reward before God is not based on what we attempt but on our faithfulness to what we are given. De Sales expounded on this:

> The King of Glory does not recompense his servants according to the dignity of the offices they hold, but according to the measure of the love and humility with which they exercise them. Saul, seeking the asses of his father, found the kingdom of Israel. Rebecca, watering the camels of Abraham, became the spouse of his son. Ruth, gleaning after the reapers of Boaz, and laying down at his feet, was advanced to his side and made his wife. High and elevated pretensions to extraordinary favors are subject to illusion and deceit; and it sometimes happens that those who imagine themselves angels are not so much as good men...
>
> We must...keep ourselves in our lower but safer way, less eminent, but better suited to our insufficiency and littleness; in which, if we conduct ourselves with humility and fidelity, God will infallibly elevate us to a situation that will be truly exalted.[11]

Forward Motion

Humility is not only the anchor that keeps us where we should be but also the wind that takes us where we might otherwise fear to sail. For though some of us use pride to escape the obligations of the present, others use pride to avoid a call to the future, as de Sales explains:

> The proud man, who trusts in himself, has just reason not to attempt anything; but he that is humble is so much the more courageous, by how much the more he acknowledges his own inability; and the more wretched he esteems himself the more confident he becomes; because he places his whole trust in God, who delights to display his omnipotence in our weakness, and to elevate his mercy upon our misery.[12]

Sometimes pride and the fear of embarrassment can hold us back. I speak quite frequently at church retreats, and during the course of five or six talks, I am virtually guaranteed to slip into at least one faux pas. One time I referred to useful lusts instead of youthful lusts. Another time I said, "God opposes the humble but gives grace to the proud." A pastor friend of mine did even worse. He welcomed people to his church, a "healing community of love, sex, and forgiveness." He meant to say "love, acceptance, and forgiveness."

Maybe you're afraid that you don't know enough, that you don't have enough experience, that you might fail, that you might end up looking like a fool...so you don't even try. If we proudly say, "I'll serve You, God, as long as You don't ask me to embarrass myself," we'll never be able to truly serve God. We'll make mistakes, but humility moves us to serve anyway. To hold back out of fear is prideful.

Humility fills our ministries with selflessness and moves us to depend on God. We must avoid the trap of basing our qualification for ministry on our own gifts rather than our calling. A person with many gifts is not necessarily qualified because of those gifts; likewise, a person lacking in many gifts is not necessarily disqualified because of that lack. Pride motivates us to evaluate God's call based on what we possess or what we lack. We forget that both the biggest human contribution and the greatest human weakness are irrelevant in the face of God's provision. God's unlimited power is neither strengthened by our contribution nor lessened by our weakness.

Francis of Assisi modeled this wonderfully when he was questioned by an early follower named Brother Masseo, who simply couldn't understand why Francis was so popular. He once asked the saint, "Why does all the world seem to be running after you, and everyone seems to want to see you and hear you and obey you? You are not a handsome man. You do not have great learning or wisdom. You are not a nobleman. So why is all the world running after you?"

Francis sat before God a long time before answering.

> You really want to know why everyone is running after me? I have this from the all-holy eyes of God...For those blessed and all-holy eyes have not seen among sinners anyone more vile or insufficient than I am. And so in order to do that wonderful work which He intends to do, He did not find on earth a viler creature, and therefore He chose me, for God has chosen the foolish things of the world to put to shame the wise, and God has chosen the base things of the world and the despised, to bring to naught the noble and great and strong, so that all excellence in virtue may be from God and not from the creature, in order that no creature should glory before Him, but "let him who takes pride, take pride the Lord," that honor and glory may be only God's forever.[13]

Do you understand the freedom in this? We don't have to defend ourselves or even prove ourselves worthy; we can spend 100 percent of our energy and time glorifying God and pointing people to His goodness and sufficiency. And if our weaknesses and limitations spotlight God's glory even more, so much the better.

John the Baptist was the quintessential example of a humble servant of God. He was willing to serve humbly and obscurely in the desert while God readied him for his ministry. He spoke forcefully when God exalted him to become a famous and powerful prophet, but then he willingly handed his ministry over to Christ when the time was right.

May God raise up many more such servants.

PART 5

Death, Suffering, *and* Spiritual Gluttony

Living in a Dying World:
The Remembrance of Death

When sportscaster Glenn Brenner died at the age of 44 in Washington DC, the city was in shock for several days. Why? After all, the city had been dubbed the murder capital of the United States, and victims of violent crime die there virtually every day—sometimes a half-dozen a night. Yet radio talk-show hosts devoted entire mornings or afternoons to Brenner's death. The newspaper covered it in every issue for a week. One television station ran a half-hour memorial program.

The city was stunned by the suddenness of the death. It forced people to remember that death doesn't always wait until we're 95. Sometimes it sneaks up on us in our forties. As people called talk shows to express their shock, they repeated a familiar refrain: "It was so sudden; so unexpected. He was so young, in such good health, and then all of a sudden...I just can't believe it."

Brenner had recently completed a marathon. He was young, healthy, humorous, and successful, but all of that became irrelevant when a brain tumor took his life. Death didn't take into account his cardiovascular capability. It didn't inquire about the number of children still depending on him or his vocational success or how beloved he was in the capital city. Death doesn't ask questions; it doesn't review résumés. It just comes.

The city was unsettled by death's rude intrusion into its life. Denial was no longer possible, and people were forced to consider that maybe there's more to life than we have been told. Maybe we need to make some inquiries and answer a few questions before death comes to knock on *our* door.

Every now and then we sneak a peek at the obituaries and look at the ages of those who have died. When we see somebody our own age or even younger, we involuntarily wince. We grope for the cause of death—please don't let it be a heart attack or cancer, we hope. We want to be immune from that, at least for now.

Our denial means nothing to death because death doesn't have to ask our permission. Death is coming. Every day is somebody's last.

The Denial of Death

In spite of the prevalence of death, we prefer not to talk about it. In this we're similar to previous generations. Fénelon wrote of this denial centuries ago:

> We consider ourselves immortal, or at least as though going to live for centuries. Folly of the human spirit! Every day those who die soon follow those who are already dead. One about to leave on a journey ought not to think himself far from one who went only two days before. Life flows by like a flood.[1]

Most of us recognize that we will eventually die—but decades from now, not today, not this week, not this month, not this year. Death is a foreigner, not a close neighbor.

We live our lives while clutching fiercely to this illusion. How else can we explain the fact that so many die without a will? We live without making a will, not because we believe we'll never die, but because we don't expect to die this week. Thus we have more important tasks to take care of, meetings to attend, things to buy, walls to paint.

Why do we deny death? Fénelon believed we avoid the thought of death so we are not saddened by it. But this, he said, is shortsighted. "It will only be sad for those who have not thought about it."[2] William Law wrote that the living world's brilliance blinds us from eternity and the reality of death. "The health of our bodies, the passions of our minds, the noise and hurry and pleasures and business of the world, lead us on with eyes that see not and ears that hear not."[3]

Part of this denial comes from the company we keep. During the seven years I studied in college and seminary, I attended a church with a congregation that was predominantly young. During those seven years, one person in the congregation died, and it was big news.

My first position after seminary was in a more historic church with a predominantly older congregation. The first church had required two rooms to break up the nursery, but this church couldn't round up enough babies to fill more than two or three double strollers. During our first six months, we had three funerals.

Young people have a distorted view of life. They can forget that funerals are waiting on the other end of weddings and baby showers. When we segregate ourselves—when we don't know anyone who is suffering from arthritis—we can be lulled to sleep.

Law insisted that most people will regret delaying the thought of death. When death approaches, it is often too late to make amends. Law demonstrated this by describing a symbolic character who, on his deathbed, bemoans his absentmindedness:

> Do you think anything can astonish and confound a dying man like this? What pain do you think a man must feel when his conscience lays all this folly to his charge, when it shall show him how regular, exact, and wise he has been in small matters that are passed away like a dream and how stupid and senseless he has lived, without any reflection, without any rules, in things of such eternal moment as no heart can sufficiently conceive them![4]

One magazine writer told the story of a shopper who died from a massive heart attack in front of the frozen pizza section of a supermarket. The writer ruminated about the woman's last thoughts. "Should I get pepperoni or vegetarian?" Or maybe, "How about triple cheese?" The shopper was seconds away from eternity, on the threshold of entering a new era, and *she didn't even know it.* Her mind was occupied with the trivial.

This unexpectedness of death should encourage us to take a second look, to reconsider our pleasant denial, to admit that, yes, death might visit us as early as this week.

The Remembrance of Death Serves Life

William Nelson, a Union general in the Civil War, was consumed with the hostilities in Kentucky when a brawl erupted in his fort and he was shot in the chest. He had faced many battles, but the fatal blow came while he was relaxing with his men. He was caught fully unprepared. As men ran up the stairs to help, the general had just one request: "Send for a clergyman; I wish to be baptized."

He never made time to be baptized as an adolescent or a young man, and he had too many pressing concerns while in command. In half a second, the general's priorities had been turned upside down. The war raged on, but suddenly his interest had been captivated by another world. Who cared about Robert E. Lee now? And it was too late to bother with a doctor. Get me a clergyman! With only minutes left before he died, the one thing he cared about was preparing for eternity. He wanted to be baptized.

Thirty minutes later he was dead.

How was this general served by the remembrance of death? Hardly at all, because he remembered it too late. To help us avoid such a gross oversight, Thomas à Kempis urged, "Thou oughtest so to order thyself in all thy thoughts and actions, as if today thou were about to die."[5] Law expounded on this:

> I can't see why every gentleman, merchant, or soldier should not put these questions seriously to himself: What is the best thing for me to intend and drive at in all my actions? How shall I do to make the most of human life? What ways shall I wish that I had taken when I am leaving this world?[6]

When we find out we have only 30 minutes left to live, as General Nelson did, we can't do much more than prepare our own souls. Even worse, the moment of death could prove that our whole life has been a lie.

As vice president, George H.W. Bush represented the United States at the funeral of former Soviet boss Leonid Brezhnev. During the secular service, Bush witnessed a silent protest carried out by Brezhnev's widow. She stood motionless by the coffin until seconds before it was closed. Then, just as the soldiers touched the lid, Brezhnev's wife performed an act of great courage and hope, a gesture that must surely rank as one of the most profound acts of civil disobedience ever committed.

Brezhnev's widow reached down and made the sign of the cross on her husband's chest.

There, in the citadel of secular, atheistic power, the wife of the man who had run it all hoped that her husband was wrong. She hoped that there was another life and that that life was best represented by Jesus, who died on the cross. She hoped that same Jesus might yet have mercy on her husband.

The thought of death came too late for an American Civil War general and a Soviet head of state—will it come too late for us? When your body is lying in the coffin, when your life is being remembered, do you want your surviving spouse or kids or friends to think, "Everything he gave his life for was a fraud. It was wasted. But now, perhaps God will have mercy for him giving his life over to such useless aims, and still usher him into His eternal kingdom."

Virtually every classic writer holds up the remembrance of death as an essential spiritual discipline. It will help us to live a life that is celebrated rather than mourned. "The man who is really concerned to live well must possess himself continually of the thought that he is not to live long."[7]

Making Death Our Servant

D avid is dead," my wife said. "His parents want you to speak at the funeral. They're burying him tomorrow."

I had spent the day with my kids at a local fair. We had been riding kiddie roller coasters, braving gravity-busting wheels, and digesting cotton candy. We got home late at night, and the funeral—a three-hour drive away—was scheduled to take place in about 13 hours. It was difficult, as you might imagine, to shift gears so suddenly.

The funeral was a particularly sad one because David died in prison. He poked heroin into his veins once too often, and on one occasion, the HIV virus was clinging to the needle. David developed AIDS and slowly wasted away. He was in his early thirties.

I tried to comfort his parents: "God knows what it's like to watch a son die in his early thirties," I said.

Lisa and I decided to take our children to the funeral. On the way, we talked to them about what we could learn from this sad passing. "If somebody tells you what you're missing out on when you refuse to take drugs, I want you to remember this," I said. "Think of a young man giving up the rest of his life, dying without a wife, without kids, locked inside a prison cell. That's where drugs will take you. That's what you're missing when you say no to drugs."

I struggled through the service, trying to find words to reach out to those who had come to say good-bye. "David is gone now," my talk began, and I searched for lessons we could learn. The classic Christian writers helped me by teaching me that even tragic deaths can provide valuable truths—if not positively, then negatively. In fact, these writers urge us to *use* death by extracting the message out of each one, thereby making death our servant. Let's see how the remembrance of death can serve us today.

Pure Perspective

> Imagine a number of men in chains, all under sentence of death, some of whom are each day butchered in the sight of others; those remaining see their own condition in that of their fellows, and looking at each other with grief and despair await their turn. This is the image of the human condition.[1]

In this quote, Blaise Pascal captured the reality of the human condition. The remembrance of death acts like a filter, helping us to hold on to the essential and let go of the trivial. Climacus pointed out that a "man who has heard himself sentenced to death will not worry about the way theaters are run."[2] His point, of course, is that all of us have been sentenced to death. It's just a matter of time, so why let trivial matters captivate our hearts?

Eternity certainly does turn everything around. I'm reminded of this every year when I prepare my tax returns. During the year, I rejoice at the paychecks and extra income, and sometimes I wince when I write out the tithe and offering. I do my best to be a joyful giver, but I confess it's not always easy, especially when I have other perceived needs and wants.

At the end of the year, however, all of that changes. As I'm figuring my tax liability, I wince at every source of income and rejoice with every tithe and offering check—more income means more taxes, but every offering and tithe means fewer taxes. Everything is turned upside down, or perhaps more appropriately, right-side up.

I suspect judgment day will be like that. The things that bother us now and force us out of our schedules—taking time out to encourage or help someone, for instance—will be the very things we deem most important. Today, we may not be too happy about having to skip a movie so we could paint an invalid's house, or we may regret missing a meeting so we could visit a prisoner or sick person. But in eternity, the movie and the meeting will seem much less important, and we will be glad we took the time to do those acts of kindness.

Perhaps this is why Fénelon writes, "We cannot too greatly deplore the blindness of men who do not want to think of death, and who turn away from an inevitable thing which we could be happy to think of often. Death only troubles carnal people."[3]

We can maintain a pure perspective on what truly matters by viewing life backward—through the lens of the reality of death.

The Passion Filter

The remembrance of death also serves us by filtering our passions. Pascal wrote, "To render passion harmless, let us behave as though we had only a week to live."[4] Notice the practical element in Pascal's teaching: Remembering death can take the heat out of sinful passions.

Climacus joined him in this counsel. "You cannot pass a day devoutly unless you think of it as your last."[5] He called the thought of death the "most essential of all works" and a gift from God.[6] "The man who lives daily with the thought of death is to be admired, and the man who gives himself to it by the hour is surely a saint."[7]

Law suggested we make moral choices based on the way we'll feel on our deathbeds. "The best way for anyone to know how much he ought to aspire after holiness is to consider not how much will make his present life easy, but to ask himself how much he thinks will make him easy at the hour of death."[8]

What man in his right mind would continue contemplating an affair if he really believed he might not wake up in the morning? What person would risk entering eternity in a drunken stupor? What fool would ignore his loved ones and his God for one last night so he could make another quick ten thousand dollars just before he died?

Thomas à Kempis took an even larger view, arguing that the remembrance of death is a powerful force for spiritual growth in general.

> Didst thou oftener think of thy death than of thy living long, there is no question but thou wouldst be more zealous to improve. If also thou didst but consider within thyself the infernal pains in the other world, I believe thou wouldst willingly undergo any labor or sorrow in this world, and not be afraid of the greatest austerity. But because these things enter not to the heart, and we still love those things only that delight us, therefore we remain cold and very dull in religion.[9]

When we schedule our priorities and follow our passions without regard to eternity, we are essentially looking into the wrong end of a telescope. Instead of seeing things more clearly, our vision becomes tunneled and distorted. We miss the big picture. Law described this skewed perspective:

> Feasts and business and pleasures and enjoyments seem great things to us whilst we think of nothing else; but as soon as we add death to them, they all sink into an equal littleness; and the soul that is separated from the body no more laments the loss of business than the losing of a feast.[10]

Only the denial of death allows us to continue rebelling against God. Only because we presume sometime in the future to set things right do we consider letting them go wrong now. Some of us will be surprised in our presumption; eventually our spirits will be dulled until we forget we are presuming, and like all the rest, death will catch us by surprise.

That's why Thomas à Kempis urged us, "Labor now to live so, that at the hour of death thou mayest rather rejoice than fear."[11] That hour is coming. If it comes tonight, will you be able to rejoice at your state? Or does the mere thought strike fear into your soul? More is involved than just our eternal destiny. God's mercy may well pass us into His eternal presence, but do we want to enter heaven after faithfully serving God to the best of our ability, or after some desperate, last-minute confession, realizing we have wasted our lives?

I want to enter death tired. I want to have spent what energy God has apportioned me. The cross-country races that were most satisfying to me when I was young were not the ones I won most easily but the ones that took everything I had to win. Weariness produced by hard, diligent labor is a reward, not a curse. An eternal rest awaits all who know Christ, so why are we preoccupied with rest now?

Death's Comfort

Death can be a *consoling* thought for those who face particularly difficult losses or trials in this world. Fénelon reminded us, "St. Paul recommends to all Christians that they console themselves together in the thought of death."[12]

Christians, above all people, have reason to be consoled through death. Although we are last on earth, we will be first in heaven. Those who mock our faith and have a sadistic pleasure in polluting our collective soul with their perversion won't have a voice in heaven. The lost loved ones we miss so much are waiting for us on the other side of time. Our disabilities or broken-down bodies won't torment us in heaven. Instead, we'll rejoice as we meet new and improved versions of ourselves without the aches and pains and without the propensity to sin.

And even more importantly, death ushers us face-to-face into the fulfillment of the cry of our hearts—fellowship with the one true God—and this is our greatest consolation of all. All sincere Christians experience at least a bit of loneliness because we long for a more intimate walk with our God—a walk that we will realize beyond our dreams once we pass the threshold of eternity.

To experience the pain of death is normal and healthy. Jesus, after all, wept at the death of Lazarus. But death can also bring hope, not for what it is, but for what God promises us on the other side. The Christian life doesn't make complete sense without the consoling thought of eternal life. Paul himself said we should be pitied above all others if the Christian faith is only for this temporal world (1 Corinthians 15:19). John Calvin said we haven't matured spiritually at all if we don't actively *look forward* to the day of our death.

Keeping Death Alive

When I lived in Virginia, I occasionally attended a Wednesday Communion service at an Episcopal church that dates back to the eighteenth century. As is common with many older churches, the building is surrounded by a graveyard. Every week I walked past the grave markers on my way in and out.

That short walk did almost as much for me as the service itself. I was reminded as I faced the second half of the week that one day, my body, *my* bones, would be lying in the ground. My work on earth will be done. What will matter then? What should matter now in light of that?

I am fond of old graveyards—not in a morbid way, but in a way that inspires me like nothing else. I want to use death the way Thomas à Kempis used it.

> Happy is he that always hath the hour of his death before his eyes, and daily prepareth himself to die...When it is morning,

think thou mayest die before night; and when evening comes, dare not to promise thyself the next morning. Be thou therefore always in a readiness, and so lead thy life that death may never take thee unprepared.[13]

William Law urged that we make the subject of death the focus of our prayers every evening.

The subject that is most proper for your [evening] prayers is death. Let your prayers therefore then be wholly upon it, reckoning up all the dangers, uncertainties, and terrors of death; let them contain everything that can affect and awaken your mind into just apprehensions of it. Let your petitions be all for right sentiments of the approach and importance of death, and beg of God that your mind may be possessed with such a sense of its nearness that you may have it always in your thoughts, do everything as in sight of it, and make every day a day for preparation for it.

Represent to your imagination that your bed is your grave… Such a solemn resignation of yourself into the hands of God every evening and parting with all the world as if you [were] never to see it anymore, and all this in the silence and darkness of the night, is a practice that will soon have excellent effects upon your spirit.[14]

Scupoli urged the remembrance of death by using one of the most common aspects of living: "When walking, think how each step brings you one step nearer to death."[15]

Another way I keep death alive is by living in the communion of saints. I'll post a picture here or a quote there of someone whose faith and life has encouraged me as a reminder that work has an end. If the world can get by without a Dietrich Bonhoeffer or a Blaise Pascal (both died in their thirties), it can get by without me—and one day it will. I have a limited time to use, and it may be much shorter than I realize.

When contemporary saints die, let's benefit from their deaths as much as we benefitted from their lives. The passing of Dr. Klaus Bockmuehl, who mentored me in seminary, gave me great pause and still touches me today, two decades later. Wise shoppers clip coupons. Wise Christians clip obituaries.

But the supreme way for a Christian to keep the thought of death alive is, of course, to remember the crucifixion of our Lord. Jesus died proclaiming, "It is finished." What a wonderful and triumphant way to die— knowing that you've completed the task you were sent here for. What is *your* "it"? Determine what you must accomplish so that at the hour of your death you can look up to heaven and echo the apostle Paul's words: "The time has come for my departure. I have fought the good fight, I have finished the race, I have kept the faith. Now there is in store for me the crown of righteousness, which the Lord, the righteous Judge, will award to me" (2 Timothy 4:6-8).

Just before my family moved from one state to another, Gordon Dunn, a dear missionary in his eighties, invited Lisa and me over for a good-bye dinner. As the night wore on, Gordon pulled me aside and opened up his well-worn Bible to Acts 26:19, where Paul tells Agrippa, "I was not disobedient to the vision from heaven."

"Gary," Gordon said as he looked me in the eye, "at the end of your life, will you be able to say, as Paul did, that you were not disobedient to the vision given you from heaven?"

I've never forgotten that conversation. I particularly try to remember it—as well as Christ's words on the cross—every time I participate in the Lord's Supper. Every time we take Communion, we should do so with the awareness that, just as Christ's work on earth had a beginning and an end (as He ministered in a human body), so the mission He has given us has a beginning and an end.

One of my editors told me of a fellow writer, not well known in the United States, who died at a relatively young age. He had worked tirelessly to get Christians more actively involved in the arts. His life was a testimony to God's grace and creativity. By all accounts, this man had been a faithful husband, a good father, and an earnest servant of the gospel.

Many tears were shed at the funeral for a man most thought should have had several more decades to live. Yet as his casket was picked up by the pall bearers and carried down the church aisle, something curious happened: Mourners turned into celebrators. The crowd erupted into a spontaneous standing ovation. This was a life well lived; a life in which death revealed a victory, not a defeat; a life marked by faithfulness and service. It deserved a raucous cheer.

May we all live in such a way that our passing evokes a standing ovation, not only by believers on earth but also by the saints and inhabitants of heaven.

Keeping death alive is one of the most fruitful spiritual disciplines we can ever practice. "Death is the destiny of every man; the living should take this to heart" (Ecclesiastes 7:2).

32

A Difficult Road

When Mary approached Joseph with her incredible news, she must have been full of wonder. God had visited her—*her!*—and chosen her and Joseph for the incredible task of raising the Son of God.

Did Mary's wonder and excitement slip into confusion and fear when she saw the doubt in Joseph's eyes and heard the disbelief in his words? We're not given any details about Mary and Joseph's encounter, but we can conclude that Mary knew two things when she left her meeting with Joseph. First, Joseph didn't believe her. He hadn't told her he was planning to break the engagement yet, but she knew that he had serious doubts.

Second, because he didn't believe her, her life was in danger. From John 8 we know that the Pharisees weren't slow to carry out the punishment for adultery (death by stoning). Joseph may have been a righteous and gentle man, but who would stop the Pharisees once Mary's pregnancy began showing?

Was that when the questions began?

"How can You do this to me, God? I said yes to You, and this is the thanks I get? I held nothing back, only to be called a liar and have my life threatened by my own people!"

God could have made it so easy on Mary. For instance, He could have rewarded Mary's willingness to bear Jesus by visiting Joseph *before* Mary told him about the child. Then Joseph could have immediately comforted her and said, "It's okay, Mary, I believe you! God visited me last night and told me all about it." Remember, Joseph had a special visit from an angel on his own *after* Mary gave him the big news. Why didn't God make it easy on Mary and visit Joseph a few days earlier? Maybe God wanted to do a work *in* Mary before He did a miraculous work *through* Mary. Perhaps. But one thing is clear: God asked Mary to travel a difficult road.

He continues to call His saints to great challenges.

Unlike some contemporary teachers, Christians in earlier centuries widely recognized that the spiritual life is very difficult. The classics speak with one voice, perhaps best typified by Johannes Tauler: "Beloved, no one can escape suffering. Wherever a person may be, he must suffer."[1]

The Life of the Cross

Those who have gone before us have left a clear witness: We may seek God or we may seek ease, but we cannot seek both. The road we travel is anything but easy. God loves us more than we can imagine and has wonderful plans for our lives, but those plans are often fraught with tension, uncertainty, and emotional, spiritual, and physical pain. John Climacus referred to this in his book *The Ladder of Divine Ascent.*

> Violence [see Matthew 11:12] and unending pain are the lot of those who aim to ascend to heaven with the body, and this especially at the early stages of the enterprise, when our pleasure-loving disposition and our unfeeling hearts must travel through overwhelming grief toward the love of God and holiness. It is hard, truly hard.[2]

Brother Lawrence lived with chronic gout that forced him to walk with a limp. At one point he was in such pain that he moved by rolling on top of barrels. This was a humbling experience for him. But he didn't spend time writing about his physical condition; to him, the *spiritual* war was the truly difficult one. Speaking of the challenge of building a never-ceasing prayer life, Lawrence wrote, "I found no small trouble in this exercise, and yet I continued it, notwithstanding all the difficulties."[3]

The anonymous author of *The Cloud of Unknowing* offered this warning of the immense challenges sure to confront anyone serious about developing a contemplative prayer life: "A difficult task indeed does he have who commits himself to his work. In fact, it will be exceedingly difficult." He urged his readers to persevere, saying they must "labor in this work with great patience, enduring the pains of it no matter how great they be."[4]

Franciscan friar Brother Giles saw the same difficulty in the area of character growth: "It is impossible to acquire virtues without trouble and effort."[5] Accordingly, Lorenzo Scupoli argued for more honesty with new believers.

> Great is the toil and struggle at the outset, which beginners experience when they resolve to amend their wicked lives and, renouncing the world and the flesh, to yield themselves up to the love and service of Jesus Christ. For the assault, which the higher will sustains from the divine and sensual wills warring on both sides of it, is so sharp and violent, that it entails much suffering.[6]

In Scupoli's mind, talking about easy virtue and painless character transformation is like talking about a peaceful war or a quiet riot—it's just not honest.

> Let no one suppose it possible to form true Christian virtues, and to serve God as he ought, unless he is ready in good earnest to do violence to his own inclinations and to endure the pain of giving up all the things that please him, both great and small, and to which he has clung with earthly affection.[7]

The truth about the difficulty of the Christian life is particularly challenging for many contemporary believers who have been told that turning to Christ should make life *easier*. From the perspective of these writers, turning to Christ is to begin an entirely new season of travail.

This is an example of the way the devotional classics can provide a needed corrective to our modern thinking. Given the range of Scriptures and the near unanimity of the historic Christian witness on difficulty—its certainty and our need for it—I'm not sure how we have developed a gospel that speaks of God lifting us *out* of trouble instead of a gospel that talks about God walking *with* us in the midst of trouble. But such a gospel is occasionally taught. We need to get rid of such surface thinking if we are ever to mature in the faith.

Saints on Sleep Number Beds

When you travel a lot, everything starts to look the same, so you notice when something out of the ordinary appears—something like a professional-looking man walking with a briefcase in one hand and a colorful pillow in the other hand. Part of him appeared to be on his way to a meeting on Wall Street, and the other half seemed to be headed for Camp Chickamauga.

The man explained as we were getting off the plane, "Hotel pillows are always too hard, so I can never get any sleep."

When I think of the cells the ancients lived and slept in and compare them with the Sleep Number bed supporting me at night, I wonder if modern believers can ever truly appreciate the classic Christian teaching on difficulty. The man on the plane couldn't bear a pillow that wasn't fluffed just right. How affluence has softened us.

The ancients would have looked at our ease as a troublesome problem, not a divine blessing! This opening sentence from Julian of Norwich's *Revelations of Divine Love* is surely one of the most shocking in the Christian classics: "I asked for three graces of God's gift. The first was vivid perception of Christ's Passion, the second was bodily sickness and the third was for God to give me three wounds."[8]

I've been in more small group prayer meetings than I can count, and I can't remember a single time when someone prayed to get sick and wounded so he or she could feel the Passion of Christ more intensely.

Julian explains why she had such a curious prayer request: "I longed to have in this sickness every kind of suffering both of body and soul... because I wished to be purged by the mercy of God and afterwards to live more to God's glory because of that sickness."[9] These words are not religiously sentimental. Julian lived through the Black Death, the famous bubonic plague that decimated the population of fourteenth-century England. She wasn't praying for an ordinary head cold.

When we face battles, disappointments, or difficulties, we tend to ask other believers to pray for their immediate end. That's because we see the difficulties as greater evils than our spiritual immaturity. John of the Cross looked at this from an entirely different perspective.

> Endeavor to be inclined always: not to the easiest, but to the most difficult; not to the most delightful, but to the harshest; not to the most gratifying, but to the less pleasant; not to what means rest for you, but hard work; not to the consoling, but to the unconsoling; not to the most, but to the least; not to the highest and most precious, but to the lowest and most despised; not to wanting something, but to wanting nothing;

> do not go about looking for the best of temporal things, but for the worst....
>
> You should embrace these practices earnestly and try to overcome the repugnance of your will toward them. If you sincerely put them into practice with order and discretion, you will discover in them great delight and consolation.

Personally, I think you can take John's advice too far. I no longer immediately assume that the difficult road, the less enjoyable road, is God's will. But we do need a willingness to embrace pain under God's providence (a providence that may also occasionally lead us to joy and pleasure).

German pastor and martyr Dietrich Bonhoeffer called suffering "the badge of true discipleship," adding, "If there is no element of asceticism in our lives...we shall find it hard to train for the service of Christ."[10] Discomfort can be a friend, not a foe, for those who truly want to grow.

Contemporary Comfort

This morning I traveled from a climate-controlled house to a climate-controlled office in a climate-controlled car. I have virtually no persistent physical pain right now, and I've never experienced true hunger.

Though Christ says I must be willing to do so, I've never been forced to choose between my family or my vocation and my faith. In fact, my vocation is directly tied to my faith. Growing up, I was occasionally ridiculed for my beliefs, but now I am usually encouraged rather than discouraged whenever I venture outside my office.

Thus, Scripture and the classics almost seem melodramatic when they refer to the difficulty of the Christian life. Sure, life was difficult for Richard Baxter, who wrote *The Saints' Everlasting Rest* with a grotesque tumor hanging on the side of his body. Of course it was difficult for Brother Lawrence, whose painful, chronic gout eventually developed into an ulcerated leg, leaving him to walk for the rest of his life with a pronounced limp (in a world without cars, wheelchairs, or bikes). Obviously it was difficult for John Climacus and other monks whose societies glorified such practices as perching for decades on sunbaked pillars, living in cells that were too small to stand up or lie down in, or cultivating leeches on their bodies—after all, they intentionally *made* life difficult. But is it that difficult for you and me?

If these saints came into a church today and saw our padded chairs, climate-controlled classrooms, acoustically perfect sanctuaries, and luxury cars, would they still teach that the Christian life is difficult? Would they still say it is "hard, very hard" to follow Christ?

In some ways, they might say it is even harder. As Baxter wrote his famous treatise on heaven, his tumor reminded him that heaven was drawing near. Being enamored with heaven was easy for him—his body wouldn't let him forget it. Our surgical and medical advancements lull us into a false security, causing us to forget that we are one missed heartbeat away from heaven. When life becomes easier, faith, to the secular mind, becomes less important.

The physical and social luxuries of our world also make it more difficult for us to face unpleasant internal issues because we don't have to—we have plenty of escapes. Radios, iPods, televisions, and the Internet keep our minds occupied from morning to midnight. The weightier thoughts of Christian commitment and sacrifice never need to bother us. By filling our lives with noise, we can hide from the truth of the gospel and our responsibility to serve God.

Maybe the luxurious world in which Western middle-class Christians live assaults our faith every bit as much as the deprivation of the Middle Ages. Former saints had nowhere to turn but to God; we can take our pick of comforts.

Our external world would be unrecognizable to someone from the Middle Ages, but the internal world remains the same. Unbelief, sin, and temptation are no less rampant for us than they were for our spiritual ancestors—perhaps even more so. The historic message that the Christian life is difficult is every bit as relevant today as it was when Jesus first spoke it. We're just a little less willing to embrace it. How do we talk about the cross to a generation that finds unfluffed pillows intolerable?

Converts or Disciples?

The Christian faith contains two elements—good news (joy and peace) and bad news (persecution, self-denial, and the cross)—that our society sees as inherently contradictory. Herein lies the temptation to transform the faith in order to make it more inviting to nonbelievers.

When the goal is to make converts rather than disciples, we are tempted to restate the Christian life according to felt needs—the peace, fulfillment, and purpose that life in Christ brings. But speaking of these things exclusively is similar to describing the feeling of winning a gold medal at the Olympics—the accomplishment, joy, and elation—without mentioning the grueling training that is required.

Scripture says the disciples "strengthened" or "encouraged" each other with these words: "We must go through many hardships to enter the kingdom of God."[11] Notice Scripture doesn't say they "threatened" each other with the possibility of suffering. No, they *encouraged* and *strengthened* each other.

Jesus chose to compare the way of Christianity with the cross, a brutal executioner's tool leading to the darkness of the tomb, not a gentle instrument leading to hours of ease. (Have you ever heard of a padded, sleep-number cross?) Such was Christ's introduction to the Christian life when He said, "If anyone desires to come after Me, let him deny himself, and take up his cross daily, and follow Me."[12]

There are at least three reasons why we should teach people about difficulties. The first reason is the most compelling one. We have an obligation to mention the difficulty of the Christian life because Jesus did, and He is the Author of our message. "In this world, you will have trouble" (John 16:33). We have no right to bear any other message. The Christian faith is meant to be unoriginal. It has been given to us. We didn't create it, nor were we given permission to edit it. To transform it in any way is arrogant presumption at best and prideful heresy at worst.

Second, when we ignore difficulty, we threaten to create disillusioned Christians who jump into the faith enthusiastically but take the next religion out as soon as the joy wanes and frustration and struggle arise. They may eventually abandon the faith altogether and thereby be inoculated against real Christianity, mistakenly believing they have already tried it, when in fact, they experienced nothing more than a caricature.

Third, we need to remember the difficulty so we can keep going. Thomas à Kempis reminds us that when we struggle, we need to know others struggle too.

> It is but little which thou sufferest, in comparison with those who suffered so much, who were so strongly tempted, so grievously afflicted, so many ways tried and exercised. Thou oughtest therefore to call to mind the heavier sufferings of others, that so thou mayest the easier bear thy own very small troubles.[13]

If we know the Christian life is difficult, we will not question our faith when difficulty arises but instead will turn to the God who will strengthen our faith. We begin to use difficulty as an encouragement to press on.

God's wonderful plan has a painful beginning and many difficult hills to climb before we reach the final resting ground. We are less than honest when we fail to mention this. Ignatius stated it this way (imagining Christ speaking): "Whoever, therefore, desires to come with Me must labor with Me, in order that following Me in pain, he may likewise follow Me in glory."[14]

In the next chapter, we're going to look at the lives of two people in particular who overcame more than their share of suffering and difficulty. For now, let's embrace a biblical and ancient truth: Christianity presents a difficult life—a glorious life, a rich life, the best life imaginable, but not an easy life. In the words of Johannes Tauler, "Our Lord always promised peace to His disciples," both before and after the resurrection, "yet they never obtained an outward peace. Nonetheless, they found peace in sorrow, and joy in tribulation. In death they found life, and to be judged, sentenced and condemned was for them a joyous victory."[15]

Two Lives, Two Triumphs

Teresa of Avila's classic treatise on prayer, *The Interior Castle*, has inspired millions of Christians to seek a deeper intimacy with God. Yet prayer was once so painful and difficult for Teresa that she gave it up temporarily.

Teresa entered the Carmelite Monastery of the Incarnation against the wishes of her father. He wanted her to have a good education after her mother died, but he certainly didn't expect her to "throw her life away" by joining a religious order. Teresa had to virtually orphan herself—her mother was dead and she was abandoning her father—to follow God's call on her life. She wrote later that the separation felt like every bone in her body was being torn apart.

A few years later, Teresa became very ill and was nearly killed by fantastic methods of treatment. After one "doctor" was finished with her, she slipped into a coma for three days without any signs of life. When she came to, she was partially paralyzed, and three years later, she was still unable to walk.

Her difficulties were more than physical, however. During her thirties, Teresa experienced severe spiritual travail. The woman whose prayer life has inspired so many actually gave up prayer for a short while because her prayer life caused her such pain. She wrote about this period with horror, believing it to be her most serious lapse into sin. But at the time, prayer was so difficult that she would have preferred heavy penance to prayer. Teresa once wrote to God, "If this is how you treat your friends, it's no wonder you have so many enemies."

Added to the physical and spiritual battles, Teresa soon found herself the cause of an enormous social battle. She wrote *The Interior Castle* while her life's work of founding reformed monasteries was being questioned and threatened by higher authorities. Italian Carmelites feared that Teresa's Spanish reform might spread and compel them to reform themselves. A dear friend of hers, John of the Cross, whom she had put in charge of some of the monasteries she had founded, was viciously treated and thrown into jail for remaining loyal to Teresa's teachings. The social battle may have resurrected Teresa's physical ills, for they once again became intense. Teresa wrote in the prologue of her classic, "I have been experiencing now for three months such great noise and weakness in my head that I've found it a hardship even to write concerning necessary business matters."

When Teresa of Avila wrote about the difficulties encountered in deepening one's spiritual life, she knew what she was talking about.

> What interior and exterior trials the soul suffers before entering the seventh dwelling place! Indeed, sometimes I reflect and fear that if a soul knew beforehand, its natural weakness would find it most difficult to have the determination to suffer and pass through these trials, no matter what blessings were represented to it.[1]

The "seventh dwelling place" was Teresa's "spiritual marriage" through prayer. When she obtained it, John of the Cross was in the room. What joy these two believers must have felt, for both of them had walked through great difficulty to get there.

John's Journey

John of the Cross also grew up in difficult circumstances. His father died when he was three, and John's family was cast into hunger and poverty. John eventually received a proper education but still chose to enter a religious order. Because of his connection with Teresa and her teachings, he was arrested, classified as a rebel, and given the usual penalties for such offenses—imprisonment, flogging, and fasting on bread and water. John was kept in a small room, six feet wide by ten feet long, with one two-inch window for his only source of light. For nine months he lived in darkness with little food and hardly a change of clothing.

Yet a divine light pierced the darkness of that prison cell, and John's teaching on the dark night of the soul has inspired many Christians to persevere through the spiritual desert. Read what John wrote about difficulty: "The darknesses and trials, spiritual and temporal, that fortunate [notice, he says *fortunate*] souls ordinarily undergo on their way to the high state of perfection are so numerous and profound that human science cannot understand them adequately."[2] He added later, "Both the sense and the spirit, as though under an immense and dark load, undergo such agony and pain that the soul would consider death a relief."[3]

Remember, John's life was not easy, but he didn't mention the physical pain, the cold, the hunger, or the loneliness. Instead, he was concerned about the difficult war within, the battle for his soul. This was the struggle he focused on.

In John's mind, internal pain became the "doorkeeper" to further growth. He wrote that often souls do not advance because they are unwilling to face the dark night that would lead to a closer walk with God.[4] He also warned of unwise counselors who do not understand the necessity of difficulty.

> [Those who suffer] will meet someone in the midst of the fullness of their darknesses, trials, conflicts, and temptations who, in the style of Job's comforters, will proclaim that all of this is due to melancholia, depression, or temperament, or to some hidden wickedness, and that as a result God has forsaken them. Therefore the usual verdict is that these individuals must have lived an evil life since such trials affect them.[5]

The counselor may then urge a general confession of sin, which John called "another crucifixion" and considered untimely.

> The director does not understand that now perhaps is not the time for such activity. Indeed, it is a period of leaving these persons alone in the purgation God is working in them, a time to give comfort and encouragement that they may desire to endure this suffering as long as God wills, for until then, no remedy—whatever the soul does, or the confessor does— is adequate.[6]

Rejecting the Cross

I am struck by John's radical perspective about the dark night. When most Christians today encounter anything anywhere near this, their counselors and pastors and friends feel compelled to fix it—to help suffering believers out of their trials. John believed precisely the opposite. In his mind, we must allow God to take believers through some soul-crushing experiences in order for them to mature. We do not "fix" these things— we learn from them and endure them.

When we find ourselves rejecting difficulty, we may find that we are actually rejecting the cross—and therefore Christ Himself. John of the Cross was not alone in writing about this. Consider Thomas à Kempis's words:

> Christ's whole life was a cross and martyrdom; and dost thou seek rest and joy for thyself? Thou art deceived, thou art deceived, if thou seek any other thing than to suffer tribulations; for this whole mortal life is full of miseries, and signed on every side with crosses. And the higher a person hath advanced in spirit, so much the heavier crosses he oftentimes findeth.[7]

Willingness to bear the cross results in our spiritual growth just as surely as a refusal to bear the cross keeps us from growing. Both Teresa and John must have been tempted to turn back many times. They were comforted, however, with the knowledge that throughout Scripture, those who followed God most closely suffered most severely. Jesus Himself was the supreme example. Teresa writes, "We have always seen that those who were closest to Christ our Lord were those with the greatest trials."[8]

Perhaps Teresa had read Julian of Norwich's description of her own experience: "The cross which stood at the foot of my bed, it was bleeding hard."[9]

If you find yourself in a time of difficulty, know that you are not alone. Be encouraged that God is treating you as He has treated so many of His saints, from Mary to Teresa to John and countless others in between. Yes, if sin is in your life, repent of it, but don't expect that to lead to an initial healing or release. Difficulty might simply be a preparatory work. Perhaps God has some significant task for you that is going to require you to be stronger, more mature, and more faith-filled than you are now. This difficult road may be the only path to take you there.

This understanding led the devotional masters to value trials. Let's end this chapter with a choice quote from Scupoli: "I entreat you to cherish a love for that which is painful and difficult, for such things will bring you victory over self—and on this, all depends."[10]

It's Not Easy to Be You

W hy is the Christian life so difficult? Five very challenging and ongoing obstacles plague us. Regardless of how mature we become, whether we are ordained ministers or recent converts, these obstacles unceasingly pursue us. They are part of the natural human condition, and we will bear them to some degree until we are ushered into eternity.

Physical Disabilities and Limitations (Romans 8:18-25)

These physical bodies we live in, so necessary and yet so burdensome, are the very first obstacles that slam into our spiritual idealism. We want to pray, but we fall asleep. We desire to fast, but our stomachs rage and urge us to break down before the hunger. We want to be patient, but stressful situations draw out our temper.

As physical beings, we are subject to plenty of limitations. We have to earn a living. We have to face pain, from arthritis to cancer. We grow tired and hungry. We fight physical compulsions and fears. Add to these the sinus problems, allergies, headaches, and any other ailments we may have, and some days can feel pretty long. These all proceed from the fall of humanity, and until Christ's return, we will live in a broken world.

Our bodies are part of us. Even in our glorified state we will not be bodiless. We will have glorified bodies, yes, but bodies nonetheless. In the meantime, we have to make do with less than perfect instruments through which to live out our faith.

Physical difficulties include financial difficulties. Taxation has increased to such an extent that Christians who are committed to tithing often live on less than half of their income (federal, state, and local taxes can add up to 40 or 50 percent of your income).

When we sense a spiritual breaking point in our own lives, we need to look at our physical condition. Have we pushed it too far? We shouldn't allow our bodies to master us, but neither should we try to live as if our bodies don't need care. "The soul has no thought or passion but the body is concerned in it; the body has no action or motion but what in some degree affects the soul."[1]

Though physical pain is a part of the fall, God can and does use it for our spiritual advancement. Brother Lawrence said, "[God] sometimes permits the body to suffer to cure the sickness of the soul."[2]

Social Pain (1 Thessalonians 2:2)

In addition to pain arising from our fallen physical condition, pain is also generated from living in a fallen social environment. We live as sinners surrounded by sinners. People hurt us; our parents, our friends, and our fellow believers all contribute to our pain.

One father told me the heartbreaking tale of his daughter returning a Christmas present to him in July, telling him she didn't want it anymore. He had purchased a cell phone, but after trying it out for seven months, his daughter said, "Nobody calls it." The phone was a symbol of her alienation from the world. During one stretch, she charged the phone three times without getting a single call, until she just felt foolish and more alone than she'd ever felt before. She didn't need a reminder that nobody wanted to talk to her.

Social pain can be as intense as physical pain. Some of this pain may be deserved, but much of it may not be. All of us are surrounded by people dealing with various neuroses, obsessions, and unhealthy attachments and needs. This social pain often sends us reeling and begging for deliverance.

When my kids were small, they loved a book about a family going on a bear hunt. The father and his children face all kinds of obstacles—a deep, dark forest; oozing mud; a swirling, whirling snowstorm. At each dilemma they conclude, "We can't go over it, we can't go around it. Oh, no! We have to go through it!"

This book holds a lesson for adults as well as children. We can't always run from social pain; sometimes we just have to go through it. We may be forced to work with unhealthy people. You might even be married to a cruel spouse or be the child of a cruel parent or the parent of a cruel child. If we run, we'll often end up with the same pain in a different situation. A friend of mine was locked into a difficult relationship with her boss but refused to leave. "I've had four bosses, and they've all been like this one. There's no use running. I just have to learn whatever it is God wants to teach me."

When social pain becomes intense, we may be tempted to dull the ache with unholy methods—the spiritual quicksand of addictions, food, gambling, television, or any of the hundred other diversions we use to escape from pain rather than learn from it—or become bitter and angry at God, insisting that He's not being fair. Our anger may be deeply buried, but healing will begin only when we're willing to accept that life is difficult.

In this light, we see that many marital situations with "irreconcilable differences" could be the seedbed of growth if we would stay in them and not give up. Jesus chose 12 disciples who would naturally have problems with the beliefs, attitudes, or dispositions of the others. If I were seeking peace and harmony, I certainly wouldn't put a tax collector with a zealot—two natural enemies. But Jesus knew that real spirituality is proven in our relationships with others, and He was willing to call people into relationships that stretched them beyond their comfort level.

Let's not forget that God is well aware of the difficulty of living in a world of sinners. In one of His most astonishing pronouncements, Jesus, on His way to the cross, told some women who were weeping at His condition, "Daughters of Jerusalem, do not weep for me; weep for yourselves and for your children...For if men do these things when the tree is green, what will happen when it is dry?" (Luke 23:28,31).

Jesus no doubt appreciates the women's sympathy, but He displays a remarkable empathy of His own, mentioning how sorry He is that they live in a world where people are treated like this. I've found great comfort in knowing that God understands this is not an easy world to live in.

The Tendency to Sin (Romans 7:14-20)

We are born in sin, and every inclination of our hearts is to do evil. According to John Owen, the rule of sin is broken in believers, and its

strength is weakened and impaired, but the law of sin is still "of great force
and efficacy." He wrote, "Indwelling sin is an exceedingly effective power
in believers, working constantly toward evil."[3]

Thus, Owen wrote, our enemy is not only upon us but also *in us*.[4] We
can pretend we are above sin, but such pretending serves Satan, not God.
Ignorance of the law of sin, wrote Owen, "breeds senselessness, carelessness,
sloth, self-sufficiency, and pride—all of which the Lord's soul abhors."[5]

Paul's honesty in Romans 7 about his constant battle against the flesh
reveals God's kindness. God inspired Paul to write honestly so we would
know *God gets it*—He understands that the battle against the flesh is fierce,
never ending, and sometimes excruciating. Through Paul, God teaches
us that a Christian is never dominated by sin, but a Christian is often
assaulted by sin.

I believe that when the Bible speaks, God speaks, so I receive Paul's
words as God's ordained message to us that He completely understands
how difficult, frustrating, and humiliating life with a forceful sin nature
can be. Yes, God hates our sin, but He inspired Paul to write so openly
about his own struggles so we would know that though God sets the standard very high, He knows it's not easy. He understands. Fighting sin is
tough.

Think about it. Sin attempts to pollute every relationship, every life
situation, every holy moment. When God provides a great meal, we have
to guard against gluttony. We love our kids, but that love can tempt us to
become fearful or express anger in inappropriate ways when they disap-
point us. Even a noble affection (a parent's love) can set us up for ungodly
action.

This has been true from the beginning of human history. God warned
the first murderer, "Sin is crouching at your door; it desires to have you,
but you must master it" (Genesis 4:7). Don't you get tired of sin crouching
at your door? Don't you grow weary of constantly battling the sin nature
that still assaults you? Of course you do. We all do.

A reminder from John Calvin has become helpful for me. After we
become God's adopted children, He doesn't treat our sin the way a judge
would, but rather as a physician would. God knows we sin, and He will discipline us accordingly, but He does so with the spirit of a doctor who wants
to make us well, not a prosecuting attorney who wants to make us pay.

This is where reading works from the Eastern Orthodox branch of

Christianity has been so enlightening and helpful to me. The Reformed tradition emphasizes that Christ's death absorbed God's wrath against us, and many biblical passages support this emphasis. The Orthodox branch, however, emphasizes the fact that Jesus died not primarily to absorb God's wrath, but to defeat the powers of sin and darkness that war against His people. Man is not only the perpetrator but also the victim. As Romans 8:3 puts it, "He condemned *sin* in sinful man." Or Galatians 1:4: "Jesus Christ...gave himself for our sins to rescue us from the present evil age."

Yes, we are guilty, so we cannot paint ourselves exclusively or even primarily as victims. But in another sense, God *does* see us as victims because He knows that on our own, we are powerless against the force of sin in our hearts.

This Orthodox perspective of God's empathy toward our battle against sin has been a great encouragement to me. Growing up in my own tradition, I was intensely aware of God's wrath and disappointment (I still am). The Eastern branch helped me to see that God is also empathetic toward my struggles, that He sent His own Son as a statement of just how sorry He is that we must bear the burden of our sin.

However, the writers of the Christian classics want us to remember the difficulty of sin not only so we will deal with it on a personal level but also so we will see how it distorts everything God gives us—even *good* things. How many of us have used a gift God has given us to serve Satan's ends rather than build God's kingdom? How many of us have used humor to cut and ridicule instead of to heal and encourage? How many of us have received the gift of earning money and then let that money waste away on selfish pursuits? How many of us have been empowered to serve but have perverted that gift by trying to make others feel indebted to us? How many of us have been equipped to lead others but have turned that gift into a tool of manipulation and control?

If we forget the law of sin in our lives and how very difficult it is to obtain mastery over it, Satan will have a field day with our self-righteous carelessness. Even our strengths can become weaknesses if we're not careful.

We are called to be holy, but our inclination is to do evil and be selfish. This creates more than mere difficulty in our lives; it can result in an internal war. Healthy Christians are somewhat suspicious of themselves. They have reason to be!

The Temptation to Sin (1 Peter 5:8)

The fourth difficulty builds on and exacerbates the third. Our natural tendency toward sin is problematic enough, but our situation is even worse. We also have a real, living being tempting us to sin—the evil one, Satan. Peter warns us that our "adversary the devil walks about like a roaring lion, seeking whom he may devour" (1 Peter 5:8 NKJV).

Climacus reiterated that fact. "There are demons to assail us after our renunciation of the world."[6] Satan doesn't watch us give our lives to Christ and then retire in frustration. He continues to try to trip us up. When we pray, he seeks to distract us. When we consider serving, he tempts us to think only of ourselves. He and his minions will do whatever is necessary to slow us down or take us off the path entirely.

Have you ever been hit exactly where you're weakest, when you're weakest, and felt as if you were set up? Ever think that maybe you *were*? This is not to excuse sin, but to help us understand that spiritual beings are actively tempting us, our family members, and our coworkers to sin. We must vigorously embrace grace, understanding, and forgiveness, or these spiritual foes will tear apart our homes, our churches, and our workplaces.

I regularly talk and visit with Christians all over the nation in various situations. The most dangerous Christians are those who have forgotten their tendency to sin—and Satan's agenda to capitalize on that tendency. When Satan is allowed to move in the shadows, forgotten and without restraint, his power can be tremendous. Thoughtful Christians have never forgotten that we have an enemy as well as a Savior.

Gaining mastery over the law of sin is difficult, as is maintaining vigilance against the devil's schemes. As Christians, we're going to fail. Our spouses and children are going to fail. Our pastors and fellow church members are going to fail. Someone, right now, is tempting these people to fail. We can either admit the difficulty, become a people of grace, and support each other in this fight, or we can tear each other apart for the slightest infraction.

I'm not suggesting we downplay the seriousness of sin. I am suggesting, however, that we drop the accusing voice, stop pretending we're above temptation, and learn the biblical admonition to restore people gently (Galatians 6:1). When I truly understand that someone who sins against me has been actively tempted to do so, I gain empathy and understanding, making the act of forgiveness a little easier and perhaps less painful.

Surprisingly enough, Christian writers from centuries past found some measure of comfort in the difficulty of satanic opposition. Climacus, who warned of the reality of demonic opposition, also reminded us that being shot at is evidence that we are fighting. The Christian should not fear this difficulty—it is a sign of progress. Instead, we should fear the lack of opposition, for its absence means the enemy has found us unworthy of opposition.

A Deceitful Heart (Jeremiah 17:9)

The heart is deceitful above all things. "There is a way that seems right to a man, but in the end it leads to death" (Proverbs 14:12). Consider this: We endure physical pain and limitations, persevere in spite of social pain, struggle with a tendency to sin, and face a fierce enemy who tempts us to sin—all in an arena in which we walk naturally blind. We deceive ourselves. Sometimes, we become our own enemy.

John Owen wrote, "We do not...know the secret intrigues and schemes, twists and turns, actions and tendencies of our own hearts."[7] We are easily led astray, often because we want to be led astray. We confuse our emotions or our fears with the voice of God. We rationalize that God will understand. We pretend the situation we face is ambiguous. We lie to ourselves and others and take the easy road. We run a hundred red lights and then wake up surprised that we have crashed.

We cannot trust ourselves to live the Christian life alone. The smug, self-confident, and solitary Christian is the deceived Christian who is about to fall or who is in the midst of a fall and doesn't know it. This is why I am so pleased to have mature Christians with whom I pray regularly and who can speak God's truth into my life. They know me well enough to detect even a hint of insincerity in my prayers, and they love me enough to mention it.

Even Paul recognized that he wasn't up to judging himself. "My conscience is clear, but that does not make me innocent" (1 Corinthians 4:4). We have been placed in the toughest battle of our lives, only to find that we are to be feared as much as the enemy. Even our own minds, hearts, and spiritual understanding cannot be trusted.

Too many Christians forget this fifth difficulty—the difficulty of self-deception—and take no steps toward protecting themselves against it. Just remember that a solitary Christian is Satan's favorite toy. When we're alone, he'll have the time of his miserable life luring us toward destruction.

Nowhere to Run

It gets even worse: There really is nowhere on earth to run from these challenges. Through the ages, the difficulty of the Christian life led believers to try many different living arrangements in a sometimes desperate attempt to find a life of less temptation.

Three living arrangements gained the most prominence: (1) solitary living—the world of the hermits, (2) a large community of monks who lived under the direction of an abbot, and (3) small groups of religious adherents who lived in fairly close-knit communities under the guidance of a spiritual father or mother (often called the "middle way").

At various points in his life, John Climacus lived in all three, but he eventually settled on the middle way. Every life situation provided different temptations; none were free of temptation. Climacus believed solitary living made men particularly susceptible to pride, and large communities could foster gossip, improper affections, and wasted time. All you could do, he said, was choose an arrangement that would make you less susceptible to different kinds of sin. He found that there was no living arrangement—absolutely none—that sin couldn't manipulate to its advantage.

Whether you are single, married, widowed, divorced, with kids or without kids, an empty nester or in the throes of raising toddlers, employed or unemployed, sick or healthy, affluent or poor, in the country or living in a city, sin will find you out and exploit your situation for its advantage. You can trade temptations, but you can't completely avoid them.

And the dirty little secret is that life tends to lead us toward *more* difficulty, not less. What usually happens when we Christians reach our twenties or thirties? We get married. Now these five realities are doubled. Not only must we deal with difficulty in our own lives, but we must also face our spouses' physical pain, which we must sometimes bear; our spouses' social pain, which we will sometimes pay for; our spouses' tendency to sin, which we will bear the brunt of; and our spouses' assaults from the devil. And our spouses, like us, may not even realize what is going on.

Hold on. That does sound difficult, but I'm still not done. When people get married, they have a tendency to bear children. Pretty soon there are four or five people who face a difficult life, who must endure physical pain and spiritual temptation, and who can bring out the best or worst in each other.

No wonder some Christians feel beaten up! I'm not surprised some families simply give up! The answer is not to give up, of course, but when we don't teach the reality of difficulty, who can blame people for thinking maybe they ought to trade in their family for a new one? They don't realize that they can't run from the human condition, because all they see on Sunday morning are smiling faces that seem impervious to the human condition.

Life is difficult, and the Christian life is even more difficult. Some creative theology has arisen to explain the difficulty away, but a new coat of paint will only hide the rot for a short time. Sooner or later we'll have to face the truth, as à Kempis noted: "If thou cast away one cross, without doubt thou shalt find another, and that perhaps a heavier one. Thinkest thou to escape that which no mortal man would ever avoid? Which of the saints in the world was without crosses and tribulation?"[8]

In the next chapter we'll explore some of the spiritual benefits of all these realities and challenges, but for now I want to affirm the biblical and historic Christian perspective: We should *expect* difficulty. To assume that the more mature we become, the easier life will get is entirely wrong. Very often, the opposite is the truth. If you're walking a particularly difficult road, rather than assume you've somehow fallen outside of God's will, at least be open to the possibility that in fact you might be exactly where He wants you to be.

35

The Sweet Side of Suffering

I used to be a vicious discipler. I never missed a quiet time, and if people I was working with did, I questioned the sincerity of their faith. Then God in His mercy crushed me for eight long years. Sins I had never faced before came roaring to life. Prayer became difficult. Ministry felt strained and awkward. I had no sense of God's power coursing through me.

At the end of this period a door flew open, the darkness was lifted, and I was changed. I realized God doesn't need someone who can preach better than anyone else, fast longer, pray more, or evangelize more. He wants somebody who loves His people. I knew a lot about discipline and commitment, but I knew nothing about love.

Difficulty teaches us to be pastoral people, something that does not come naturally to us. If we deny our own pain, we must also blind ourselves to the pain of others. We need difficulty because without it we become proud, self-centered, and uncaring monsters who are full of ourselves.

Difficulty is not to be feared or denied, but to be used. I've never heard someone say, "It was only after I made my first million that I finally understood the meaning of life, that my priorities were put in order, and my relationship with God was deepened." But many of us have heard people say, "As much as I dislike the disease and the treatment, this cancer (or this unemployment or this betrayal) has taught me a lot about life."

When we pray for ease and comfort, we are asking that God will allow us to remain shallow in our personalities and our faith. When we learn to see difficulty as the path of growth, our relationships will change. When we remember that difficulty can be positive, challenging relationships become a vital part of Christian spirituality. Difficult work, church and family relationships, hurdles in ministry...all can be treasures if we place them in God's hands. Don't run from a relationship simply because it is demanding. Relationships should end for various reasons, but mere difficulty is not one of them.

Precious Pain

Amid Teresa of Avila's numerous travails, she discovered that when we open our eyes to the benefits of difficulty, the pain can become precious.

> Lord, how you afflict your lovers! But everything is small in comparison to what you give them afterward. It's natural that what is worth much costs much. Moreover, if the suffering is to purify this soul...it is as small as a drop of water in the sea... The soul feels that the pain is precious; so precious—it understands it very well—that one could not deserve it...With this knowledge, the soul suffers the pain very willingly and would suffer it all in life, if God were to be thereby served.[1]

References to this apparent irony—the sweetness of suffering—are widespread in the literature of Christian spirituality. Climacus wrote, "If individuals resolutely submit to the carrying of the cross, if they decidedly want to find and endure trial in all things for God, they will discover in all of them great relief and sweetness."[2]

The key to understanding the sweetness of suffering is a will fully submitted to the sovereignty of God and a clear understanding that, as Paul wrote, "our light affliction, which is but for a moment, is working for us a far more exceeding and eternal weight of glory" (2 Corinthians 4:17 NKJV). The difficulty is temporary; the benefit is eternal. À Kempis expressed a similar sentiment:

> The more the flesh is wasted by affliction, so much the more is the spirit strengthened by inward grace. And sometimes he is so comforted with desire of tribulation and adversity, for the love of conformity to the cross of Christ, that he would not wish to be without grief and tribulation; because he believes

that he shall be unto God so much the more acceptable, the more and heavier things he can suffer for him.[3]

Something about an absolute demand for comfort, even in the littlest things, wrecks our communion with God. My natural man tells me I have a right to live in total comfort, so whenever this comfort is threatened because of climate control malfunctions or because a meal is pushed back for an hour or two, I get a true picture of the demanding nature of my heart and the bitterness and anger that cause my spirit to growl like an untamed beast at the slightest discomfort or inconvenience.

Seasoning

Jonathan Edwards saw various trials as a benefit to true religion. "They not only manifest its truth but they also enhance its genuine beauty and attractiveness. True virtue is loveliest when it is oppressed. The divine excellency of real Christianity is best exhibited when it is under the greatest trials."[4] He goes on to say that such trials "purify and increase" true faith.

In the history of the church, the desire for suffering at times became extreme, but perhaps we have gone too far the other way today. Fénelon provides a healthy balance by reminding us that we are not to seek difficulties, but when they come, we should "never let them go by without result."[5]

The sweetness of pain can woo us from the world if we are determined to learn from it rather than complain about it, as Teresa of Avila explains: "The soul is left with greater contempt for the world than before because it sees that nothing in the world was any help to it in that torment, and it is much more detached from creatures because it now sees that only the Creator can console and satisfy it."[6]

And that's the key: In what or in whom do we find our ultimate satisfaction?

The Christian life will not be easy, but glory awaits us. When the love of Christ grips our hearts, we will suffer anything for His sake, endure any difficulty, or persevere through any trial. We will begin to understand these words from William Law: "How many saints has adversity sent to Heaven? And how many poor sinners has prosperity plunged into everlasting misery?"[7] And perhaps we will even embrace the final wisdom of John of the Cross: "I would not consider any spirituality worthwhile that wants to walk in sweetness and ease and run from the imitation of Christ."[8]

Spiritual Gluttony

From his youth, Francis de Sales appeared destined to become a great saint. He was involved in the occasional boyish prank, but he never approached the worldliness of, say, a young Ignatius or Augustine. In particular, Francis was set apart from his contemporaries by his unusual spiritual sensitivity. During part of his eighteenth and nineteenth years, Francis's sensitive soul became tormented by a vicious temptation toward despair. "A morbid conviction grew upon him that he was destined by God for damnation—and naturally enough, this neurotic nightmare quickly induced an invalidism in body and soul."[1]

Francis lived with this torment for several weeks until he was finally able to pray, "If I may not love Thee in the other world—for in hell none praise Thee—let me at least spend every moment of my brief life here in loving Thee as much as I can." After this prayer left his lips, every trace of Francis's spiritual disease "fell at his feet like the scales of a leper." Biographer Katherine Bregy writes, "The only legacy of his anguished temptation was to be in ever patient sympathy with other tortured souls."

As I have read spiritual biographies and talked with other Christians, I've noticed how many earnest believers share Francis de Sales's experience. The only thing unusual about Francis's experience is that it was so short. Usually, we enter a period of legalistic dryness, and we leave that season of dryness inspired by grace and love. Before, we were quick to condemn; now we are quick to intercede. The previous chapters explored many difficulties in the Christian life, but this section will focus on the internal spiritual challenge known as the "dark night of the soul," or a desert experience. De Sales describes it this way:

> Sometimes you shall find yourself so absolutely destitute of all feeling of devotion that your soul shall seem to be a wild, fruitless, barren desert, in which there is no trace of a pathway to find her God, nor any water of grace to refresh her, on account of the dryness which seems to threaten her with a total and absolute desolation.[2]

Scupoli notes, "At times dryness is accompanied by such great and thick darkness of mind that you know neither which way to turn nor what step to take. Do not be dismayed, but remain alone and firm upon the Cross."[3]

I dedicate this section to those courageous contemporary believers who are facing or who have faced such dryness, wondering what was wrong with them, feeling so alone in churches filled with happy saints. I want you to know that you are *not* alone, that in fact, some of the most brilliant souls have passed through something very similar to your own experience. In the words of Jeanne Guyon, "If you set forth for the spiritual lands…you must realize that times of dryness await you…You *will* have times of spiritual dryness. It is part of the Lord's way."[4]

The Beginning

At the beginning of the spiritual journey, the new believer often seeks nothing more than to be in church, in prayer, or in Scripture, for nothing else brings such great pleasure. This euphoric stage is part of growing up spiritually and should be respected. It's sort of like being infatuated with God.

However, like Francis, we may eventually find that we will be plunged from the exhilaration of exciting worship, prayer, and evangelism into months or years of spiritual lethargy, boredom, frustration, and confusion.

The wise spiritual adviser will eventually need to tell the new believer, ever so gently, that maturity will one day demand that the euphoric feelings on which he or she is becoming dependent must come to an end. Feelings, even spiritual feelings, can become a roadblock to further spiritual growth. Sooner or later, God in His mercy seems to begin a weaning process to mature the believer's faith.

Julian of Norwich believed this "stepping back" was universal and was not only expected but even essential: "It is necessary for everybody to have such experiences."[5]

Scupoli took a somewhat different view. He saw such dryness as evidence of a mature lover of God persevering in the faith. Superficial believers can avoid such dryness: "But we never find that sinners, and those who have given themselves to the things of the world, have to lament such trials. From this, it is clearly manifest that this is a precious food with which God feeds those whom He loves."[6]

Few writers understood this spiritual need as clearly as did John of the Cross, who coined the famous phrase "dark night of the soul." John noted that shortly after a person's conversion, God often "nurtures and caresses the soul…like a loving mother who warms her child with the heat of her bosom, nurses it with good milk and tender food, and carries and caresses it in her arms."[7] New believers, says John, find their joy in spending lengthy periods in prayer, "perhaps even entire nights." Even fasts provoke happiness, and the sacraments bring a special joy.

The ecstasies of life in Christ have been widely understood and documented. Consider this example from anonymous author of *The Cloud of Unknowing*:

> God…will give man his reward in bliss both in body and in soul. In giving that reward, he sometimes inflames the body of his devout servants with wonderful pleasures here in this life, not only once or twice, but very often in some cases as he may wish…Such pleasures are not to be held suspect.[8]

Fénelon agreed. "This witness by sensation is the support of beginners. It is the milk of tender new-born souls. They have to suck a long time. It would be dangerous to wean them."[9] According to Francis de Sales, God uses these "foretastes of heavenly delight" to withdraw us from "earthly pleasures" and encourage us in the "pursuit of divine love."[10]

As unregenerate people, we operate in a sensual realm, so God tends to use the senses to draw us to Him. In time, however, He often withdraws the sensual support, and the fierce weaning process begins.

Why God Steps Back

If intense spiritual sensations lasted too long in believers' lives, several problems could result.

Lost focus. "Spiritual caressing," if left unabated, would eventually cause us to lose focus. Thus we could begin to enjoy the fruits of worshipping God (our feelings) more than we enjoyed the God we worship. Augustine wrote, "Whosoever seeketh of God anything besides God, doth not love God purely. If a wife loved her husband, because he is rich, she is not pure, for she loveth not her husband, but the gold of her husband."[11]

Pride. Furthermore, ongoing spiritual euphoria can lead to spiritual pride. John of the Cross warned that a certain kind of pride is generated in us when the feelings remain intense. We "develop a desire somewhat vain—at times very vain—to speak of spiritual things in others' presence, and sometimes even to instruct rather than be instructed." John added that we can become so "evil-minded" that we do not want anyone except ourselves to appear holy, and so by both word and deed we "condemn and detract others whenever the occasion arises."[12]

Most pastors have noticed this pride rising up and gripping baby believers in their churches. These beginners, having been Christians for a relatively short time, think they could pastor better than the pastor, lead better than the elders, teach better than any of the teachers, and lead worship better than the worship leader.

Complacency. Johannes Tauler taught that spiritual feelings can also lead to complacency.

> As soon as a man experiences this pleasure and feels this extraordinary well-being, he thinks he can rely upon it. He leans on it and does not work with the same zeal and fidelity as before. He becomes self-indulgent and pampered, imagining that he [need not] suffer and work as he used to…As soon as the devil sees a man in such a condition, he invests it with a false sweetness in order to keep him in his state of treacherous tranquility.[13]

"Treacherous tranquility"—what a phrase! It makes sense, doesn't it? We usually visit a doctor only when something seems wrong, when we can't sleep, a pain won't go away, or something itches or makes us uncomfortable. When we feel healthy and happy and full of energy, we don't think about going to the doctor.

In the same way, "spiritual sweetness" can lead us to a false sense of maturity and spiritual well-being. We don't *feel* arrogant, we don't *feel* selfish, we don't *feel* as if we're neglecting God, so we stop paying attention. According to Tauler, that is precisely when we stop growing. He urges us to use spiritual sweetness as something that will spur us on instead of put us to sleep.

> When God strengthens and feeds us with sweet comfort and spiritual joys, everything should increase: our love, our gratitude, our praise, our intention to live according to His will. We should stretch toward God and in sweet longing and ardent love and be so consumed in this service that God would rightfully multiply His gifts of comfort and spiritual [delight].[14]

Anger. Spiritual gluttony can also lead to a deep anger once the delight and satisfaction of spiritual worship pass. We can feel angry at God because we think He left us, angry at ourselves for losing the feelings, angry at the worship leader or pastor we believe is blocking the sensual satisfaction, or angry at others who seem to be experiencing the feelings we miss.

If we do not become impatient with others, we may become impatient with ourselves and thus reveal our pride. We mistakenly believed that the spiritual feelings were a reward for our exceptional spiritual commitment, so we now mistakenly believe that by somehow increasing our spiritual heroics we can bring the feelings back. John of the Cross said we need patience to humbly wait for God to do His work in our souls, but we, addicted to spiritual highs, refuse to wait for God and instead try to push through the desert with a desperate thrust of the will.

Unwise counselors may try to tell us we should try to regain the lost feelings. Yet spiritual gluttony—lust for spiritual feelings—opens a wide door to the other appetites, including greed, overeating, sexual lusts, the hunger for power, and the like. When feelings become the focus of our faith, religion becomes not a friend but an enemy, concealing the true state of our hearts. We wonder why we fall into sin so soon after a seemingly powerful encounter with God. We fail to realize that our hearts were stolen by spiritual gluttony, not real reverence. We have been misled into believing that these feelings indicate the temperature of our hearts and the commitment of our will. They do not.

So God steps back. He stubbornly denies us the spiritual feelings to which we've grown so familiar. This is frequently accompanied by very dry periods, times when our prayers seem to bounce off the ceiling and our hearts feel like hot, dry sand. God does this so He can irrigate our deserts with the cold water of pure faith, so He can break our addiction to the sensual and call us to the truly spiritual, and so we can humbly say, without doubt or need for reinforcement, "O God, You are my God, and I will follow You all of my days."

Before we move on, I want to make this clear: The desert is real, it is difficult, and it is to be expected. God is not singling you out, He is not punishing you or even necessarily disciplining you. He is training you, strengthening you, purifying you, and *loving* you.

Let's explore this dark night a bit more in the next chapter.

Understanding the Desert

Although the coming and going of the desert experience is largely an act of God's sovereign care for us, spiritual dryness in general can have many causes, including some we create ourselves.

For instance, according to Francis de Sales, we can bring on something like a dark night by overexerting our bodies in an attempt at heroic spiritual growth.

> It sometimes happens that spiritual dryness proceeds from an indisposition of body, as when, through an excess of watching, labor, or fasting, we find ourselves oppressed by fatigue, drowsiness, lassitude, and the like infirmities, which, though they depend on the body, yet are calculated to [inconvenience] the spirit also, on account of the intimate connection that subsists between both…So St. Francis [Assisi] ordained that his religious [friars] should use such moderation in their labors so as not to oppress the fervor of their spirits.[1]

De Sales went on to give six additional reasons for the onset of dryness.

The first reason is the classical teaching on God's breaking us of spiritual gluttony. "As a mother refuses to gratify the appetite of her child, when such gratification might increase its indisposition, so God withholds consolations from us, when we take a vain complacency in them, and are subject to the spiritual maladies of self-conceit and presumption."

Second, Francis warned that when we neglect to "gather the sweetness and delights of the love of God at the proper season," then God will remove the feelings from us "in punishment of our sloth." Just think what is available to us as believers—receiving God's wisdom, His blessing, His affection, His insight—and yet how lackadaisical we can be in taking advantage of such opportunities. God may pull back the feelings to alert us to our taking Him for granted.

Jeanne Guyon agrees. "He hides Himself for a purpose. Why? His purpose is to rouse you from spiritual laziness. His purpose in removing Himself from you is to cause you to pursue Him."[2]

The third cause of spiritual deserts is that we can become overly pleased "in the bed of sensual consolations," and God thus needs to wean us from them. Instead of seeing spiritual feelings as a delightful gift, we start to act like addicts, craving the benefit of God's presence instead of God Himself. We're sort of like those who eat dinner only to get at dessert.

The fourth reason is that if we are not honest with our spiritual directors, if we mislead them with half-lies and deceits, God will send dryness to call us into truth. In contemporary terms, we may start to compromise morally, to get lax in our pursuit of God, and yet present ourselves to others as growing more than ever. God hates hypocrisy and insincerity; He is a God of authenticity and will often pull back the feelings to wake us up to the truth.

A fifth reason deserts sometimes occur is that we may have immersed ourselves in worldly pleasures and therefore are unable to enjoy "spiritual delights" because they are distasteful to us. Our hearts can be groomed to enjoy inappropriate pleasures. Modern neurologists have found that our brains adapt to repeated experience and will crave the familiar. If we learn to deal with stress by knocking back a cocktail instead of seeking God, we'll eventually come to depend on the cocktail more than we depend on God.

Finally, if we have been careful to preserve the fruits of the consolations we have already received, we can expect to receive new ones. But if we have carelessly lost what was given us, we may not receive any more.[3] It's a matter of stewardship. If we have not been faithful in the little things, God withholds the great.

Increased Temptation

Keep in mind that the loss of spiritual feelings is often accompanied by increased temptation. In fact, this is a common pairing in ancient writings, which make a direct connection between spiritual dryness and spiritual enticement. On one hand, God seems distant, and on the other, the world suddenly seems so appealing, in an assaulting way. Johannes Tauler speaks for many when he comments on the "terrors *and temptations* of spiritual darkness," when one "no longer experience[s] the emotional comfort of God's closeness."[4]

Increased temptation and the loss of spiritual feeling may seem like a double hit, which is likely to make you feel even worse. But according to Scupoli, that is exactly the point: growth in humility.

> For it generally happens that the servant of God who is thus tried by thoughts such as these, by lack of devotion and dryness of spirit, concludes that they arise from his imperfections, and that there cannot be another soul so imperfect and so lukewarm as his own. And he believes that such thoughts come only to those who are forsaken by God and that he himself, therefore, deserves to be forsaken by Him. It follows, then, that he who once thought himself to be something is now brought, by this bitter medicine, sent to him from God, to regard himself as the most depraved person in the world and as one unworthy to be called a Christian. And he never would have arrived at this low opinion of himself, nor would he have attained to such a depth of humility, had he not been sorely tried and forced to it, as it were, by these extraordinary temptations.[5]

Notice that Scupoli speaks of "extraordinary temptations." He isn't referring to just a few trifles, but a new level and depth of spiritual assault.

If we truly value humility as much as God, Scripture, and these early Christian writers do, we won't reject the very tool God uses to create that humility—even when the remedy is so severe.

Christian, you are not being forsaken or punished. You are being shaped, sanctified, and blessed. The same God who shepherded Julian of Norwich, Francis de Sales, Lorenzo Scupoli, Teresa of Avila, and John of the Cross through this time of dryness and increased temptation is more than capable of leading you through it as well.

Before we go on, however, we need to consider a certain type of Christian who is acutely aware of spiritual feelings and therefore may feel the dark night even more acutely than most—the sensual Christian.

Sensual Christians

We have seen that spiritual feelings are common in an early stage in the Christian life, but the rising and falling of spiritual feelings can also be related to our spiritual temperaments. Some of us are primarily motivated by ideas, others by action, and still others by emotions. We can call this latter group the "sensual Christians." These believers are likely to have ongoing and intense struggles with spiritual gluttony. We are most vulnerable to whatever feeds us, and some of us, by temperament, are fed more by sensual feelings than others. We can even become addicted to the feelings and thus think we need them. When they are withdrawn, we immediately lapse into sin. *The Cloud of Unknowing* speaks to this.

> Some persons are so weak and tender of spirit that if they were not comforted by some feelings of pleasure they would not be able to bear the diversity of temptations and troubles that they encounter at the hands of their physical and spiritual enemies in this life...On the other hand, there are some persons who are so strong in spirit that they can derive sufficient pleasure for themselves within their own souls by offering this reverent and meek stirring of love and their will in accord with God. They do not need to be sustained by pleasures in their bodily feelings.[6]

God treats His children as individuals. Christians cannot follow one universal timeline or fit a single spiritual temperament. Jonathan Edwards acknowledges this when he writes, "The zeal of the excessive worker could be simply a disposition of the temperament and not necessarily any grace at all."[7]

God created us individually, and He treats us accordingly. This should cause us to respect the differing needs of Christians for spiritual feelings. Fénelon uses this analogy:

> The invalid who cannot walk without a cane cannot let anyone take it away from him. He feels his weakness. He fears to fall, and he is right. But he ought not to be upset to see a healthy and strong man who does not need the same support. The healthy man walks more freely without a cane. But he should never be contemptuous of him who cannot do without it.[8]

In other words, if we are discipling or directing others, we shouldn't look down on those who need spiritual feelings to fight sin. On the other hand, those who have a very sensual faith shouldn't look down upon those whose faith seems boring compared to their own. Church life should never become a competition. It's a school of discipleship in which we encourage, respect, and build up each other, knowing that all of us face different challenges along the way.

Our Response

Once we realize we are in a state of persistent spiritual dryness and not simply tired, overworked, or in the middle of a long winter and thus emotionally downcast, we would do well to examine whether any of De Sales's six reasons apply to our own lives. But he warned, "This examination is not to be made either with [anxiousness] or too much curiosity." If we can't find a reason for our lack of spiritual feelings, we shouldn't trouble ourselves, but should "with all simplicity"…

- humble ourselves before God, acknowledging our own "nothingness and misery,"

- call on God and ask Him to comfort us, and

- go to our confessor, and "opening to him the several plaits and folds" of our souls, "follow his advice with the utmost simplicity and humility."

(Unfortunately, few people can find an experienced confessor or spiritual director. We'll deal with this later in this book.)

If you have considered all the possible causes and still find yourself mired in a state of dryness, and if you can't determine the cause, receive comfort and guidance in these words from de Sales:

> There is nothing so profitable, so fruitful, in a state of spiritual dryness, as not to suffer our affections to be too strongly fixed upon the desire of being delivered from it. I do not say that we ought not simply to wish for a deliverance, but that we should not set our heart upon it…In the midst of our spiritual dryness, let us never lose courage, but wait with patience for return of consolation.[9]

Making our desires known to God is vastly different from impatiently demanding that He fix whatever it is we think is broken. As in every aspect of the Christian life, when facing a spiritual desert, humility is our truest friend. We can be especially encouraged by holding on to the wisdom and insight of Jonathan Edwards:

> It is the duty of God's people to trust in Him when in darkness...It may look as though God has forsaken them and does not hear their prayers. Many clouds may gather and many enemies may surround them formidably, threatening to swallow them up. All events of providence seem to be against them and all circumstances seem to render the promises of God too difficult to be fulfilled. Yet God must be trusted when He is out of sight, when we cannot see how it is possible for Him to fulfill His word. When everything but God's Word makes it look so unlikely, it is then that people must believe with hope against hope.[10]

38

Surviving and Thriving in the Desert

The Christian classics teach to consider our spiritual feelings the way we check the daily weather forecast. The weather can make our work more pleasant or more difficult, but it should never define our task. Likewise, feelings may make our spiritual lives easier or harder, but they should never direct our devotion.

Scupoli is strong in his warnings about letting dryness become an excuse to avoid times of devotion: "But on no account leave off any of your devotions, but pursue them with all your might, however fruitless and distasteful they may appear to you, drinking willingly the cup of bitterness, which in this dryness the loving will of God holds out to you."[1]

As a runner who enjoys training for marathons, if I let the weather dictate my daily workout, I'd never be fit to tackle 26.2 miles. Sometimes it rains, sometimes the heat seems unbearable, and sometimes the cold is frightening. I can dress for the weather, but I can't let it beat me. It may affect my expectations for a workout, but I must not let it hinder my ultimate progress.

In fact, Brother Giles emphasized the benefit of learning to pray even when you don't feel like it. He was once asked, "What can I do to go willingly to prayer when I feel dry and lacking devotion?" This was his response:

> Suppose a king has two servants, one of whom is armed, but the other is unarmed, and they have to go to war. The one who is armed goes bravely to war, but the other who is unarmed

says this to his lord: "My lord, as you see, I have no weapons. But because I love you I will go into battle even without weapons." Now the king on seeing the faithfulness of that servant says to his attendants: "Go and prepare armor to adorn this faithful servant of mine, and place on him the emblem of my own armor." So too if someone goes into the battle of prayer as if without arms, because he feels dry and lacking devotion, God sees his faithfulness and places the emblem of His armor on him.[2]

What a beautiful image! The next time you feel dry, consider blessing God by going to prayer even without your armor. What inspiring faith and devotion!

At times we'll be virtually singing as our prayers flow from a heart full of God's joy. At other times each word will require the most severe labor. Feelings will make prayer and devotion seem easier or harder, but that's about all the thought we should give to them. The author of *The Cloud of Unknowing* put it this way:

> Toward…sweetness and pleasures, physical or spiritual, no matter how pleasing nor how holy they may be, we should have an attitude of unconcern. If they come, welcome them; but do not depend on them lest it weaken you, for it will take up a great deal of your strength if you remain with these sweet pleasures for a long time.[3]

We must avoid the trap of equating good worship with good feelings. The two are unrelated. De Sales noted, "Devotion does not always consist in that sweetness, delight, consolation, or sensible tenderness of heart, which moves us to tears, and causes us to find satisfaction in some spiritual exercises."[4]

In fact, as we've already learned, spiritual feelings can actually be our enemies if they mislead us to believe something that is false or cause us to overestimate our maturity or level of commitment. They can not only mislead us into false teaching but also fool us into thinking we have some secret knowledge or a special relationship with God that exalts us above the rest.

Feelings are never the yardstick of truth. They will betray the truth far more often than they will confirm it.

The Journey of the Dark Night

The dark night of the soul can come in many different forms and in varying degrees. It can be a cyclical experience, returning as God ordains, or go on for days, months, or years without abating. We all have different needs and different attitudes and addictions that need to be burned up within us. Keeping some of the wisdom of the ancients in mind will help you survive and even thrive in a desert experience.

Silence Is Necessary

Earlier, I wrote about my son receiving stitches in his forehead, and I imagined how Graham would feel if a man whispered in his ear, "If your father really loved you, he wouldn't let this man do this to you. If you were my son, I wouldn't abandon you this way."

Satan often does exactly this during a dark night. God is leading us through a hard but necessary journey, and His silence is a vital aspect of this journey. But Satan will tempt us to believe that God is being cruel, that God is abandoning us, that we have somehow pushed God away, that we have somehow lost the Holy Spirit, or similar lies. The truth is, God is simply helping us mature. He is preparing us to drive blind, without sensual support, through the night of faith.

Scupoli believed "innumerable benefits are derived from dryness and the absence of devotional feelings," which is why he calls a desert season a "marvelous help, although at the time we are not conscious of it."[5]

Think about it. We cannot learn certain lessons unless God allows our feelings to settle. Therefore, His silence is not abandonment or agreement with the accuser's twisted logic. It is a necessary weaning of sensual support.

You Are Not Alone

When we begin to sense we are entering a dry spell, we need to know that this is how God has always treated His saints, as Thomas à Kempis pointed out.

> If great saints were so dealt with, we that are weak and poor ought not to despair, if we be sometimes fervent and sometimes cold; for the Spirit cometh and goeth, according to the good pleasure of his own will...I never found any so religious and

devout, that he had not sometimes a withdrawing of grace, or felt not some decrease of zeal. There was never a saint so highly rapt and illuminated, who first or last was not tempted.[6]

The barrenness of these spiritual deserts can be excruciating, but we can be encouraged by remembering that most Christians have endured them to some degree. We are not abnormal or less committed Christians for going through dry spells. We do not need to uncover buried sins that are stealing our joy. We are simply average Christians going through a normal spiritual process.

God Is Not Judging You

Spiritual feelings are not a gauge of our maturity, and God will not judge us when the spiritual feelings wane. Thomas à Kempis urged us not to lose heart when the feelings fly.

> All therefore is not lost, if sometimes thou hast less feeling for Me…than thou wouldest. That good and sweet affection which thou sometimes feelest, is the effect of grace present, and a sort of foretaste of thy heavenly home; but hereon thou must not lean too much, for it comes and goes.[7]

Don't let self-accusation create a wall between you and God. The feelings weren't a reward, and their withdrawal is not a punishment.

Feelings Have a Limited Role

Some Christians grow so dependent on spiritual pampering, they would rather remain comfortable in their immaturity than press on to true faith. When God takes the feelings away, we need to remember that spiritual feelings are the beginning of Christian living, not the end. Fénelon put it this way: "How many souls, having had too tender a childhood in Jesus Christ, too delicate, too dependent on so mild a milk, draw back and give up the life within, when God begins to wean them!…They make the sanctuary of what was only the porch of the temple."[8] Scupoli is very practical in this regard. "When you are unable to meditate, through confusion of mind, and cannot pray as usual, meditate as best you can."[9] We can't control the feelings, but we can control the actions, and that is all that God will hold us accountable for.

Take Up Your Cross

Fénelon urged that as God steps back from us, we should follow Him and thus step back from ourselves. Dying to self, after all, is one of the primary purposes of this weaning.

> We never so need to abandon ourselves to God as when he seems to abandon us. So let us take light and consolations when he gives them, but without becoming attached to them. When he plunges us into the night of pure faith, then let us go into this night, and let us lovingly suffer this agony. One moment is worth a thousand in this tribulation.[10]

When we love Christ only for what He brings us, including spiritual feelings, we are loving ourselves, not loving Him, regardless of the sacrifice we think we are offering. The dark night of the soul purifies our motivation and keeps us from becoming like the crowds in the New Testament who followed Jesus, not for His teaching, but for the miraculously supplied bread.[11]

Rather than fight the withdrawal of spiritual feelings, therefore, we should let the loss call us to the cross. God's "tough love" is far more stubborn and enduring than our petty rebellion anyway. Instead of anger or rebellion, our attitudes should reflect humility. We never deserved the spiritual feelings in the first place, so we can hardly claim them as our right when they are taken away.[12] Teresa of Avila gently but firmly cuts us to our knees. "It's an amusing thing that even though we still have a thousand impediments and imperfections and our virtues have hardly begun to grow...we are yet not ashamed to seek spiritual delights in prayer or to complain about dryness."[13]

One of the great temptations during the desert is to arrogantly demand that God end the dryness at once. We remind God how much we have left for Him when we should actually be praising Him for how much He delivered us from. We remind God how zealously we have served Him when we should actually be thanking Him for giving us purpose. We live with a distorted view of our own spirituality. If we do not embrace humility—if we do not go to the cross—we will very likely embrace anger, and instead of maturing in our walk with Christ, we will be stuck in a spiritual cul-de-sac.

Beware of New Circumstances

When we begin to notice the sensory delights slipping away, the worst thing we can do is to try to recreate them by running to some new spiritual experience. Doing so can not only lead to a counterfeit faith but also fight against God's work in our souls.

The temptation to flight can be great. People who are mad with thirst can run circles in the desert and drink water from a rancid pond just to wet their throats. John of the Cross warned of those who refuse to accept God's withdrawal of the delight.

> All their time is spent looking for satisfaction and spiritual consolation; they can never read enough spiritual books, and one minute they are meditating on one subject and the next on another, always in search for some gratification in the things of God. God very rightly and discreetly and lovingly denies this satisfaction to these beginners. If He did not, they would fall into innumerable evils because of their spiritual gluttony and craving for sweetness. Wherefore it is important for these beginners to enter the dark night and be purged of this childishness.[14]

Fénelon advised Christians to "remain serene in the trial, and not torment [yourself] by dwelling on what God is taking away from [you]."[15] How sad it is when Christians seek out one church after another and attend one conference or seminar after another in a desperate search for the delight God is purposefully holding back. Such people are particularly vulnerable to new teachers who seem exciting and who promise the experience they so desperately seek—and there is no shortage of teachers who will gladly reinforce this exciting element to encourage people to transfer membership to their church or television ministry.

Surrender

If you have found yourself in a desert and continue to argue with God about it, I urge you to surrender. May I be honest with you? Nobody wins against God. He is far more patient than we are rebellious. Often He will bring us out only when we submit and learn what He wants us to learn, but even this is a dangerous statement. If we submit only to be relieved of our desert, we're not learning our lesson. We're simply bargaining. Scupoli urges us to adopt the attitude of our Lord.

> Remember also your Christ, who, in the garden and on the Cross, was, to His great pain, abandoned by His heavenly Father, as far as the feeling of comfort was concerned. And bearing the cross with Him, with all your heart say, "Thy will be done." By doing so, your patience and prayer will raise the flame of your heart's sacrifice into the presence of God, leaving you truly devout—true devotion consisting in a lively and firm readiness of will to follow Christ with the cross on your shoulder, by whatever way He invites and calls us to Himself.[16]

The dark night is a fearsome journey, but it eventually produces a new depth of intimacy worth every bit of agony. The darker the night, as the saying goes, the brighter the dawn.

A New Depth

Teresa of Avila said that when we live by faith and not by feelings, when we persevere regardless of how dry we feel, we show we are among those souls who "would want the Lord to see that they do not serve Him for pay."[17] That is, we want the Lord to see that we will serve Him regardless of whether it gives us pleasure or pain. We will serve Him because He is God and Lord and because He has captured our hearts and our wills. "The desires these souls have are no longer for consolations or spiritual delight, since the Lord Himself is present with these souls and it is His Majesty who now lives."[18]

This ushers us into a new depth, a new freedom, a new strength. The path to get there was far fiercer than we could have imagined, but the view at the destination is more wonderful than we could have conceived. For the rest of our lives, spiritual feelings will no longer be our Seeing Eye dogs. Rather, they will be comforting friends who occasionally appear by our side.

PART 6

Seasons *and* Surgery *of the* Soul

Seasons of the Soul:
The Passages of the Spiritual Life

laise Pascal possessed one of the greatest mathematical minds of his day. In fact, in many circles, he is more well known for his contributions to math and science than for his Christian devotion. Pascal's father planned to guide his son through language studies before introducing him to mathematics, but that stopped the day he found Blaise drawing figures on the floor. When he asked Blaise what he was doing, Blaise answered that he was trying to express the relationship between the angles of a triangle and two right angles. In other words, Pascal was working on the thirty-second proposition in Book 1 of Euclid's *Elements of Geometry.*

By the time he was 20, Pascal had gained national notoriety by creating a math machine that performed the four basic functions of arithmetic. He later became famous for his work in physics.

Near the end of his short life, Pascal wrote in a letter that the study of geometry is a valuable way of learning to reason correctly and the highest exercise of the mind, but it is only a *métier*, or trade, and is ultimately useless.[1] Pascal had found a subject to study that was even more difficult than math: humankind.

"Fewer people study man than mathematics. It is only because they do not know how to study man that people look into all the rest."[2] *Pensées*, perhaps more than any other Christian classic, studies the nature of people. In this study, Pascal came up with several provocative thoughts. "If we are too young our judgment is impaired," he wrote, "just as it is if we are too old." Or this: "Man is so made that if he is told often enough that he is a fool he believes it. By telling himself so often enough he convinces himself, because when he is alone he carries on an inner dialogue with himself which is important to keep under proper control."[4]

Taking our cue from Pascal, we will use the next several chapters to explore what it means to be a person on a spiritual journey. Like Pascal, we want to explore what moves us and what makes the spiritual life difficult and exciting. Fortunately, as we look back, we have much help.

One of my first delights after my initial forays into the spiritual classics was the realization that these ancient writers understood human nature far more than many of the modern psychologists I studied in college. As I continued reading, I began to understand that this is what makes the difference between a book that lasts for hundreds or thousands of years and one that is out of print within months.

I remember being astonished when Johannes Tauler demonstrated how slowly true Christian maturity grows. In an age in which young thirty-something pastors are the hottest commodities around, Tauler speaks to us with a clear warning:

> Until a man has reached his fortieth year, he will never attain lasting peace, never be truly formed into God, try as he may. Up to that time he is occupied by so many things, driven this way and that by his own natural impulses; he is governed by them although he may imagine that he is governed by God. Before the proper time has arrived, he cannot achieve true and perfect peace, nor can he enter into a God-seeing life.[5]

I read this in my forties and started to feel pretty good about myself until I read further. "After that he shall wait *another ten years* before the Holy Ghost, the Comforter, the Spirit Who teaches all things, is truly his."

According to Tauler, it takes *decades* to die to ourselves and at least another decade to truly learn how to surrender to the work of the Holy Spirit, after which a person "may receive the Holy Spirit in the loftiest and most sublime manner, that Holy Spirit Who will teach him all truth."

This is not to say young people don't have much to teach us. I love listening to sermons from thirtysomething pastors. But the warning is worth heeding. We must not mistake charisma, enthusiasm, and youthful energy for the Spirit's work and touch. The depth of God's mark takes time to root itself in our thinking, our hearts, our ambitions, our pride, and our view of God, others, and self. Keep in mind that Tauler is speaking to a group of religious people who dedicated *every waking hour* to the spiritual life. Even in this circumstance, he noted, only after four or five decades did authentic Christian maturity take root in people's souls.

Studying spiritual growth requires that we understand the human condition—not just its difficulties, which we've already discussed, but also the stages, conditions, and challenges of the Christian life. Those who have gone before us have recognized that the spiritual life has a natural progression of highs and lows, peaks and valleys. I've identified three elements of the Christian life that express this progression—spiritual *climates, terrains,* and *stations.*

Too many Christians suffer from the illusion that one spiritual prescription fits every Christian, yet the devotional classics consistently remind us that we all face different spiritual climates, terrains, and stations, and therefore we have different needs and capabilities.[6] Furthermore, the spiritual life is so fluid that no one program will fit anyone for his or her entire life. Our spiritual terrains, climates, and stations will change, so our spiritual understanding must change as well. Let's look at each of these elements carefully.

Spiritual Climates

Spiritual climates are the environments in which we serve God. If we live in religious communities as monks or nuns, our climate will be much different than if we live in college fraternities or sororities. A woman who lives with a believing and supportive husband exists in a very different climate from a woman who is berated and mocked by an unbelieving husband. A child growing up in a warm and supportive atmosphere has a different climate from one growing up in a household driven by alcoholism and blatantly immoral behavior.

We choose some of our climates, but not all of them. For instance, we choose whom we want to marry, and this choice greatly affects our spiritual climate in the years to come. But children do not choose the homes they are born into. The five main climates in our lives are our homes, our work, our social relationships, our churches, and our self-thought (or "personal" climate). Most of us can't choose every one of our climates, and we can't even improve some of them. On the other hand, most of us can change one or two climates to create a better foundation on which to build the rest of our spiritual lives.

The importance or relevance of a healthy spiritual climate may never have occurred to us, but the concept itself shouldn't be a surprise. Northerners often travel south in the winter to improve their physical health, so why shouldn't Christians consider changing spiritual climates to improve their spiritual health?

Home

A courageous woman was working to offer the gospel and practical assistance to women facing unplanned pregnancies. One day, as she was leaving her home to go to a meeting, her husband broke her heart by cruelly calling out, "When are you going to realize that you're just throwing your life away?"

She was stunned. Was that what her husband truly believed?

"Abortion is always going to be here," he said. "Nothing you do will ever change that."

Of course, she knew better. The babies who lived and the women who found new life through her work confirmed that her labor was decidedly not in vain. All the same, she was devastated by her husband's degrading remark.

If you are married to a drug addict, an extremely negative person, or an unbeliever, or if you're the parent of a sad, angry, or rebellious child, you're going to face some spiritual issues that others don't.

Let me ask you this. Does your home life make your faith easier or harder? Are you faced with more temptation than encouragement to grow in holiness? Is prayer made more difficult or easier? If you need someone to talk to about spiritual matters, is someone available? If you need encouragement, can you find it?

If you're living with a roommate, you can readily address issues of climate. If you're married or have dysfunctional parents, changes may not be so simple. But many Christians never even think about this. Take the time to evaluate the spiritual climate of your living arrangement. Once you've evaluated it, ask God what you can do to improve it. You might not be able to move, but can you and the people you live with talk about creating a better environment? Why force yourself to stay in a spiritual winter when you can create a spring?

For example, if you're married to a nonbeliever, you might able to say, "Look, I'm going to be a better spouse for you if you will support my need to spend a quiet hour with God each morning. I know you may think it's a waste of time, but I think you'll agree I am more loving when I get that time. Is that something you'd like to support?"

Spiritual growth doesn't happen in a vacuum. If we truly want to grow, we should wisely consider the climate in which we live. Of course, sometimes a difficult living situation can actually foster spiritual growth, but in such circumstances the wise Christian will also make sure she can receive support and encouragement outside the home. It's one thing to serve at a church where you don't feel like you're being fed when you have a supportive family, but if you're in a church body that feels dead while you're also in a difficult living situation at home, you could be setting yourself up for a fall.

Because we each live in several different climates at the same time, we would do well to strengthen those climates we *can* change so we can better endure those climates we must endure. Our home climate is particularly crucial. It is the foundation to every other climate.

Work

Many professional athletes and soldiers have come to my Sacred Marriage seminars. During these times, team and base chaplains have explained to me that it is virtually impossible for professional athletes and soldiers to so organize their lives that they won't come across some tempting salacious material. It's hanging around the locker room or barracks on a daily basis.

As a Christian writer, I can so organize my work climate that temptation is cut to the bare minimum, but many people don't have that luxury. If you are weak toward gossip and you work in an office where watercooler talk is the favorite pastime, you're going to face some difficult challenges. You may feel as if you are struggling to lose weight while working in front of a candy jar.

I'm not suggesting you run from such a challenge by changing your place of employment. If every Christian sought a pleasant work climate, we might be happier Christians, but the world wouldn't be evangelized. And some people must put up with the degrading attitudes and speech of others because they need the paycheck and no other job is available. The way to improve our work climates may not be to flee them but to prayerfully transform them.

I wrote earlier in this book about my experiment with "positive gossip" that helped make a very negative work environment somewhat more positive. In prayer, perhaps you can come up with some similarly positive remedies. The key is to try to be an agent of transformation instead of becoming complacent. If your spiritual life is being depleted and yet the people around you aren't being changed, your effectiveness may have come to an end, and you may need to seek a new place of employment.

If your home climate is strong, your church is supportive, and your social base is enriching, you can survive and even thrive in a negative work climate. But if you are hurting in the other areas, a damaging work climate could be the final burden that pulls you down. At least consider whether your support base in the other climates is strong enough for you to face particular challenges in *this* one. Or do you need to seriously explore changing your job because you have little support in other areas and the negative influence of this one is simply too great for you to bear?

Social Relationships

Our call to evangelism may lead us to live and work in unfavorable climates. But we can choose whom we socialize with, and we should choose carefully. In fact, the apostle Paul and the writers of Proverbs expressly urge us to be discerning in our social relationships.

- "Do not make friends with a hot-tempered man, do not associate with one easily angered, or you may learn his ways and get yourself ensnared" (Proverbs 22:24).

- "I have written you in my letter not to associate with sexually immoral people—not at all meaning the people of this world who are immoral, or the greedy and swindlers, or idolaters. In that case you would have to leave this world. But now I am writing you that you must not associate with anyone who calls himself a brother but is sexually immoral or greedy, an idolater or a slanderer, a drunkard or a swindler. With such a man do not even eat" (1 Corinthians 5:9-11).

- "If anyone does not obey our instruction in this letter, take special note of him. Do not associate with him, in order that he may feel ashamed. Yet do not regard him as an enemy, but warn him as a brother" (2 Thessalonians 3:14-15).

Few Christians can thrive if every climate is adverse, and this climate is relatively easy to change because it is part of our leisure time. Are your friends true friends? Do they encourage you, or do you find yourself continually following them into unhealthy practices? Does someone invariably lead you to gossip? Does someone else always speak negatively and lead you to respond the same way?

We shouldn't necessarily end such relationships, though in some cases we may need to be willing to. But we should aggressively seek out positive, mutually edifying relationships so we can grow in the faith together.

I want to be around men who inspire me to be a better husband, a more involved father, a more creative worker, a deeper lover of God, and someone who truly enjoys life. We need friends we can laugh with but also friends who will lovingly warn us if they see us going astray. We need to be intentional about pursuing friendships and occasionally letting some die. This climate is one of the most fluid and the easiest to change.

Church

Increasing attention is being paid to churches that abuse and congregations that use rather than build up the body of Christ. Are you in a church that supports the role God has called you to, or is your church more concerned with meeting the needs of the institution? Are you in a place where you can exercise the gifts God has given you? Does your church prepare you to interact with the world, or is it keeping you so preoccupied that you have no time to reach out?

Does your church create a climate in which your personal growth is inevitable, or is it putting stumbling blocks in your way? Has your church created a warm, caring, and supportive environment, or does it operate on fear, guilt, secrecy, and manipulation?

As I've gotten older, I've watched some Christians grow and mature in their personal lives, at home, and at work. But I've seen others slowly languish and ease out of the faith. In almost every instance, the health of their church had a huge impact. When you hear God's truth proclaimed on a weekly basis and rub shoulders with others who love God and carry an infectious faith, your own life is built up. Choose your church carefully.

Personal Self-Talk and Behavior

You can influence this environment more than any other. What type of climate are you creating for yourself with your self-talk and your daily actions? Think again about Pascal's earlier statement. Are you continually telling yourself you're a fool, or are you learning how to have a healthy inner dialogue?

I'm learning that as I go through the day I'm bringing either light or discouragement into my life by the way I talk to myself and others. By evaluating what I'm thinking and saying, I can determine whether I'm encouraging myself or making myself more miserable. Primarily, I want God's perspective because mine is never balanced.

Scupoli warns that well-meaning believers can fall into "the Devil's snare" by becoming discouraged or overanxious when they sin. Such a response is based in pride and leads to anxiety and restlessness. On the other hand, God's peace leads to intimacy, fellowship, and obedience.

Grace and humility aren't just concepts—they are the very marrow of our spiritual lives. Falling in love with mercy doesn't lead us to excuse our sin. On the contrary, it leads us to God, who convicts us of our sin, removes our shame, and fills our hearts with gratitude. As a result, we are better equipped to resist future temptation.

Negative self-talk is based on pride. "How could I? I'm such an idiot. There's no hope." How could I? I'm a sinner, that's how! But we have a Savior, a Healer, a Redeemer, and a Friend. Instead of berating yourself, find refuge in His forgiving arms, plead for His assistance, and receive His acceptance and affirmation.

Putting the Climates Together

Take some time to evaluate each climate we've discussed. Which is your strongest one? Which is your weakest? Can you improve any of them? Just as gardeners sometimes construct greenhouses to create premium environments in which to grow plants, can you construct a spiritual greenhouse to nurture your soul?

As you undertake this exercise, remember that God has designed many of the circumstances in our lives. We need a healthy respect for God's sovereignty. We cannot simply say, "This climate is difficult, so I'm going to change it." If we've made it difficult, or if we've chosen the difficult climate, evaluating it makes perfect sense. But when God has designed the climate, we shouldn't try to run away from it.

Olympic athletes often intentionally train in difficult climates to get the greatest benefit from their training. Runners may purposely flock to the higher altitudes. Similarly, God may place His sons and daughters in adverse climates that will test them to the very limit in order to prepare them for a particular work.

In these seasons, remembering these two things has helped me: Climates change, and God is aware of my situation. The rainy season passes, and winter eventually turns to spring. Just as importantly, God doesn't expect me to run as fast or as far in a snowstorm as I might run on a beautiful autumn day. Fénelon urged patience. "Wait until the winter is past, and until God has made all die which ought to die, then the spring revives all."[7]

Spiritual climates do not predetermine our spiritual growth, but they do affect it. We have to allow for them. Our thirst for God should motivate us to create and maintain supportive climates that will encourage our quest.

40

Spiritual Terrain

Spiritual terrain is the road on which we're traveling. You may have tremendously supportive spiritual climates, but if the road gets bumpy—your business crashes, you get laid off, you contract a serious disease, or a loved one dies—your spiritual life will be affected. Supportive climates are tremendously helpful, but they don't make you impervious to difficulties.

Francis de Sales was particularly sensitive to these issues. As a skilled spiritual director, he often received letters from people battling illness and feeling guilty because their prayer lives were suffering accordingly. De Sales assured them that God looks not only at our actions but also at our hearts. He knows, for instance, that depression is real and that a person who is battling a chemical depression is going to have a more difficult time praying than someone whose brain is producing sufficient amounts of dopamine.

God knows that the hormonal response to giving birth can play havoc with a woman's emotions. He knows (and the young mother should too!) that the postpartum state of flux is not the best time to evaluate her heart's affections or commitment toward Him. She needs to let her body heal and adapt.

Many of the things that make spiritual devotion more or less difficult are out of our control. God is aware of each of them, and we would be wise to remember this. If you're planning a wedding, moving across the country, burying a parent or a child, struggling with a disability, or laboring under high vocational demands, you're walking a difficult road.

The Inner Terrain

Experienced runners don't get discouraged by difficult hill workouts. Their pace is slower and requires more effort, but they attribute those things to the terrain, not to their fitness. When these runners crest a hill and begin cruising down the other side, they don't assume they are suddenly in better shape simply because they begin running faster with less effort. Rather, they recognize that the terrain has changed. When we don't take our spiritual terrain into account, we may be doing better or worse than we think. Our walk with Christ may feel like a struggle simply because of the difficulties we're going through.

In the same way, we can't make direct comparisons between our experiences and the experiences of others because we all face different spiritual terrains. We can wreck sincere hearts by asking for things that people are not capable of giving, or by wanting them to advance too quickly, or by allowing them to proceed too slowly. Christians who seek ministries of healing and counsel and who want to participate in soul surgery must therefore take great care to broaden their experience by listening to others.

When faced with a difficult terrain, we need to remember that just as seasons change, so do trails eventually level out. God rarely leaves believers in periods of doubt, for instance, for their entire lives. Even something like depression is usually cyclical.

On the other hand, those who are having it particularly easy should remember that around the corner, the trail may lead uphill. Ignatius urged those fighting "desolation" or difficulty to remember that they will one day be in a state of "consolation" and ease. He urged those in the joyous state of consolation to remember that one day they will be back in desolation.[1]

The temptation to teach others when we are on a spiritual high is great—but dangerous. We often have an idealized view when we feel so well, and we run the danger of disillusioning other Christians by speaking as if we floated on this earth rather than walked. On the other hand, if we are facing particularly difficult struggles, we may mistakenly assume that every Christian struggles the same way.

Do you see the great danger here? If we do not objectively recognize the valleys and hills, the summers and winters, we run a great risk of subjectifying the faith—interpreting everyone's faith by our own particular and seasonal experiences. Our teaching, preaching, and counsel will always be out of balance as we struggle from one season to the next.

This is why we should be cautious and judicious about asking young Christians to teach. Until we have walked over several hills and through many valleys and have a feel for the broad timeline of the Christian journey, we are liable to lose perspective and balance in our teaching. We will imprison our hearers in our own experience rather than launch them into the experience that God has for them. The author of *The Cloud of Unknowing* warned against this tendency.

> Those who are able to see or experience the perfection of this work only after a long labor and then but seldom may easily be deceived if they speak, think, or judge other men in terms of their own experience, thinking that other men are like them able to achieve it only rarely, and then not without great labor.[2]

Some people may find prayer easier than we do; others may find it much more difficult. Some may drop sin at will and never look back; others may have to slowly grow out of sin's habits. Wise teachers will remember that their experience is one story among millions. Let's not force every other Christian into our own custom-made box.

To adequately serve God's church, then, we must become learners and observers as Blaise Pascal did. Let's study common patterns of the Christian life, talk to each other, encourage each other, and learn from each other so that we can support each other with practical advice in the journey of faith.

41

Stations in Life

I once was blessed to spend an evening with a wise and godly Christian lawyer. He's the kind of guy who applies his faith in the marketplace and at home. When his kids went off to college, he wrote them a letter every day. Yes, *every* day. And though some of his Christian stands made other partners in the law firm uncomfortable, he was so skilled at what he did and so gifted in bringing in clients, they couldn't afford to cut him off.

He was 15 years older than me. My kids were just going off to college, so I asked him what I could expect and what I should anticipate about life, family, and faith. I'll not share his answer, as some of it was personal and affected other members of my family, but I'll never forget how astonished I became when I realized just how accurate he was. His advice proved to be invaluable because he had been there.

The classics can provide this same perspective as we face the spiritual implications of our stations in life. Our stations in life include our roles as husbands and wives, sons and daughters, fathers and mothers, brothers and sisters, hired or retired, single or widowed. And no two individual's stations are identical, but they do include many similarities that we can learn from.

Necessary Adjustments

As you have encountered the writings of John Climacus, William Law, Thomas à Kempis, and the others I have referenced in this book, you may have occasionally felt frustrated and even discouraged. Their words are intended to instruct and inspire you, but these saints may seem so far above you and me in their spiritual lives, you may feel tempted to just give up.

Understanding the stations of the spiritual life is crucial to maintaining a proper perspective. A young mother with three children under the age of six cannot expect to have the same spiritual opportunities as Teresa of Avila, who lived as a celibate woman and who wrote *The Interior Castle* in her later years after decades of walking in close communion with Christ. A working man with a wife and children cannot expect to fully enter into the same experience as John of the Cross, a member of a religious order who was not married and had no children. If we try to leap stations, we won't glorify God and will just frustrate ourselves. Even William Law, who called for a very demanding spirituality, understood the need to tailor our spirituality to our station in life.

> Those who have most leisure seem more especially called to a more eminent observance of these holy rules of a devout life. And they who by the necessity of their state and not through their own choice have but little time to employ thus must make the best use of that little they have.[1]

A woman working 60 hours a week as a stockbroker and a college student taking 12 credits and going home on the weekends will have very different spiritual programs. Each individual has his or her own particular temptations and challenges.

Chapters

Elton Trueblood is a bit too contemporary to be called a classical writer (he died in 1994), but he put everything into perspective for me when he wrote about our lives being written in chapters. God looks at the entire story of our lives, not the particular chapter we're in. For instance, the average married couple experiences the chapter of their singleness, the chapter of the early years of marriage, the chapter of the tired years of raising their kids, the chapter of being empty nesters, and the chapter of their retirement.

An empty nester can assume certain responsibilities and duties that a young parent cannot or should not. We are freer to put more time into study and prayer in some seasons than in other seasons. We are not judged by any one moment; a faithful life is one that is lived thoughtfully throughout all the seasons.

If you're a young mom whose child rearing or employment is wreaking havoc on your devotional life, you can be assured that (unless you have a dozen kids or more) the season of actively raising children is shorter than most of us realize. Be faithful to the task at hand, doing what you can in terms of devotion.

Look at it like warfare. A solider goes through seasons of basic training, deployment and waiting, battle, and recovery. No one would criticize a wounded soldier recovering from a battle injury as lazy. And one would rightly warn a soldier who wanted to skip basic training and go right to battle. A successful soldier lives each season in its time and for its purpose.

In the same way, when we enter a life of faith, God may take us through seasons of preparation, seasons of active ministry, and seasons of recovery before cycling us through all three again. We'll go farthest when we learn how to prepare when He wants us to prepare, work when He wants us to work, and recover when He wants us to recover.

Sin in the Seasons

According to Francis de Sales, even our sins should be evaluated in light of our station.

> Young beginners in devotion…commit certain faults…That low and servile fear which begets excessive scruples in the souls of new converts from a course of sin, is commendable in beginners, and a certain foreboding of a future purity of conscience; but the same fear would be blamable in those who are far advanced, in whose heart love ought to reign, which by imperceptible degrees chases away this kind of servile fear.[2]

Excessive ethical sensitivity is actually fairly common after new believers' conversion or rededication—not only in the lives of those who had much to repent of, such as an Ignatius or Augustine, but also in the lives of people such as Francis de Sales, who lived relatively clean lives and would not appear to be naturally subject to such a tortured conscience. Maturity, however, eventually led each of these men to a deeper faith based on love and relationship rather than guilt and regulations.

So we shouldn't attempt to cure new believers with an overactive conscience if they need it to develop lives of obedience. On the other hand, if
people are long past the time they need to move on, we can step up and
challenge them toward a greater maturity.

The classics are both honest and practical. At certain stages in our lives,
we are more vulnerable to some appetites that lead to various temptations. Augustine talked about this when he separated the temptations he
faced as a young man from those he faced as the mature man who wrote
Confessions. As an elder churchman, Augustine was able to remove himself from the sexual temptation (and failure) of his youth by abstaining
from all sexual activity. However, this was replaced by the temptation of
gluttony. Augustine realized he could only manage this temptation, not
escape it. He had to eat, and therefore the temptation to abuse food was
ever present.

A young woman may be overly concerned with physical appearances,
but an older woman might be more predisposed toward materialism. Your
greatest temptation now probably won't be your greatest temptation ten
years from now.

A young couple raising a family have to work and earn money, and this
necessarily cramps their schedules. Prayer, Bible study, meditation, and
fellowship must somehow fit into a day that already has many of the best
hours spoken for. Having a family involves affection for each other and
for children, which can bring tremendous blessing as well as numerous
complications and stresses.

Older couples with grown children have temptations of their own.
For the first time in their lives, they may have significant disposable income. Being frugal and responsible was easy when every penny had to be
accounted for, but will materialism steal their hearts in a time of abun-
dance? Different stations in life have different danger zones. We'll eventually be a safe distance from some of these zones, but usually that just means
we'll happen upon new ones.

The apostle Paul spoke of the many different stages, especially as they
relate to age groups.[3] Paul expected different things from different generations. In New Testament times, *elder* was more than a title. The early
church used this chronological word to signify an official office because
it recognized that the office would be filled by those who were not young.
There were occasional exceptions, but the general rule was that the office

of an elder would be filled by a Christian who had walked through a good part of the Christian life, had grappled with its difficulties, had overcome the basic appetites of particular stations, and could now give guidance in hindsight.

If elders are struggling through life or even burdened down with young families, jobs that require extra hours, or children who demand extra attention, they are not free to minister to the church. So stations have practical ecclesiastical significance as well as individual spiritual significance.

Accepting Your Station

The apostle Paul makes clear that God respects the stations. Paul wrote in 1 Corinthians 7:33, "He who is married cares about the things of the world—how he may please his wife" (NKJV). This being so, should we leave our marriages and therefore become undistracted? Paul said no. "Each one should retain the place in life that the Lord assigned to him and to which God has called him" (1 Corinthians 7:17).

If we ignore our responsibilities in life because we want to live "spiritually," we are mocking God, not serving Him. True spirituality has practical ramifications. Providing for your family is spiritual (see 1 Timothy 5:8). Expressing physical intimacy in marriage is spiritual (see 1 Corinthians 7:3-5; Hebrews 13:4).

We need an honest, realistic, and objective view of our lives with their seasons and stations. We can enjoy young children. We can enjoy without guilt the thrill of working hard at a new vocation. We can slow down a little in retirement. A truly Christian spirituality will incorporate these stations and not fight them. Yet all of them must be held loosely, for all of them are transient. Each of the stations will pass, but our relationship with God will remain.

People often confided in Francis de Sales because he was a master spiritual director. One woman, Madame Brulart, desperately sought after the Christian perfection talked about in her day, but de Sales gently reminded her that perfections "vary according to the diversity of vocations." He further warned Madame Brulart not to alienate her husband or her family due to excessive devotions. "Not only should you be devout yourself and love piety," he wrote, "but you should make it lovable to others." [4]

In other words, if Madame Brulart ignored her family in an attempt to heroically serve God and get to know Him, she might inadvertently make piety unlovable to her family. They would resent her faith instead of being attracted by it.

Another woman, Jeanne Chantal, longed to become a nun so she could devote herself entirely to her faith. De Sales was gentle but firm with her, finally saying, "Nothing so impedes our progress in perfection as to be sighing after another way of life."[5]

God called Jeanne into marriage, and she would most please God by surrendering to the demands and obligations of marriage rather than pining for the life of a celibate nun. God would receive her changing diapers as enthusiastically as He receives a nun working in a hospital, bandaging up a wound.

The Unchanging God Who Lives Above It All

Every aspect of a truly Christian spirituality points us to the glory of God, and a discussion of the spiritual climates, terrains, and stations is no exception. We are challenged by the changes in our lives, but God is not. We worship Him and place all our hope in Him in every circumstance.

God is enthroned in heaven, above all the changing climates. He roams over the earth, above all terrain. He is eternal, above all stations in life. Therefore, we base our confidence on the finished work of Christ, we draw our strength from the limitless power of the Spirit, and we gain our sense of acceptance from the mercy and grace of the Father, who has made provision for our shortcomings and limitations in the person of His Son.

If we base the success of our faith on ourselves, we will be disillusioned in the winter and unduly smug in the spring. Even though we are called to cooperate with God's work in our lives, our spiritual existence rests securely in the finished work of our triune God.

The ever-changing spiritual climates, terrains, and stations cry out for an unmovable foundation. If we carefully attend to our cry for intimacy, purpose, and meaning, it will lead us to God alone. We will not always be active parents or be working in a vocation, but we will always be walking with the God who made us, the rock of our faith, the anchor of our souls.

Soul Surgery:
A Guide to Spiritual Direction

When Augustine finally began his famous turn toward the Christian faith, he soon realized he needed help. Great Christians are rarely produced in isolation. The most effective route to mature growth is to work one-on-one with a more mature Christian. Augustine wrote, "To Milan I came, to Ambrose the Bishop.... To him was I unknowingly led by Thee, that by him I might knowingly be led to Thee. That man of God received me as a father.... I hung on his words attentively."[1] Augustine's humility and wisdom in seeking spiritual direction helped to make him one of the most influential Christian bishops of all time.

The beginning of Augustine's spiritual journey wasn't the only time he sought counsel, however, and in this we can learn an even greater lesson. Later in his life, Augustine wrote this:

> And Thou didst put into my mind, and it seemed good in my eyes, to go to Simplicianus [Ambrose's successor as bishop], who seemed to me a good servant of Thine; and Thy grace shone in him. I had heard also, that from his very youth he had lived most devoted unto Thee. Now he was grown into years; and by reason of so great age spent in such zealous following of Thy ways, he seemed to me likely to have learned much experience; and so he had. Out of which store, I wished that he would tell me which were the fittest way for one in my case to walk in Thy paths.[2]

Augustine was not a self-made Christian. Very few who go far are. We need spiritual coaching, which is quite different from sermons delivered to hundreds or even thousands of people on Sunday mornings. Christian writers throughout history have urged Christians to find one-on-one relationships in which they could be challenged, corrected, and inspired to press on in the faith. Three more of the most influential classical writers are in complete agreement on this.

- Thomas à Kempis: "Consult with him that is wise and conscientious and seek to be instructed by a better than thyself, rather than to follow thine own inventions."

- John Climacus: "Those who have given themselves up to God but imagine that they can go forward without a leader are surely deceiving themselves. The fugitives from Egypt had Moses, while those escaping from Sodom had an angel for a leader…We must have someone very skilled, a doctor, for our septic wounds."

- Francis De Sales: "Wouldst thou walk in earnest towards devotion, seek some good man, who may guide and conduct thee; this is the best advice I can give thee."

Why Do We Need Spiritual Direction?

Why do we need help with spiritual direction? Four reasons help explain the importance of this need.

Our Hearts Are Deceitful

We shouldn't be surprised that early Christian writers, who took Scripture seriously, usually agreed on the need for wise, objective advice (see Proverbs 14:12). We lack the objectivity to see things accurately, so we gain clarity by sharing our soul with other, wiser Christians. Alone, we are in danger of leading ourselves astray.

The unknown author of *The Cloud of Unknowing* writes, "As long as the soul dwells in this mortal body the accuracy of our understanding in perceiving spiritual things, most particularly God, is mingled with some manner of fantasy that tends to make our work unclean."[3]

Even the most mature Christian, according to John Climacus, hasn't outgrown the need for the input of others. Any one of us could be led astray. "A man, no matter how prudent, may easily go astray on a road if he has no guide."[4]

We Need Humility

More than mere prudence calls us to seek the counsel of others. Humility also moves us to get good advice. Thomas à Kempis wrote, "Who is so wise that he can fully know all things? Be not therefore too confident in thine own opinion; but be willing to hear the judgment of others."[5]

Notice that he said, "Be willing to hear the judgment of others." We may not always agree with the input we receive, but humility demands we at least listen to the counsel of others. This is particularly important for those à Kempis calls "inexperienced."

> They that are yet but novices and inexperienced in the way of the Lord, unless they govern themselves by the counsel of discreet persons, may easily be deceived and broken to pieces. And if they will rather follow their own notions than trust to others who are more experienced, their end will be dangerous, at least if they are unwilling to be drawn away from their own fond conceit.[6]

We need direction to weed out those prejudices and attitudes that block further spiritual growth. A broken attitude can hold us down for years if we never realize its power over us, but a wise spiritual director might be able to spot such an attitude or faulty assumption within minutes. Why limit our growth to our own wisdom? Why not explore the fullness of life in Christ by learning from those who walk the journey with us?

We Have an Enemy

We also need a spiritual friend because we have a vicious and cunning spiritual enemy. The Bible says Satan is actively opposing us.[7] He wants us to sin. He plots to see our downfall. Plans are being made right now for you and me to fall. With such an enemy plotting our destruction, shouldn't we also cultivate a friend who will plot our growth?

Our modern culture has lost sight of spiritual realities that earlier Christians took for granted. Ignatius understood hell's individual attention to the believer. He realized that Satan and his cohorts look at us as individuals, working to exploit our own personal weaknesses.

> The enemy observes very narrowly whether the soul be gross
> or delicate; and if it is delicate he strives to make it delicate
> to an extreme, that he may the more easily disturb and ruin
> it…If he sees a soul consent to no sin…then the enemy, since
> he cannot cause it to fall into what has the appearance of sin,
> contrives to make it judge that there is sin where there is not,
> as in some word or insignificant thought. If the soul is gross,
> the enemy contrives to render it still more gross.[8]

In other words, we need a spiritual director who not only points out where we're sinning but also comforts us when we fear we are sinning but actually are not. I tend to be what Ignatius called "delicate to an extreme" and often feel condemned. A friend of mine once summarily dismissed my frustration by saying, "Well, I'd rather suffer the way *you* do than the way *I* do," but for those of us besieged with accusations, the spiritual warfare feels real and can make us miserable. "Were you gentle like Christ in that conversation? Were you completely, absolutely truthful? Might that interaction have included just a little bit of pride?"

Ignatius wants us to see that our perception of our spiritual growth can be rooted in error. Satan will manipulate our feelings. He can use our own emotions against us—even our desire to please God.

Because of such possibilities, we need objective voices speaking truth into our souls. Ultimately, the Holy Spirit and the Spirit-inspired Scriptures will be that voice, but those same Scriptures encourage us to get many counselors. Ignatius was convinced that Satan is defeated when we bring our concerns into the light.

> When the enemy of our human nature obtrudes on a just soul
> his wiles and deceits, he wishes and desires that they be fur-
> tively received and kept secret, but he is very displeased when
> they are discovered to a good confessor or some other spiritual
> person who knows his frauds and malice, because he infers
> that he cannot succeed in the wicked design he had conceived,
> as his evident frauds are laid open.[9]

If we really believe hell exists, we must learn to live accordingly and protect ourselves against it. Satan has limits. He cannot overpower us, but he can deceive us. The best way to fight deception is to discuss our spiritual concerns with another believer who is objective, who is acting within the gifting of the Holy Spirit, and who is therefore less likely to be deceived. We should also seek someone who is aware of the mechanics of temptation and who has the ability to hear and be led by God.

> We should submit ourselves to the direction of a faithful friend, who, by the prudence and wisdom of his counsels, may guide us in all our actions, and secure us from the ambushes and deceits of the wicked one. Such a friend will be to us as a treasure of wisdom and consolation, in all our afflictions, our sorrows, and relapses; he will serve as a medicine to cure, and as a cordial to comfort our hearts in our spiritual disorders; he will guard us from evil, and make us advance in good; and should any infirmity befall us, he will assist in our recovery, and prevent its being unto death.[10]

Secrets Are like Cancer

Yet another blessing of having a spiritual director is the death of secrets. Secrets are spiritual cancers. They allow sinful actions to become habits until hell has a feast on what started out as "one little sin." Confession keeps us uncomfortable in our sin and forces us to seek a resolution.

Lying is the doorway to spiritual destruction. Jesus called Himself the truth (John 14:6) and Satan "a liar and the father of lies" (John 8:44). When we become mired in deceit, we are following Satan, not Christ.

Scripture calls us to be people of the truth, and I've found that both truth and deceit are habits. A spiritual director helps us develop the habit of truth. When we begin to live in the light in front of one, it is easier to live in the light in front of all.

One of the church's main needs today is authenticity, especially in its leaders. Any type of ministry is intense, and when you add secrets, particularly secrets of sin, ministry can become almost unbearable. Secrets allow Satan to blackmail us. Rather than ministering in the freedom of Christ, we will forever be looking over our shoulders to cover that one little corner.

Earlier in my life, I couldn't have been as honest as I have been in sharing some of my own history and failings in this book. Slaying the glittering image has been incredibly freeing! The story of my life could be summed up like this: God has done some very good things in my life and I have done some very bad things, but through it all, God's grace has prevailed.

My willingness to be honest began when I was first honest with just one person. When that person's love and respect remained constant, I was able to be more open with a slightly larger circle. When we engage in this process, we may very well experience occasional betrayals, but usually we will find walking in the light so freeing that we can simply pray for those who betray us and ask God to grant them His mercy. Soon we no longer want to be adored as much as we want to be real. Secrecy and deceit create a burden no Christian should have to bear.

This call to authenticity doesn't include baring our souls to anyone who cares to listen. Some things need to remain between us and only one or two other people, but very few things need to remain between us and God alone. Remember, the heart is deceitful, and secrecy provides a ripe atmosphere for sin to grow from an event to a habit and then a character trait.

A healthy spiritual life has no secrets, no deceit, and no cover-ups. God has provided for our forgiveness in Jesus Christ, so believers have no reason to suffer the pangs of conscience in isolation. Confession is not a duty as much as it is God's gift to renew us and make us strong.

I want to speak a special word particularly to those who have been victimized in any way. Be wary about letting a secret remain between you and your victimizer. An ongoing secret can be a form of ongoing abuse, for it gives the abuser power over you. The abuser may even derive a certain sadistic pleasure from the false intimacy of knowing something about you that nobody else knows. Prayerfully consider sharing your secret with a mature believer who loves you. You may be amazed at the liberating power of truth and love. When you get to choose the people you share this secret with, and when they pray with you and assure you, you will experience a newfound freedom. Even more, you will be released from the abuser's grip forever and experience the joy of being liberated by the love of God.

43

Choosing a Spiritual Director

S piritual directors can play an important role, so we need to be very careful about the people we choose. Those who have problems with power or control, incorrect theology, or a lack of humility can do more harm than good.

Thomas à Kempis urged that we seek those who are "wise and conscientious" and "better" (or more mature) than ourselves.[1] In other words, we should choose people we can look up to.

Teresa of Avila urges us to find people who can inspire us to do the impossible. When we see the ease with which these people do the impossible, we will be encouraged and made "bold to fly." In this, little by little, we can imitate the parent. "Receiving this help is most beneficial; I know."[2] Knowing her history, I can't help but wonder if she is referring to John of the Cross, who served as her spiritual director for three years.

Teresa also urged that we seek after both wisdom and spiritual perception—though we may not necessarily find both of these in the same people.

> It is good that at the beginning you speak about this vision under the seal of confession with a very learned man, for learned men will give us light. Or, with some very spiritual person, if there be one available; if there isn't, it's better to speak with a very learned man. Or with both a spiritual person and a learned man if both are at hand.[3]

Do you understand what Teresa is saying? Some have great academic understanding and can parse any Scripture backward and forward, but they may lack a spiritual awareness of how to apply that Scripture or how God's life works its way into our soul. Others may have a prayerful aware-ness of God's ways but could be deficient in their understanding of basic theology and Scripture. Study is an essential part of maturity, but it doesn't necessarily result in true understanding. Some may study with a hard or undiscerning heart. Teresa urges us to choose someone well versed in Scripture who is also well aware of the spiritual journey and human expe-rience. If we find someone who is both wise and spiritually perceptive, we should be particularly thankful.

The directors we choose should not be the kind of people who will be threatened by our growth or who will imprison us within their own lim-itations. Teresa warned, "If the confessor is a person whom, although he practices prayer, the Lord has not led by this path, he will at once be fright-ened and condemn it. For this reason I advise you to have a confessor who is very learned and, if possible, also spiritual."[4]

Different Strokes

The director should also be able to appreciate diversity. Spiritual disci-plines, such as fasting, can be very helpful for some, but they can be dan-gerous if they foster pride or are used as an attempt to gain God's favor. A director who treats every believer the same way is like a doctor who only prescribes one medicine regardless of the ailment. Such a director can actually poison one's faith.

> One man's medicine can be another man's poison, and some-thing can be a medicine to the same man at one time and a poison at another. So I have seen an incompetent physician who by inflicting dishonor on a sick but contrite man pro-duced despair in him, and I have seen a skillful physician who cut through an arrogant heart with the knife of dishonor and thereby drained it of all its foul-smelling pus.[5]

I was at a Christian retreat where two men were discussing marriage, and one of the men was really hurting. The other one immediately began telling him he must be ignoring his wife, failing to build her up, taking her for granted, and so on. When I asked a few simple questions, how-ever, it became abundantly clear that this wasn't the case at all. An entirely different dynamic was at work. This brother needed healing and encouragement, not condemnation. The one doing the counseling, we found, was admittedly going through a time of conviction from God about his own sin toward his wife, and he was transferring it to this other brother.

People who are full of themselves can't direct others. A director must be as liberated as possible from his or her own experience in order to enter the experience of another. (And please understand, all of us can be full of ourselves at various points in our life. We all need to guard against this tendency.)

You may find, as I have, that when you first seek out someone to make a confession, he or she confesses the same sin to you and then asks you for counsel! Press on and find another director, for such a person has not matured enough to care for someone else. I'm all for mutual sharing as long as both parties are getting the care they need. If the situation becomes one-sided, however, we need to find someone strong enough to help us in our weakness. (Incidentally, the possibility of receiving a confession is a good reason to live in holiness and full repentance. We don't want to be caught ashamed and unhealed if someone brings a confession to us and we have not addressed our own sin in that area.)

A director should also have an understanding of the devotional classics. Such an understanding frees the director from being a one-dimensional Christian who has only one answer. De Sales and Fénelon, for example, have much to teach us about temptation, but because they both lean toward quietism and (in Fénelon's case) mysticism, I'd have someone read John Owen's *Sin and Temptation* in between reading de Sales and Fénelon to give him or her a more systematic understanding of fighting sin and a more varied perspective. If people who come to me are legalists, I wouldn't let them near Law's *A Serious Call* until they understood the reality of grace. And if they're just flat-out uninformed or apathetic about temptation, I'd steer them toward Lorenzo Scupoli's *Spiritual Combat*. In the right hands, the classics represent an amazing arsenal of spiritual weapons to defeat ignorance, apathy, and temptation.

John Climacus urged us to choose a spiritual director who is "old in wisdom rather than years,"[6] He also advised that we consider our own strengths and weaknesses and match those with the appropriate director. A director who does wonders for your friend may not serve you well at all.

We should analyze the nature of our passions and of our obedience, so as to choose our director accordingly. If lust is your problem, do not pick for your trainer a worker of miracles who has a welcome and a meal for everyone. Choose instead an ascetic who will reject any of the consolation of food. If you are arrogant, let him be tough and unyielding, not gentle and accommodating. We should not be on the lookout for those gifted with foreknowledge and foresight, but rather for those who are truly humble and whose character and dwelling place match our weaknesses.[7]

Choosing a soft director is a particular temptation for those who have a problem with control. A high-powered manipulator may purposefully choose a mushy yes-man so he can feign accountability. A good director (or accountability group) should not be easily manipulated or intimidated by us.

Love the One You're With

Climacus urged us to thoroughly check out our spiritual director, but once we've made our choice, to respect his or her role.

When humbly and with true longing for salvation we resolve to bend the neck and entrust ourselves to another in the Lord, there is something to be done before we start. If there happens to be any cunning in us, any prudence, then we should question, examine, and...put to the test our master, so that there is no mistaking the sailor for the helmsman, the patient for the doctor...with the resulting shipwreck of our soul. But having once entered the stadium of holy living and obedience, we can no longer start criticizing the umpire, even if we should notice some faults in him. After all, he is human and if we start making judgments, then our submissiveness earns no profit.

If we wish to preserve unshaken faith in our superiors, we must write their good deeds indelibly in our hearts and preserve them in our memories so that, when the demons scatter distrust of them among us, we can repel them by what we have retained in our minds...When the thought strikes you to judge or condemn your superior, leap away as though from fornication.[8]

One of Satan's favorite ploys to keep us from truth is to make us despise the messenger of truth. If our director speaks a difficult word to us, we will be tempted to ignore the truth by trying to find the same or a similar fault in our director. This is nothing but evasion. Other people may have the same faults we do—even our spiritual directors—but that doesn't mean we don't need to address our own shortcomings. Imperfections don't disqualify people from being used by God to speak truth, conviction, and healing into our souls.

Spiritual directors have a demanding role to play, so we obviously should not choose them casually. Francis de Sales quoted Teresa in this regard:

> "For this end, choose one amongst a thousand," says Avila; but I say, choose one amongst ten thousand; for there are fewer than can be imagined who are capable of this office. He must be a man of charity, learning, and prudence. If any of these three qualities be wanting in him, there is danger.[9]

44

Growing Together

Once we've found suitable spiritual directors, we can make their job easy or difficult. As soon as we decide to become accountable to someone else, our spiritual enemy will do all he can to get us to be less than honest during our time together. In the grips of conviction, we might seek out a spiritual director with great earnestness, but as conviction fades, we may visit the director with much less sincerity. We may even wonder why we are visiting a director in the first place or feel as if we were just overreacting when we initiated the process. Be prepared for this; it is nearly universal.

Getting a spiritual director is like receiving a prescription. The prescription itself won't cure you until you actually take the medicine. If you leave that little white slip in your glove box, your visit to the doctor will have been a complete waste. So don't just decide to visit a director; make the best use of your visit.

Confessing Sin

Once we've found an able director, what is the proper process for sharing our sins and temptations? First, we must determine to be absolutely honest. To believers who would confess to their spiritual directors, Francis de Sales gave this advice:

> [Tell] how long a time you have continued in your sin; for the length of time is an aggravation of the evil. We must...

tell the fact, the motive, and the continuance of our sins. For though we are not bound to declare venial sins [slight or accidental offenses], nor absolutely obliged to confess them, yet those who desire to cleanse their souls perfectly and attain to holy devotion, must be careful to make their spiritual physician acquainted with the evil of which they desire to be cured, no matter how small it may be.[1]

Think of sin as a disease that is slowly destroying your health. You would tell a physician about every symptom, every nuance, every complication, to give him or her as accurate a description as possible. Have the same attitude toward sin. It is different from a disease, but if anything, it is even more deadly, for the potential complications are spiritual as well as physical. Don't give sin any place to hide. If nothing else, this is an excellent exercise in humility.

The second way we must confess is face-to-face. Confession forces us to face the reality of our sin. Why is confession with God so easy, but confession to a brother or sister in Christ is so hard? The problem is that our grasp of God's presence and power is so pitifully small. We aren't really confessing to God; we're confessing to ourselves. When we confess to another believer face-to-face, we sense Christ's presence in that person, and then we see the true nature of our sins. This helps to break the hold of repeated sins. John Climacus wrote, "Confession is like a bridle that keeps the soul which reflects on it from committing sin, but anything left unconfessed we continue to do without fear as if in the dark."[2]

As I write this, a famous athlete's personal life has been exposed on a world stage, leading him to put his career on hold to address the root behavioral issues that are threatening his family. His actions have been going on for years, but he hadn't seen how horrible they were and hadn't taken action until they came into the light. He had grown so comfortable with his sin that it didn't seem so bad, but when it was exposed and he saw how others reacted, he finally realized he needed some help.

In this sense confession is a spotlight, forcing us to look at our sins in the full light of God's truth, not letting us pretend they are merely slight indiscretions. We need to face the one to whom we're confessing, look him or her in the eyes, and be humiliated as we state our sins and admit our wrongdoing. We need to let the intensity of the moment burn the sin out of us.

We need to be honest about our temptations as well as our sins. God does not want us to suffer in silence, alone and isolated, as we carry out an unseen battle with Satan. When we are tempted, we need encouragement, perspective, and instruction. De Sales emphasized the need for openness.

> The sovereign remedy against all temptations, whether great or small, is to lay open your heart, and communicate its suggestions, feelings, and affections to your director; for you must observe, that the first condition that the enemy of salvation makes with a soul which he desires to seduce is to keep silence…Whereas God, on the other hand, by his inspirations, requires that we should make them known to our superiors and directors.[3]

Building Strengths

A skillful spiritual director will understand that the Christian life is about far more than what we don't do. He or she will encourage you to grow in positive virtues and active service. A wise director will focus on building your prayer life, fortifying your times of devotion, and cultivating the life of Christ in your soul.

At the risk of sounding like I'm offering a shameless plug, my book *Sacred Pathways* lists nine different spiritual temperaments (or "pathways") that Christians have used to build personal lives of devotion and to connect with God. The best spiritual direction spends more time building up a life of prayer than it does dealing with the consequences of sin. If your times become mere confessions, you'll begin to view your spiritual life through the lens of an avoidance mentality—"Please help me to stop doing x, y, or z." Far more beneficial is the approach of growing in prayer, heart, mind, and service, and letting those advances create an ever more impressive defense against sin and temptation.

Confession is inevitable and vital in spiritual direction, but it shouldn't become the only aspect or even the primary aspect of the relationship. Keep the focus on growth, and you'll actually grow.

45

The Call to Be a Spiritual Director

Themodel of church life is tantamount to a physician lecturing 1000 cancer patients in the same room with the same advice. Some might have cancer of the esophagus, some might have lung cancer or cancer of the liver. But everyone gets the same lecture, the same information, the same application.

This doesn't appear to be the way of the early church. The Didache, an ancient Christian document that the early church used as a primer when training new believers, *assumes* a personal teacher-disciple relationship. It addresses a single novice and encourages him to honor and model his life after the one who is doing the training (4:1).

Spiritual direction may seem relatively new, but it is actually an ancient practice being renewed. Unfortunately, the church has plenty of servants who are skilled at talking to large crowds but suffers from a virtual famine of Christians who can perform soul surgery, dealing with confused and struggling Christians one-on-one as spiritual directors.

How then can we find one if they are so rare? To be honest, this is one of the most frequent inquiries I receive. The demand for spiritual direction far exceeds the supply. Francis de Sales urged that we make it a matter of earnest prayer. "Beseech God, with the greatest importunity, to furnish you with one who may be according to his own heart; and be assured that he will rather send you an angel from heaven...than fail to grant your request."[1]

The good news is that God is raising up many individuals who are seeking to address this need. Training opportunities for those who wish to become spiritual directors may be more readily available now than any in other time since the end of the reformation. Books and programs directly addressing this need are multiplying. Even so, you may simply have to be a pioneer, admitting the need and doing the best you can to fulfill it, even if you don't believe you are fully prepared or adequately trained to do so.

A Labor That Refreshes

Where are the brave souls who will plunge into this private work of spiritual direction? In the first part of this book, we considered spiritual goals. Becoming a skilled spiritual director is a very laudable goal. It will mean being ruthless with our own failings and honest with others about our own faults, and it will mean we need to draw ever closer to Christ. I have found, however, that as fulfilling as rapturous prayer is, releasing someone else to enjoy that same prayer is even more so. Being healed from a troublesome sin or trait is thrilling, but helping another be healed of a sin or character weakness is even more so.

Francis de Sales, the great bishop who took the time to minister to individuals—and who, despite his fame, was willing to preach to fewer than half a dozen at a time—wrote of the laborers' reward.

> It is painful, I confess, to direct souls in particular; but it is a pain that gives a comfort like that which is felt by the laborers in the harvest and vintage, who are never better pleased than when they have most to do, and when their burdens are the heaviest. It is a labor which refreshes and revives the heart by the sweet delight it excites in those who are engaged in it. [2]

Henry Drummond cut his teeth on spiritual direction. He was a primary counselor following Moody's crusades, and Drummond's work with individuals gave him the insight into the human heart that few other writers have matched. There is no substitute for dealing with real lives and real issues. Beware the teacher who masks a lack of understanding by speaking general platitudes to huge crowds that can never talk back.

Don't get me wrong. Preaching is a vital service, but preaching itself can be fed, energized, and strengthened with active individual work. That is part of the reason why I and so many others are drawn to de Sales and Drummond time after time. Both were known for their ability to direct individuals and address real problems with realistic, insightful suggestions.

Are You Ready?

Here's another reason to take the time to get involved in spiritual direction, as God leads: Directing others requires us to keep building lives of authenticity and progress. Signing up for marathons motivates me to be faithful with my training. Too many Christians never run any real spiritual race, so they never see the need to truly train. But when they step out and God begins to use them, they see their need to understand the Scriptures better, they are more intent on God purifying their hearts, and they want to keep walking in grace. They pay heed to their own growth so they can bring others along.

Parenting, of course, is one of the earliest and most natural training grounds for spiritual direction. What an ideal way for people to introduce themselves to the process—by naturally directing their children. At that stage, they needn't feel any guilt or obligation to take time away from the home to direct others (though they might well benefit from direction themselves). If they give themselves fully to raising their kids, by the time their children are grown they will be that much more experienced and skilled at helping others grow in grace.

I'm not suggesting everyone is called to this work in an official capacity. That would be foolish. But most of us want to be more helpful and earnest friends, parents, spouses, or coworkers, and adopting some of the aspects of spiritual direction could deepen these relationships and increase our effectiveness. This is a high calling and an exciting work for those who will listen to God's leading.

PART 7

Radically
Changed Lives

46

Cooperating Christians

O ne of the great problems with Christians today is that they try too hard. They just don't rest in grace."

I've heard dozens of pastors say something like this in various sermons, books, and interviews, and every time I hear it, I'm *astonished*. The notion that today's believers try too hard or that there is actually something wrong with that seems ridiculous on its face.

Consider the monks John Climacus addressed, who went to great lengths to get rid of sin—the penance chamber, extreme fastings, strict obedience, and more. Consider the hours Teresa of Avila, John of the Cross, and their followers spent on their knees in order to explore contemplative prayer. How many today follow even half of the daily meditations and study times William Law prescribed or a portion of the devotional exercises Ignatius of Loyola offered? Who has accomplished even a slice of the ministry narrated by John Wesley in his journals or a fraction of the mortification of sin practiced by John Owen and Ralph Venning and other Puritans? Where do we see even a touch of the simplicity and poverty of the Franciscans captured in *The Little Flowers of St. Francis*? If these things were common, I might begin to believe that today's believers try too hard. But I see none of this.

In fact, I think Dietrich Bonhoeffer's lament applies to many in our day: "The word of cheap grace has been the ruin of more Christians than any commandment of works."[1]

An Old Foe

We are concerned about legalism, and rightly so, but the classic case of New Testament legalism—relying on circumcision and statutory works of the Old Testament law for acceptance with God and justification—is all but dead today. What contemporary Christian thinks he can find peace with God by being circumcised? We rightly reject the legalistic attempt to win or maintain God's acceptance through our behavior, but the Christian classics preserve the scriptural truth that once we are saved by grace through faith, we are actually compelled to be more active in our faith than ever before—not to earn God's favor, but because the Holy Spirit Himself motivates us.

Most pastors nobly want to preserve the precious truth of salvation by grace through faith (to which I subscribe fully, completely, and without reservation). With the best of intentions, these pastors uphold the finished, completed work of Christ for our justification, to which we can add nothing. Bravo for that. But the notion that subsequent effort, on its own, discounts this or somehow even undercuts it, is a modern one. It is diabolically clever, and it has kept many believers in a state of immaturity and ineffectiveness. We fear the very thing that would usher in a greater maturity.

Jonathan Edwards, often called the last of the Puritans and thus Reformed to the core, points out that conversion launches the *beginning* of our efforts.

> The Scriptures often represent the search, effort, and labor that occur in a Christian chiefly after his conversion. Yet his conversion is only the beginning of his work. From then on he has to stand, press forward, reach out, continue instant in prayer, and cry to God day and night.[2]

An Earnest Effort

In the classics, we see the same cooperative blend that the apostle Paul upheld: "Continue to work out your salvation with fear and trembling, for it is God who works in you to will and to act according to his good purpose" (Philippians 2:12-13). Johannes Tauler embraced the cooperative nature of the transformation process, writing without any fear of contradiction, "One way is active, in which we are seeking; the other passive, in which we are sought."[3]

Lorenzo Scupoli captures this brilliantly in this prayer: "This conflict, then, is chiefly Thine, and it is from Thee alone that I can hope for victory, although I must do my part."[4] In the evangelical framework, this is not about adding to justification, for that would be impossible. Rather, it's about cooperating with God's work in our souls so that we not only experience redemption in our hearts but also live it out every day. To use the apostle Paul's language, we "fan into flame" the gift that God has given us.

Calvin is emphatic that both human inclination and the power to carry it out come from God, but he references the Philippians 2 passage we just read to emphasize that "working out our salvation with fear and trembling" "represses drowsiness as well as confidence."[5] I love that take—the same truth that rejects self-confidence also attacks "drowsiness." We were not saved to go to sleep. "By the term *work*," Calvin writes, Paul "reproves our indolence."

Edwards is even stronger: "In order to be true Christians, it is necessary that we pursue the business of religion and the service of God with great earnestness and diligence. All Christ's saints not only do good works, but they also are zealous of good works (Titus 2:14)."[6]

Paul wrote, "To this end I labor, struggling with all his energy, which so powerfully works in me" (Colossians 1:29). Scupoli embraces the same cooperative effort. "Then, make a vigorous attack upon the passion, and wait in faith upon God for the victory, who will never fail you (although for a while He may seem to delay), if you, on your side, make every possible effort."[7] Dallas Willard offered one of the most succinct and yet powerful explanations of this dichotomy ever written: "Grace is opposed to earning, not effort."

We have no hope apart from God, and we have no power apart from God. Many believe we also have no inclination apart from God. But to say that there is no *labor* or *effort* on the human side once redemption recaptures our souls is to distort a precious truth into an absurdity that plays right into Satan's hands. Jonathan Edwards' take is classic: "True religion intensely exercises the will."[8]

Even Jeanne Guyon, who tends toward passivity in a way I find questionable, admits that at least in the beginning, earnest effort is essential to grow out of the old way of life. She has a wonderful analogy of "working our way" into being carried along by God's tide. It goes something like this.

> When sailors first take a ship out of port, it is very difficult to
> head her out to sea. They must use all their strength to get that
> ship clear of the harbor. But once she is at sea she moves eas-
> ily in whatever direction the seamen choose.
>
> It is the same with you as you begin to turn within to God.
> You are like that ship. At first you are very strongly bound by
> sin and by self. *Only* through a great deal of repeated effort
> are you turned within.[9]

God alone can give us the power, but we can choose to turn our
thoughts toward Him. We can choose, by His grace, to spend time building up our minds, fortifying our souls, taking in spiritual nutrition, choosing to confess our sins, and taking advantage of opportunities to serve and
grow in humility.

This is *work*. It requires a can-do attitude of intention, purpose, and
yes, effort. Julian of Norwich puts it this way: "It is God's wish that…our
search should be committed and diligent, with no laziness."[10]

Receptivity

Tozer brilliantly defined this dualistic work, in which God, the active
agent, empowers us, but His work increases rather than diminishes our
effort or "receptivity."

> I venture to suggest that the one vital quality which [the great
> saints] had in common was spiritual receptivity. Something in
> them was open to heaven…They had spiritual awareness and
> they went on to cultivate it until it became the biggest thing in
> their lives. They differed from the average person in that when
> they felt the inward longing *they did something about it.* They
> acquired the lifelong habit of spiritual response.[11]

Tozer warned that this receptivity "may be increased by exercise or
destroyed by neglect."

We can choose to study Scripture, read the classics, and build a mind
open to God's wisdom. We can choose to pray, perhaps even to fast, and
to ask others to hold us accountable. We can develop disciplines that will
help us practice the presence of God throughout the day. We can use the
common events of everyday life as a school of character, listening to God's
voice along the way.

Apart from God's presence, such activities would be as fruitless as planting a dead stick in the ground. But with God's dynamic touch, such activities are like putting a flame at the bottom of a pile of kindling—we will soon witness a raging fire.

I recognize the danger of legalism, but in some ways, I've moved on. The notion that I can make God love me more or accept me more based on anything I might do is so far removed from my way of thinking that it's absurd. You might as well tell me I'm capable of high jumping over the moon. But I am compelled—by God's Spirit within me, I believe—to put forth an increased effort to press on toward maturity, to take seriously the actual transformation Scripture calls us to.

- "Be perfect, as your heavenly Father is perfect" (Matthew 5:48).

- "Be imitators of God" (Ephesians 5:1).

- "You may participate in the divine nature...Therefore...be all the more eager to make your calling and election sure" (2 Peter 1:4,10).

- "So I tell you this, and insist on it in the Lord, that you must no longer live as the Gentiles do...You were taught...to put on the new self, created to be like God in true righteousness and holiness" (Ephesians 4:17,22,24).

Let's be honest. How in the world can we imitate God without trying? How do you obey the directive to make your calling and election sure if you fear effort more than sin? How can we consciously put on the new self if we believe effort leads us toward legalism?

None of us will ever get within a light-year of perfection, but that doesn't mean we should simply stop trying. To do so is to take God's Word lightly, and to take God's Word lightly is to undercut His authority.

We are woefully deficient in every way, but when we take transformation seriously, we will become more grateful for and aware of God's grace. Serious Christians depend on grace more than cheap-grace Christians do because serious believers never forget how far short they fall from God's high standard, which makes them even more grateful that God has made provision for their shortcomings. In this sense, trying harder does more to remind us of God's unmerited favor and grace and mercy than simply resting in laziness and sloth, taking God's provision for granted.

Let's end this chapter with a stirring call from one of my favorites, Henry Drummond: "No man who feels the worth and solemnity of what is at stake will be careless as to his progress...A religion of effortless adoration may be a religion for an angel, but never for a man."[12]

Radical Transformation

I s it possible to put a drop of red dye in a glass of water and not turn
the entire glass of water pink? Can you drop one lit match into a pool
of gasoline without starting a raging fire? Similarly, can the dynamic
presence and power of Christ enter a soul without effecting a major life
change in attitude, action, thought, word, and deed?

Of course not.

Scripture and the classics both make this vividly clear: True Christianity results in true change. Without change, there is no true faith.

- "If anyone considers himself religious and yet does not keep a
  tight rein on his tongue, he deceives himself and his religion
  is worthless" (James 1:26).

- "They claim to know God, but by their actions they deny him"
  (Titus 1:16).

- "What good is it, my brothers, if a man claims to have faith
  but has no deeds? Can such faith save him?…Show me your
  faith without deeds, and I will show you my faith by what I
  do…Faith without deeds is useless" (James 2:14,18,20).

Building on the foundation of this biblical truth, the classic devotional
writers stressed the importance of deep, abiding change in people who follow God. Thomas à Kempis led the charge. "Many there are who count
how long it is since their conversion; and yet full slender oftentimes is the

fruit of amendment in their lives." Chronology (how long you've been a believer) is no substitute for maturity.

Johannes Tauler warns, "We observe such a great difference between those who live the Scriptures and those who merely study them."[1]

During a time of supposed revival, Jonathan Edwards wrote this to distinguish *real* faith from *apparent* faith: "True spiritual discoveries are life-changing and are more than temporary experiences. They are powerful enough to alter the very nature of the soul."[2] He went on to suggest that a lack of change reveals a lack of faith.

> If there is no great and abiding change in people who think they
> have experienced a work of conversion, they are deluded...A
> man may be restrained from sin before he is converted. But
> when he is converted, he is not only restrained from sin, but
> his very heart and nature are turned away from it toward a life
> of holiness.[3]

This doesn't mean Edwards taught perfectionism; far from it. But many Christians make the important mistake of assuming that because perfectionism isn't possible, change isn't necessary. They seem to think the only two options are perfectionism or nothing! The apostle Paul avoided this trap by telling Timothy, "Be diligent in these matters; give yourself wholly to them, so that everyone may see your progress" (1 Timothy 4:15). People would never see a perfect Timothy, but Paul wanted them to see a Timothy who was growing toward maturity. Edwards provides some marvelous pastoral counsel in this regard.

> Of course, even true Christians still have remnants of a con-
> trary spirit and may even be guilty of behavior offensive to
> such a spirit. But this I affirm, there are no true Christians
> who live in the prevailing power of such a spirit so that it
> becomes truly their character. The Scripture speaks of no real
> Christians who have an ugly, selfish, angry, and contentious
> spirit. Nothing can be more contradictory than a morose,
> hard, closed, and spiteful Christian.[4]

Sin may assault us Christians, but it does not control us. It may scar us, bite us, wound us, and trip us up, but it does not, cannot, and will not stop the victorious, resurrected, and ascended Christ from raising our souls from the dead. Just as important, Jesus does far more than merely keep us breathing spiritually. He takes us by the hand, lifts our head, and empowers us to serve with passion, authority, and enthusiasm.

Many of us today are so obsessed over what we don't want to do, or so embroiled in coddling a particular sin, that we have completely lost touch with what we can become. This is particularly sad. Being dominated by any one sin creates a spiritual blindness that steals from us the joy and freedom of extensive transformation. Letting go of that sin is like cutting the string that holds down a helium balloon—we can start soaring when we are not tethered to the world.

Instead of transformation, the church gets lost in lesser pursuits, particularly mere intellectual assent (mind games).

Mind Games

If we're not careful, we can reduce evangelism to an intellectual argument. Agree with us, and you'll go to heaven. Disagree, and you'll go to hell. Mental assent to the truth of the gospel is essential for salvation, but on its own, it is not sufficient evidence that salvation has occurred. Think of our legal system. I can admit that the state has authority to prosecute me if I murder someone. I can even agree that murder is wrong. But if I still commit murder, my mental agreement and acceptance of the state's rightful authority won't save me from the jury's verdict or the judge's sentence. That's what James was talking about when he said, "You believe that there is one God. Good! Even the demons believe that—and shudder" (2:19).

I love Tozer's take on those who teach that merely assenting to the truth is all that's needed. Paraphrasing Thomas à Kempis, he writes, "I had rather exercise faith than know the definition thereof."[5]

Tozer lamented the church's lukewarm attitude about real transformation: "Ignoble contentment takes the place of burning zeal…For the most part, we bother ourselves very little about the absence of personal experience."[6] Where faith exists, according to Tozer, we will also find not only zeal, but *burning* zeal.

Sincerity

The other substitute in our day for true faith, in addition to mere mental assent, is sincerity. We can be fooled into thinking that as long as we are sincere in our pursuit of God and feel sorry when we dishonor Him, our faith must be genuine. This allows us to circumvent the objective evidence of changed lives.

Edwards is ruthless in fighting this excuse. "Godliness consists not merely in having a heart intent on doing the will of God, but having a heart that actually does it…It is absurd then to pretend to have a good heart while living a wicked life."[7]

We must be passionate about actually becoming like Christ, progressively changing in a way that others can see. Henry Drummond puts this pursuit in particularly inspiring terms. "To become like Christ is the only thing in the world worth caring for, the thing before which every ambition is folly, and all lower achievement vain. Those only who make this quest the supreme desire and passion of their lives can even begin to hope to reach it."[8]

Becoming like Christ is not easy. We will expend much effort and often fail as we seek to grow in wisdom, learn to mortify our sin, have our hearts shaped toward holiness, and gain a greater understanding through many trials and numerous falls. Therefore, if we are not enamored by the possibility of actually living the way Jesus did, we will give up long before we reach even the outskirts of maturity.

It comes down to this. Today's Christian values his *salvation*. Yesterday's Christian valued his *holiness*, and that makes all the difference. Drummond was clear on this.

> It is not necessary that we should be prosperous or famous, or happy. But it is necessary that we should be holy; and the deepest moments of our lives give us glimpses sometimes of a more tender reason still why God says, "Be ye holy"—it is for our own sakes; because it would be hell to be unholy.[9]

The invitation to holiness is the greatest ever given to humankind. It is better than the greatest job offer one could imagine. It is vastly more precious than any sexual favor ever granted. It is more nurturing than the best meal cooked by the best chef the world has ever known. It is worth far more than a lifetime vacation on any island nation with an ideal climate.

Holiness goes beyond our moral choices and struggles to become a part of who we are—changed people who see differently, think differently, and feel differently. Tozer describes this transformation.

A new God-consciousness will seize upon us and we shall begin to taste and hear and inwardly feel God, who is our life and our all...More and more, as our faculties grow sharper and more sure, God will become to us the great All, and His presence the glory and wonder of our lives.[10]

Merely improving our former selves is not enough. We are called to something much higher—to communicate the very presence of Christ through what we say and do. "If we cooperate with Him in loving obedience, God will manifest Himself to us, and that manifestation will be the difference between a nominal Christian life and a life radiant with the light of His face."[11]

This keeps our faith pure. When sincerity becomes the measuring stick, we tend to exalt occasional mystical experiences or an emotional conversion and then add intellectual assent. But the ancients held up an entirely different standard: not sincerity, but transformation. "Christian practice is much more to be preferred as evidence of salvation than sudden conversion, mystical enlightenment, or the mere experience of emotional comfort that begins and ends with contemplation."[12]

The Bottom Line: Remarkable Change

Eastern Orthodox spirituality is known for stressing true change to an extent that makes many evangelicals uncomfortable, especially when the Orthodox speak of *deification* with a little *d*. But the Orthodox tradition is not alone in teaching actual, experiential change. A broad tradition of Christians throughout all ages of the church has stressed the need for extraordinary transformation. Johannes Tauler describes it this way: "The soul becomes God-hued, divinized, reformed in the form of God. It possesses everything by grace which God possesses by nature by way of its union with Him and by sinking into Him. Thus the soul soars far above itself, right into the very core of God."[13]

Two elements keep such notions from slipping into some form of mystical heresy. First is the notion mentioned by Tauler that we possess such change only by grace, not by nature. This transformation is a gift given through the ongoing work of the Holy Spirit, not something we can possess in ourselves or apart from God's continuing touch. That's a crucial distinction. The other element anchoring us to biblical truth is that we should rightly reject the notion of being joined or subsumed into the divine. Christian teaching makes a clear distinction that there is only one God. We will always be the creatures, He will always be the Creator, and the two will always be distinct.

Even with these caveats, today's church settles for so very little. Why is that so? With even a *touch* of change, a whiff of holiness, we're in danger of becoming arrogant because we see so little change around us. Contrast this with Christians from past centuries who pursued not just change, but a *remarkable* change, interspersed with a lifelong battle against the old sin nature.

> Allowances must be made for our natural human temperament...If those who were once wolves and serpents are now converted, there is a remarkable change in their spirit even though it is not yet complete. Yes, indeed there is brought about the grace of the gospel that alters the former self...We see that in the early church converts were remarkably changed.[14]

When we lose this passion for personal transformation, we can easily get lost on political or social crusades because addressing the evil of others is easier than addressing the evil within our own hearts. Drummond makes precisely this point. "It is idle to talk of Christ as a social reformer if by that is meant that His first concern was to improve the organization of society, or provide the world with better laws. These were among His objects, but His first was to provide the world with better men."[15]

You and I can be those men and women, called to testify to the power of the gospel through remarkably changed lives. This is a slow and imperfect process, but it is vital, and we should settle for nothing less.

More Love

S ince I initially wrote *Seeking the Face of God* (the original and substantially shorter version of this book), one of the greatest insights I have gained from the classics has to do with the way our faith directly increases our love for others. Yes, this may be elementary, self-evident, and obvious to you. As a younger man, however, I focused on avoiding sin. In other words, my faith was concentrated on *piety* rather than *service*. As I've gotten older, spending more time in prayer and the classics, my heart has gravitated toward wanting to *love* more and more. I've come to believe that the ability to love people of all kinds, and to love them well, is the true definition of spiritual maturity. Tauler writes, "Our capacity to love…is indeed the measure with which our work and our life and our eternal happiness are measured…Everything depends on love."[1] Augustine famously said, "What matters is not the time spent in prayer or the amount of good works, but the greatness of your love."

Earlier in my life, to my great shame, I actually avoided people who were difficult to love. Scupoli would say I was avoiding the very thing that would bring the most maturity.

> If the agitation is caused by a person for whom you have such an aversion that every little action annoys and irritates you, the remedy then is to force yourself to incline your will to love him and to regard him, not only because he is a creature like yourself, formed by the almighty hand…but also because he affords you an opportunity, if you will accept it, of becoming like unto your Lord, who was loving and kind unto all.[2]

How this teaching could transform the way we look at marriage and parenting, not to mention the daily stresses of working with some people who are sometimes very annoying!

Here's the scandalous truth of Christian teaching: Jesus and His followers make it abundantly clear that we do not have the luxury of loving some people but not others. Anybody can love selectively. Choosing to be good and kind toward someone who is generous toward you is a natural reaction, not a mark of God's supernatural touch. Jesus says we should love even our enemies, and so Tauler rightly says, "Beloved, take very good care that your love embraces everyone. Show charity toward all and deprive no one of his peace!"[3]

Love's Transforming Power

This is the understanding that led me to write *Sacred Marriage*. Loving people is the laboratory for becoming like Christ. If I value true transformation, I'll value the opportunity to have my ability to love tested, tried, and refined. Scupoli writes, "If you desire…to grow in the habit of patience, it is not good to keep away from the persons, deeds, or thoughts that try your patience."[4]

Today's church desperately needs a renewed conviction that to be a Christian who doesn't love is impossible. Love is an active, energetic, enthusiastic, initiating force—it is anything *but* a feeling. When Jesus said we should love our neighbor, He was not scolding us to have fond feelings for everyone. Rather, He was calling us to put ourselves at others' service. In this sense, *unloving Christian*—referring to someone who says he or she believes in God but who is not committed to helping others—is an oxymoron. We are not Christians if we are not growing in the grace of love. "If anyone says, 'I love God,' yet hates his brother, he is a liar. For anyone who does not love his brother, whom he has seen, cannot love God, whom he has not seen. And he has given us this command: Whoever loves God must also love his brother" (1 John 4:20-21).

Love doesn't mean we are always nice. True love can call us to speak difficult, firm words. But of course when we do, we speak with a tender heart, a redemptive attitude, and an eye to our own shortcomings. Sometimes we express love through what we withhold rather than through what we give. We must love people more than we love being considered compassionate, particularly if our misguided compassion would lead someone toward unhealthy dependence. The motivation behind Christlike love is always the same: What best serves this person's God-prioritized interests?

The presence of love marks the presence of God, and the true presence of God always expresses itself in love. "Whenever a man feels kind compassion with love for his fellow Christian, it is Christ within him."[5]

Earthy Love

All this talk about love may sound spiritual, but it has a firm earthly application. God created the physical earth, and He deeply loves what He has created. These simple facts have enormous implications. God is invested in the creation, He takes great joy in it, and He is deeply concerned about every part of it—especially our fellow humans. The Christian faith must always be rescued from those who downplay these truths.

And yet, even in the classics, you occasionally read that God wants to separate us from the world, that He wants us to have nothing to do with it, and that the closer we get to Him, the less we have to do with the world. If we understand the world to be the systems in rebellion against God, as some Scriptures describe it, then these warnings are well-placed. But if the world is understood to be the earth God created and called into His service, an earth God himself called "good" just after He created it, the call to separation dishonors the Creator.

Henry Drummond wisely avoided the "mystical separation" trap. The call to love all but *demands* that we have a proper understanding of God's love for the world and of the way His presence actually calls us to actively engage the world rather than avoid it. "We hear much of love to God; Christ spoke much of love to man. We make a great deal of peace with heaven; Christ made much of peace on earth."[6]

If holiness is primarily about becoming like Christ, we would do well to study Jesus's life to determine what true holiness is. Christ did not spend most of His time on solitary retreats, contemplating heavenly joys. Here's where Drummond is so insightful.

> Have you ever noticed how much of Christ's life was spent in doing kind things—in *merely* doing kind things?...He spent a great proportion of His time simply in making people happy, in doing good turns to people. There is only one thing greater than happiness in the world, and that is holiness; and it is not in our keeping; but what God *has* put in our power is the

happiness of those about us, and that is largely to be secured by our being kind to them. "The greatest thing," says someone, "a man can do for his Heavenly Father is to be kind to some of His other children." I wonder why it is that we are not all kinder than we are. How much the world needs it.[7]

This means our faith is proven not just when we get on our knees in the morning to pray, open up our Bibles to read, or stand up in church to sing, but also when we are driving down the road and allow a driver to cut in front of us, when we speak a word of encouragement to the receptionist, when we liberally tip the person cleaning up our hotel room, when we notice if the checker at the grocery store is having a bad day, or when we ask, with all sincerity, how a coworker is doing and perhaps even inquire, "May I pray for you?"

Drummond puts it this way: "Is life not full of opportunities for learning Love? Every man and woman, every day has a thousand of them. The world is not a playground; it is a schoolroom. Life is not a holiday, but an education. And the one eternal lesson for us all is how better we can love."[8] He shows that a dedication to love—to express love, to grow in love, to share love—results in a meaningful and fulfilled life.

> You will find as you look back upon your life that the moments that stand out, the moments when you have really lived, are the moments when you have done things in a spirit of love. As memory scans the past, above and beyond all the transitory pleasures of life, there leap forward those supreme hours when you have been enabled to do unnoticed kindnesses to those around about you, things too trifling to speak about, but which you feel have entered into your eternal life. I have seen almost all the beautiful things that God has made; I have enjoyed almost every pleasure that He has planned for man; and yet as I look back I see standing out above all the life that has gone four or five short experiences when the love of God reflected itself in some poor imitation, some small act of love of mine, and these seem to be the things which alone of all one's life abide.[9]

If you want to live a life with few regrets and much fulfillment, live a life dedicated to love. Drummond points out, "Where love is, God is. He that dwelleth in love dwelleth in God. God is love. Therefore *love*. Without distinction, without calculation, without procrastination, love."[10]

In fact, he goes so far as to say (and this is worth writing down and meditating upon), "It is the deliberate verdict of the Lord Jesus that it is better not to live than not to love."[11]

In the end, according to the magisterial passage in 1 Corinthians 13, all the study in the world is worthless without love. The ability to work miracles, to understand the mysteries, to command a crowd's attention with spellbinding oratory doesn't mean a thing if we aren't growing in our ability to love.

Without love, we are without Christ. "The withholding of love is the negation of the spirit of Christ, the proof that we never knew Him."[12]

Love *always*, in every way, in every situation.

Just love.

Afterword

Near Walden Pond, just outside of Boston, you can see what remains of the foundation of Henry David Thoreau's cabin. Next to the foundation site is a pile of rocks—by now a fairly large one. Out of respect for Thoreau's life and writings, visitors have taken their turn adding one stone to the pile. No sign invites people to do this. If you just walked by, you might wonder, *What's that pile of stones for?*

Seeking the Face of God—the first incarnation of this book—was actually the first book I ever wrote, and in some ways I felt that writing a book would be like adding a stone to that pile. What's the use? There are already so many; can one more make any difference? But I went ahead and wrote the book, just as I added a stone to the pile. Here's why.

Thoreau was a nature mystic who uncovered a portion of truth but became so enamored with the beauty of what God had made that he missed the God behind it. I share Thoreau's respect for the outdoors. His prescription that everyone should spend several hours outside every day could only do us good. Indeed, when I'm outside, surrounded by what God has made, I feel truly alive.

I feel alive, though, because the Creator surrounds me, and that's the difference. Thoreau came close, but he kept his eyes too low. So why pay him any respect? Like few of us, he uncovered an important truth. Like many of us, however, he let a smaller truth eclipse the larger truth.

Thoreau's relinquishing the eternal for the created could be compared to parents who become so enamored with the beauty and life of their child, or their desire for the child that God seems to be withholding, that they begin worshipping the created instead of the Creator. Or the pastor who becomes so fulfilled by serving God that he begins worshipping his church rather than the God who makes the church. Or the business person who is so energized using his or her gifts to build a business that friends and family suffer. They have allowed the temporal to eclipse the eternal.

This world is full of good quests that can pull us away from our first love because we live with bent hearts. Christian bookstores carry numerous helpful books, and I've read many of them. We need to know how to handle our finances, be committed to our families, stand up for righteousness in the public square, and build our churches. But these quests will do nothing but sap our strength if our roots are not sunk deep into an intimate walk with our heavenly Father. Why wash the windshield of a car that won't run? Why water a seed that's never been planted?

The purpose of this book is to echo the words given to us by God through Jeremiah: "Who is he who will devote himself to be close to me?" (Jeremiah 30:21). Is a close, continuing walk with God really the desire of our hearts? Do we long, more than anything else, to know Him and be known by Him?

The struggle of the Christian life is really a struggle to maintain the centrality of God in our day-to-day lives. Peripheral matters are always pushing in, trying to steal our hearts away. That's why, if we're not consciously seeking the face of God and striving to know Him, we're likely falling away. We're told that King Rehoboam did evil because "he did not prepare his heart to seek the LORD" (2 Chronicles 12:14 NKJV).

As I mentioned earlier in this book, what we really need, and what the world is really waiting to see, is a group of people dedicated to living the Christian life. This is the true calling of a mail carrier, a university professor, a pastor, or a homemaker. We need to discuss various theological points, but the way we live them is even more precious in God's sight. I'll never forget the time I saw two seminary students nearly get into a fist-fight over the precise meaning of the Greek word *phileo*, which translates into *brotherly love*.

If the wisdom of the ancients has awakened any heart toward this end and moved that heart a little further along the way, then writing this book has not been like adding a stone to that pile of rocks. It is like picking up the stone from the pile, walking down the hill to Walden Pond, and dropping the stone in the middle. The rock will soon be swallowed and forgotten, as this book will eventually be, but the ripples it created as it touched the surface will continue for a little longer, perhaps until somebody else comes along and drops another rock.

The ripples might be hidden. They may be seen only in a locked room as a believer pours out her heart to God in a new and fresh way, or in a silent forest as a man renews his vows of love and commitment to his Creator, or in an empty church as a pastor or church member returns to his or her first love. But I am confident that God wants to drop the rock. I believe He wants to call us back. I'm certain He is reaching out for those who will devote themselves to be close to Him. And I have great confidence in God's ability to make ripples effective—even more effective than the dropped rock that caused them.

I placed the stone on the pile. It will be up to you, the reader, to see whether it gets moved to the pond, creating the ripples. You hold the rock in your hand now.

A Brief Annotated Reference List of Christian Classics

Anonymous, The Didache (first century). Originally an oral tradition, this collection of teachings focuses on incorporating Gentile converts into the Christian fold. A fascinating look at early Christian life.

Saint Augustine, *The Confessions of Saint Augustine* (c. 400). This has long been considered the classic of all time. Many modern readers will find this book difficult reading with scattered wisdom. The genre itself will seem unfamiliar and slightly wordy to many evangelicals. A contemporary translation might help.

John Climacus, *The Ladder of Divine Ascent* (c. 640). This classic of Eastern Christendom, written to monks, calls for a high commitment. The message may seem harsh, but the book is worthy of the attention it has received.

Brother Ugolino, *The Little Flowers of Saint Francis* (Late thirteenth or early fourteenth century). *Little Flowers* is a narrative account of Francis of Assisi and his early followers. The historicity of many accounts is suspect, but the model of devotion and the earnest application of a spirituality emphasizing poverty, simplicity, and prayer is truly inspiring.

Johannes Tauler, *Sermons* (mid-fourteenth century). Tauler, a Dominican monk, was a disciple of Meister Eckhart and a key voice of the influential German mystics. He spent the bulk of his life in the Order of Preachers, and his writings had a significant impact on Martin Luther.

Anonymous, *The Cloud of Unknowing* (late fourteenth century). This book is very mystical but with real gems sprinkled throughout. Evangelicals might find the full "program" of little interest or benefit, but those who take the time to read it will find considerable wisdom.

Julian of Norwich, *Revelations of Divine Love* (late fourteenth century). This is the first English book that we can be sure was written by a woman. As an evangelical, I must confess my own uneasiness with a book based on "divine revelations," particularly when some of those seem to go against evangelical understandings of Scripture. Accordingly, I read this book like poetry—not to get doctrine, not to take it literally, but to benefit from and be inspired by the fine prose and passionate surrender to God that are hallmarks of feminine spirituality.

Thomas à Kempis, *The Imitation of Christ* (c. 1418). This is probably one of the most popular spiritual classics of all time, and for good reason. À Kempis focused on rigorous spiritual training as a necessary part of Christian living. His work is a good counter to "soft" Christianity.

Lorenzo Scupoli, *Spiritual Combat* (sixteenth century). A practical primer on the nature of sin, temptation, and spiritual warfare, this fine book was immediately recognized as a masterpiece of holy wisdom. Though written in the midst of the Counter-Reformation, it was soon adopted by the Orthodox church as well, where it was published as *Unseen Warfare.*

Ignatius Loyola, *The Spiritual Exercises of Saint Ignatius Loyola* (1548). Full of very practical advice for monks, this book also offers many helpful insights for evangelicals.

John of the Cross, *Ascent of Mount Carmel* and *Dark Night of the Soul* (c. 1587). John of the Cross was recognized as a highly gifted spiritual director (he was Teresa of Avila's director for three years). In these mystical classics he provides many helpful insights into the spiritual life, especially the stages that Christians go through. One of my favorite writers, John of the Cross wrote with an unparalleled passion for God.

John Calvin, *The Institutes of the Christian Religion* (sixteenth century). Rewritten and updated throughout his life, this is one of the premier works on the Christian life. You don't have to be Reformed in theology to enjoy the spiritual insights and commentary that fill this work of spiritual genius.

Teresa of Avila, *The Interior Castle* (1588). This relatively short book on prayer emphasizes spiritual visions leading to spiritual betrothal and marriage.

Francis de Sales, *Introduction to the Devout Life* (1609) and *Spiritual Conferences* (post 1610). *Introduction* is unique because Francis wrote it for laypeople, not a religious community. His desire was to see ordinary tradesmen learn to grow spiritually, recognizing that they needed different advice than do members of a religious community. This book is very practical with several helpful meditations. *Spiritual Conferences* is a series of talks given to the Visitation nuns, so you can compare the way Francis speaks to different groups of people. The modern version is entitled *The Art of Loving God.*

John Owen, *Sin and Temptation* (1656–1667). This is actually a compilation of three of John Owen's treatises that have now been collected by Dr. James Houston. Owen's teaching on sin and temptation should be considered must reading for every Christian.

Ralph Venning, *The Sinfulness of Sin* (1669). A classic Puritan work, written in a classically Puritan style, developing an applicable and insightful theology of what sin is, why it is so serious, and how it affects the Christian life. Originally published as *Sin, the Plague of Plagues.*

Blaise Pascal, *Pensées* (1670). Pascal was a brilliant man in both science and devotion. The *Pensées* comprise an unfinished collection of his random thoughts. It's haphazard reading but includes some real gems for those who wade through the collection.

Jeanne Guyon, *Experiencing the Depths of Jesus Christ* (late seventeenth century). Originally published as *A Short and Easy Method of Prayer, Experiencing the Depths* explores a life of unceasing prayer, meditation, and contemplation, emphasizing abandonment and union with God.

Brother Lawrence, *The Practice of the Presence of God* (1692). Brother Lawrence was a very humble man with an extraordinary sense of living in God's presence. This little book includes several letters and conversations Brother Lawrence had with others who wanted to learn from his experience.

Francois Fénelon, *Christian Perfection* (1704–1717). Along with John of the Cross, Fénelon is one of my favorites. Fénelon wrote as a wealthy mystic living in the upper strata of French society. The temptations faced by the elite several hundred years ago are remarkably similar to those faced by middle-class evangelicals today. This is one of the most helpful spiritual classics I've read. You may want to read it over and over.

William Law, *A Serious Call to a Devout and Holy Life* (1728). This is a rigorous treatise written by a devout Puritan. It is very helpful and challenging but could be dangerous for a person who isn't rooted in grace because it might lead some into an unhealthy legalism.

Jonathan Edwards, *A Treatise Concerning Religious Affections* (1746). Discusses those who are "truly pious" by examining and discussing various religious affections. Edwards is another of my favorites.

John Wesley, *Wesley's Journal* (eighteenth century). An astonishing, convicting, inspiring, and compelling day-to-day account of a man on fire for God. He earnestly sought to build God's kingdom and invited us to share the journey.

Henry Drummond, *The Greatest Thing in the World* (late nineteenth century). Drummond was one of D.L. Moody's favorite counselors for those who responded to the famous evangelist's appeals. Drummond received considerable fame in his own right for his work applying the theory of evolution and natural laws to the spiritual life. This work consists of a series of addresses given by Drummond between 1876 and 1881, originally published under the title *The Ideal Life*.

Oswald Chambers, *My Utmost for His Highest* (twentieth century). We may be premature to call a book less than a hundred years old a classic, but this treasured devotional is surely deserving of the title. Chambers was renowned for his work with the YMCA, and his daily thoughts breathe an astonishing depth of insight and devotion.

Dietrich Bonhoeffer, *The Cost of Discipleship* (1937). A ringing indictment of cheap grace and a call to experiential faith. Bonhoeffer warned that cheap grace was ruining more Christians than legalism, and he called the church toward the costly grace of discipleship.

C.S. Lewis, *The Screwtape Letters* (1944). Among the most creative of all classics, this book brilliantly exposes the nature of temptation, spiritual warfare, human nature, and a life of faith.

A.W. Tozer, *The Pursuit of God* (1948). A classic call to an experiential, intentional, and transformational faith. I'm holding the line at books written prior to 1950 to deserve the title *classic*, but I believe Tozer will still be read 100 years from now.

Notes

Chapter 1: The Journcy of Faith: Knowing God More Intimately

1. A.J. Russell, *For Sinners Only* (London: Hodder and Stoughton, 1932), 215.

Chapter 2: Good Intentions

1. Julian of Norwich, *Revelations of Divine Love,* trans. by Elizabeth Spearing (New York: Penguin, 1998), 55, 57.
2. Henry Drummond, *The Greatest Thing in the World* (London: Collins, 1953), 155.

Chapter 3: An Intentional Pursuit: The Development of Spiritual Goals

1. The biblical exhortations to grow are too numerous to document here, but see Philippians 2:12-13; Colossians 1:10-12; 2 Thessalonians 1:3; and 2 Peter 1:5-8; 3:18 for a sampling.
2. Thomas à Kempis, *The Imitation of Christ*, ed. Paul Bechtel (Chicago: Moody Press, 1980), I:11:5.
3. John Climacus, *The Ladder of Divine Ascent*, trans. by Colm Luibheid and Norman Russell (New York: Paulist Press, 1984), 239.
4. Climacus, *The Ladder of Divine Ascent*, 259.
5. John Wesley, *John Wesley's Journal* (London: Isbister, 1902), 347.

Chapter 4: Hell Breaking Apart at His Feet

1. The Greek word is *exeplessonto*. The options chosen are taken from Zerwick and Grosvenor, *A Grammatical Analysis of the Greek New Testament* (Rome: Biblical Institute Press, 1981), 102.
2. Just ask the seven sons of Sceva (Acts 19:13-16).
3. H.A. Walters, *Soul Surgery* (London: Blandford Press, 1919), 19-20.
4. Ibid., 18.

Chapter 5: Training the Heart, Body, and Soul

1. Blaise Pascal, *Pensées*, trans. A.J. Krailsheimer (London: Penguin, 1966), 323.
2. "My son, thou art never secure in this life, but as long as thou livest, thou shalt always need spiritual armor. Thou dwellest among enemies, and art assaulted on the right hand and on the left.

If therefore thou defend not thyself on every side with the shield of patience, thou wilt not be long without a wound." (À Kempis, *The Imitation of Christ*, III:35:1.)

3. Climacus, *The Ladder of Divine Ascent*, 258.

4. À Kempis, *The Imitation of Christ*, I:3:3.

5. Ibid., I:19:2.

6. Pascal, *Pensées*, 347.

7. William Law, *A Serious Call to the Devout and Holy Life* (New York: Paulist Press, 1978), 66.

8. Based on observations made by Austin Warren in "William Law: Ascetic and Mystic," in William Law, *"A Serious Call to a Devout and Holy Life" and "The Spirit of Love,"* The Classics of Western Spirituality (New York: Paulist Press, 1978), 11.

9. Law, *A Serious Call*, 204.

10. Ibid., 205.

11. Ibid., 270.

12. Ibid., 67.

Chapter 6: Pious Readings

1. Law, *A Serious Call*, 206-7.

2. Ralph Venning, *The Sinfulness of Sin* (Carlisle, PA: The Banner of Truth Trust, 1997), 14-15.

Chapter 7: Imitation of Living Examples

1. 1 Corinthians 11:1 (NKJV). See also 1 Corinthians 4:16; Philippians 3:17; 1 Thessalonians 1:6; 2 Thessalonians 3:9; Hebrews 6:12; 13:7.

2. À Kempis, *The Imitation of Christ*, I:25:5.

Chapter 8: Cultivation of Virtues

1. Lorenzo Scupoli, *Spiritual Combat* (Manchester, NH: Sophia Institute Press, 2002), 139.

2. Ibid., 142.

3. Ibid., 45.

4. Teresa of Avila, *The Interior Castle*, trans. Kieran Kavanaugh and Otilio Rodriguez (New York: Paulist Press, 1979), VII:4:9.

5. Climacus, *The Ladder of Divine Ascent*, 77.

6. Scupoli, *Spiritual Combat*, 142.

7. À Kempis, *The Imitation of Christ*, I:25:4.

8. Scupoli, *Spiritual Combat*, 98.

Chapter 9: Early Rising

1. Law, *A Serious Call*, 189.

2. Ibid., 192.

3. Ibid., 195.

Chapter 10: A Life of Reflection

1. À Kempis, *The Imitation of Christ*, I:19:6.

2. Venning, *The Sinfulness of Sin*, 121.

3. Johannes Tauler, *Sermons*, trans. by Maria Shrady (New York: Paulist Press, 1985), 120.

Chapter 11: Learning to Live with Grace

1. See Romans 5:20–6:2.
2. Brother Lawrence, *The Practice of the Presence of God* (Cincinnati: Forward Movement Publications, n.d.), 37.
3. Climacus, *The Ladder of Divine Ascent*, 225, 254.
4. Law, *A Serious Call*, 68.
5. Francis de Sales, *Introduction to the Devout Life* (Rome: Frederick Pustet, n.d.), 241.
6. Law, *A Serious Call*, 67.

Chapter 12: Holiness of the Heart: Avoiding Sin and Facing Temptation

1. The word *mystic* has often caused great concern to many Christians because it reminds them of occult practices or Eastern religions. Certainly there are occult mystics, but historically and academically the word has also been used to describe Christians who seek a direct experience of God. Whenever a Christian says he or she wants to know God, not just know about Him, this person is approaching the world of a Christian mystic.
2. Paul Janet, *Fénelon, His Life and Works*, trans. Victor Leuliette (Port Washington, NY: Kennikat Press, 1970), 47.
3. Ibid., 28-29.
4. Ibid., 48.
5. Ibid., 235.
6. Louis Sempe, *St. Francis de Sales* (Milwaukee: Bruce Publishing, 1933), 20.
7. Katherine Bregy, *The Story of Saint Francis de Sales* (Milwaukee: Bruce Publishing, 1958).

Chapter 13: The Absurdity of Sin

1. Julian of Norwich, *Revelations of Divine Love*, 26.
2. François Fénelon, *Christian Perfection*, trans. Mildred Whitney Stillman (Minneapolis: Bethany House, 1975), 40.
3. Venning, *The Sinfulness of Sin*, 170.
4. Law, *A Serious Call*, 149.
5. Venning, *The Sinfulness of Sin*, 21.
6. Ibid., 20.
7. Julian of Norwich, *Revelations of Divine Love*, 98.
8. Law, *A Serious Call*, 155. Compare with Augustine's statement: "The soul lives by avoiding what it dies by affecting" (*Confessions*, XIII:30).
9. Ibid., 158.
10. Ibid., 160.
11. Ibid., 148.
12. Venning, *The Sinfulness of Sin*, 31.
13. Ibid., 36.
14. Ibid., 123, 197.
15. Jeanne Guyon, *Experiencing the Depths of Jesus Christ* (Auburn, ME: SeedSowers, 1975), x.
16. Julian of Norwich, *Revelations of Divine Love*, 27.

Chapter 14: Counterfeit Holiness

1. Pascal, *Pensées*, 135.
2. Fénelon, *Christian Perfection*, 35.
3. Teresa of Avila, *The Interior Castle*, VII:3:9.
4. Pascal, *Pensées*, 242.
5. Venning, *The Sinfulness of Sin*, 119.
6. Ibid., 120.

Chapter 15: When Temptation Strikes

1. Fénelon, *Christian Perfection*, 24.
2. De Sales, *Introduction to the Devout Life*, 299.
3. Climacus, *The Ladder of Divine Ascent*, 173.
4. Fénelon, *Christian Perfection*, 97.
5. Ibid., 127.
6. À Kempis, *The Imitation of Christ*, I:13:2.
7. Ibid., I:20:4.
8. De Sales, *Introduction to the Devout Life*, 107.
9. Venning, *The Sinfulness of Sin*, 169.
10. De Sales, *Introduction to the Devout Life*, 300.
11. Julian of Norwich, *Revelations of Divine Love*, 79.

Chapter 16: Consistent Climbing

1. Fénelon, *Christian Perfection*, 8.
2. De Sales, *Introduction to the Devout Life*, 212.
3. Ibid., 301-2.
4. Law, *A Serious Call*, 191-92.
5. De Sales, *Introduction to the Devout Life*, 303-4.
6. Ibid., 304.
7. Ibid., 306.
8. Law, *A Serious Call*, 111.

Chapter 17: Soul Sadness

1. De Sales, *Introduction to the Devout Life*, 307.
2. Ibid., 307-8.
3. Ibid., 308.
4. Ibid., 159.
5. Fénelon, *Christian Perfection*, 186.
6. Tauler, *Sermons*, 121.
7. Fénelon, *Christian Perfection*, 41.

Chapter 18: Joyful Surrender: Christian Submission

1. Hugh Davidson, *Blaise Pascal* (Boston: Twayne, 1983), 20-21.
2. Scupoli, *Spiritual Combat*, 122.
3. Fénelon, *Christian Perfection*, 64-65.

4. John of the Cross, "The Ascent of Mount Carmel," in *John of the Cross: Selected Writings*, ed. and trans. by Kieran Kavanaugh (New York: Paulist Press, 1987), II:7-8.

5. Tauler, *Sermons*, 72.

6. Drummond, *The Greatest Thing in the World*, 125.

7. Ibid., 236-37.

8. Ibid., 263.

9. Ibid., 262.

10. Ibid., 268.

11. Law, *A Serious Call*, 47.

Chapter 19: The Two Essential Questions

1. À Kempis, *The Imitation of Christ*, III:17:1-2.

2. Law, *A Serious Call*, 322.

Chapter 20: The Death of Complaining

1. Law, *A Serious Call*, 317, 319.

2. Ibid., 324.

Chapter 21: The Birth of Thanksgiving

1. Law, *A Serious Call*, 321.

2. Ibid., 327.

3. À Kempis, *The Imitation of Christ*, III:15:1.

4. Law, *A Serious Call*, 256.

5. Fénelon, *Christian Perfection*, 168.

6. À Kempis, *The Imitation of Christ*, II:3:1.

7. Ibid., IV:8:1.

8. De Sales, *Introduction to the Devout Life*, 51-52.

Chapter 22: Cultivating the Quiet: Simplicity

1. Fénelon, *Christian Perfection*, 155-56.

2. Pascal, *Pensées*, 38.

3. Augustine, *Confessions*, I:15.

4. Pascal, *Pensées*, 71-72.

5. Ibid., 48.

6. Ibid., 69.

7. Scupoli, *Spiritual Combat*, 76.

Chapter 23: Entering the Quiet

1. John of the Cross, "The Ascent of Mount Carmel," in *Selected Writings*, III:16:2.

2. Augustine, *Confessions*, VIII:11.

3. Fénelon, *Christian Perfection*, 28-29.

4. Ibid., 199.

5. Ignatius Loyola, *Spiritual Exercises*, 17.

6. Climacus, *The Ladder of Divine Ascent*, 158.

7. Ibid., 273, 106.
8. À Kempis, *The Imitation of Christ*, I:20:1.
9. "In the multitude of words sin is not lacking, but he who restrains his lips is wise" (Proverbs 10:19 NKJV).
10. Scupoli, *Spiritual Combat*, 36.
11. À Kempis, *The Imitation of Christ*, III:25:1.
12. Climacus, *The Ladder of Divine Ascent*, 273.
13. À Kempis, *The Imitation of Christ*, III:44:1.
14. De Sales, *Introduction to the Devout Life*, 75.
15. Ibid., 84-85.
16. Ibid., 351.
17. Á Kempis, *The Imitation of Christ*, III:26:1-2.

Chapter 24: The High and the Low: A Double-Sided Truth
1. John Owen, *Sin and Temptation* (Portland: Multnomah, 1983), 28.
2. Fénelon, *Christian Perfection*, 205.
3. À Kempis, *The Imitation of Christ*, II:10:4.
4. Teresa of Avila, *The Interior Castle*, VII:4:8.
5. Climacus, *The Ladder of Divine Ascent*, 204.
6. Law, *A Serious Call*, 228.

Chapter 25: Christian, Know Yourself!
1. Scupoli, *Spiritual Combat*, 7.
2. Climacus, *The Ladder of Divine Ascent*, 210.
3. À Kempis, *The Imitation of Christ*, I:2:1.
4. Teresa of Avila, *The Interior Castle*, I:2:9.
5. John of the Cross, "The Dark Night," in *John of the Cross: Selected Writings*, ed. and trans. by Kieran Kavanaugh (New York: Paulist Press, 1987), I:12:7-8.
6. Anonymous, *The Cloud of Unknowing*, trans. by Ira Progoff (New York: Dell Publishing, 1983), XIV:2:5.
7. Scupoli, *Spiritual Combat*, 13.
8. Guyon, *Experiencing the Depths of Jesus Christ*, 16.
9. Scupoli, *Spiritual Combat*, 91.
10. Guyon, *Experiencing the Depths of Jesus Christ*, 86.
11. Fénelon, *Christian Perfection*, 22-23.

Chapter 26: Spiritual Cosmetology
1. Pascal, *Pensées*, 270.
2. Law, *A Serious Call*, 260.
3. Jonathan Edwards, *A Treatise Concerning Religious Affections*, ed. James Houston (Minneapolis: Bethany House, 1984), 148.
4. De Sales, *Introduction to the Devout Life*, 138.
5. Guyon, *Experiencing the Depths of Jesus Christ*, 129.

Chapter 27: Christian, Know Your God

1. Anonymous, *The Cloud of Unknowing*, XXIII:4.
2. John of the Cross, "The Dark Night," in *Selected Writings*, I:2:4.
3. Edwards, *A Treatise Concerning Religious Affections*, 132.
4. Fénelon, *Christian Perfection*, 145-46.
5. Ibid., 146.
6. Owen, *Sin and Temptation*, 84-85.
7. Teresa of Avila, *The Interior Castle*, I:2:9-10.
8. Pascal, *Pensées*, 133.
9. Edwards, *A Treatise Concerning Religious Affections*, 127.
10. Scupoli, *Spiritual Combat*, 21-22.
11. Edwards, *A Treatise Concerning Religious Affections*, 129.
12. Calvin, *Institutes of the Christian Religion*, book 2, chapter 2, paragraph 11.

Chapter 28: Humility in Community

1. Owen, *Sin and Temptation*, 29.
2. Fénelon, *Christian Perfection*, 44.
3. Ibid., 60.
4. Ibid., 61.
5. À Kempis, *The Imitation of Christ*, II:2:2 and I:7:3.
6. De Sales, *Introduction to the Devout Life*, 254.
7. Law, *A Serious Call*, 234.
8. Ibid., 294.
9. Ibid., 294-95.
10. Edwards, *A Treatise Concerning Religious Affections*, 160.
11. Law, *A Serious Call*, 294.
12. Ibid., 337.
13. Ibid., 338.
14. Cited in Brother Ugolino di Santa Maria, *The Little Flowers of Saint Francis*, trans. by Raphael Brown (New York: Image Books, 1958), 283.
15. Ibid., 314.

Chapter 29: How Do Humble People Lead?

1. Law, *A Serious Call*, 229.
2. Edwards, *A Treatise Concerning Religious Affections*, 134.
3. Ugolino di Santa Maria, *The Little Flowers of Saint Francis*, 52.
4. Ibid., 54.
5. Teresa of Avila, *The Interior Castle*, VI:10:6.
6. Augustine, *Confessions*, X:58.
7. Ugolino di Santa Maria, *The Little Flowers of Saint Francis*, 268.
8. De Sales, *Introduction to the Devout Life*, 148-49.
9. Teresa of Avila, *The Interior Castle*, VII:4:14.

10. De Sales, *Introduction to the Devout Life*, 257-58.
11. Ibid., 126-27.
12. Ibid., 140-41.
13. Ugolino di Santa Maria, *The Little Flowers of Saint Francis*, 62-63.

Chapter 30: Living in a Dying World: The Remembrance of Death
1. Fénelon, *Christian Perfection*, 85-86.
2. Ibid., 104.
3. Law, *A Serious Call*, 69.
4. Ibid., 73.
5. Á Kempis, *The Imitation of Christ*, I:23:1.
6. Law, *A Serious Call*, 282.
7. Drummond, *The Greatest Thing in the World*, 250.

Chapter 31: Making Death Our Servant
1. Pascal, *Pensées*, 165.
2. Climacus, *The Ladder of Divine Ascent*, 143-44.
3. Fénelon, *Christian Perfection*, 104.
4. Pascal, *Pensées*, 143.
5. Climacus, *The Ladder of Divine Ascent*, 135.
6. Ibid., 132.
7. Ibid., 132-33.
8. Law, *A Serious Call*, 68.
9. À Kempis, *The Imitation of Christ*, I:21:5.
10. Law, *A Serious Call*, 70.
11. À Kempis, *The Imitation of Christ*, I:23:6.
12. Fénelon, *Christian Perfection*, 105.
13. À Kempis, *The Imitation of Christ*, I:23:1.
14. Law, *A Serious Call*, 339-40.
15. Scupoli, *Spiritual Combat*, 70.

Chapter 32: A Difficult Road
1. Tauler, *Sermons*, 122.
2. Climacus, *The Ladder of Divine Ascent*, 75.
3. Brother Lawrence, *The Practice of the Presence of God*, 22.
4. Anonymous, *The Cloud of Unknowing*, XXVI:1 and XXIX:1.
5. Ugolino di Santa Maria, *The Little Flowers of Saint Francis*, 270.
6. Scupoli, *Spiritual Combat*, 38.
7. Ibid., 39.
8. Julian of Norwich, *Revelations of Divine Love*, 3.
9. Ibid., 43.
10. Dietrich Bonhoeffer, *The Cost of Discipleship* (New York: Simon and Schuster, 1995), 91, 169.

11. Acts 14:22.
12. Luke 9:23 (NKJV).
13. À Kempis, *The Imitation of Christ*, III:19:1.
14. Ignatius Loyola, *Spiritual Exercises*, 34.
15. Tauler, *Sermons*, 75.

Chapter 33: Two Lives, Two Triumphs

1. Teresa of Avila, *The Interior Castle*, VI:1:1-2. See also John Climacus, *The Ladder of Divine Ascent*, 79: "The Lord has concealed from those in the world the tough, but fine, nature of this struggle. Indeed, if people really understood it, no one would renounce the world."
2. John of the Cross, "The Ascent of Mount Carmel," in *Selected Writings*, 1.
3. John of the Cross, "The Dark Night," in *Selected Writings*, II:5:6.
4. For a similar opinion, see *The Cloud of Unknowing*, LV:I:2: "I maintain that whoever will not go the hard way to heaven will go the easy way to hell."
5. John of the Cross, "The Ascent of Mount Carmel," in *Selected Writings*, 4.
6. Ibid., 5.
7. À Kempis, *The Imitation of Christ*, II:12:7.
8. Teresa of Avila, *The Interior Castle*, VII:4:5.
9. Julian of Norwich, *Revelations of Divine Love*, 32.
10. Scupoli, *Spiritual Combat*, 40.

Chapter 34: It's Not Easy to Be You

1. Law, *A Serious Call*, 215.
2. Brother Lawrence, *The Practice of the Presence of God*, 44.
3. Owen, *Sin and Temptation*, 5.
4. Ibid., 7.
5. Ibid., 9.
6. Climacus, *The Ladder of Divine Ascent*, 81-82.
7. Owen, *Sin and Temptation*, 11.
8. À Kempis, *The Imitation of Christ*, II:12:5-6.

Chapter 35: The Sweet Side of Suffering

1. Teresa of Avila, *The Interior Castle*, VI:11:6.
2. Climacus, *The Ladder of Divine Ascent*, 96.
3. À Kempis, *The Imitation of Christ*, II:12:8.
4. Edwards, *A Treatise Concerning Religious Affections*, 3.
5. Fénelon, *Christian Perfection*, 93.
6. Teresa of Avila, *The Interior Castle*, VI:11:10.
7. Law, *A Serious Call*, 291.
8. John of the Cross, "The Ascent of Mt. Carmel," in *Selected Writings*, II:7:8.

Chapter 36: Spiritual Gluttony

1. Bregy, *The Story of Saint Francis de Sales*, 18-19.

2. De Sales, *Introduction to the Devout Life*, 322.

3. Scupoli, *Spiritual Combat*, 162.

4. Guyon, *Experiencing the Depths of Jesus Christ*, 27-28.

5. Julian of Norwich, *Revelations of Divine Love*, 15.

6. Lorenzo Scupoli, *Of Interior Peace, or the Path to Paradise* (Manchester, NH: Sophia Institute Press, 2002), 208.

7. John of the Cross, "The Dark Night," in *Selected Writings*, I:1:2.

8. Anonymous, *The Cloud of Unknowing*, XLVIII:2.

9. Fénelon, *Christian Perfection*, 48. The the writers of the Christian classics understood that God can easily "outpleasure" the world and Satan and that, under His sovereign direction, this can be a powerful antidote for sin. À Kempis wrote, "Spiritual comforts exceed all the delights of the world and the pleasures of the flesh" (*The Imitation of Christ*, II:10:1).

10. De Sales, *Introduction to the Devout Life*, 331.

11. Augustine, *Sermon 137*, cited in *Confessions*, 46. See also Augustine's words in *Psalm 72*, Section 32, cited in *Confessions*, 46: "Whoso seeks from God any other reward but God, and for it would serve God, esteems what he wishes to receive, more than Him from whom he would receive it. What then? Hath God no reward? None, save Himself. The reward of God is God Himself."

12. John of the Cross, "The Dark Night," in *Selected Writings*, I:2:1-2.

13. Tauler, *Sermons*, 87.

14. Ibid., 87-88.

Chapter 37: Understanding the Desert

1. De Sales, *Introduction to the Devout Life*, 332-33.

2. Guyon, *Experiencing the Depths of Jesus Christ*, 27.

3. De Sales, *Introduction to the Devout Life*, 323-24.

4. Tauler, *Sermons*, 75.

5. Scupoli, *Of Interior Peace, or the Path to Paradise*, 209-10.

6. Anonymous, *The Cloud of Unknowing*, L:3.

7. Edwards, *Religious Affections*, 58.

8. Fénelon, *Christian Perfection*, 141.

9. De Sales, *Introduction to the Devout Life*, 324-26.

10. Edwards, *Religious Affections*, 65-66.

Chapter 38: Surviving and Thriving in the Desert

1. Scupoli, *Spiritual Combat*, 162.

2. Ugolino di Santa Maria, *The Little Flowers of Saint Francis*, 276.

3. Anonymous, *The Cloud of Unknowing*, L:1.

4. De Sales, *Introduction to a Devout Life*, 315.

5. Scupoli, *Of Interior Peace, or the Path to Paradise*, 207-8.

6. À Kempis, *The Imitation of Christ*, II:9:5, 7.

7. À Kempis, *The Imitation of Christ*, III:6:2.

8. Fénelon, *Christian Perfection*, 152.

9. Scupoli, *Spiritual Combat*, 162.

10. Fénelon, *Christian Perfection*, 56.
11. See Fénelon, *Christian Perfection*, 151.
12. "O Lord, I am not worthy of thy consolation, nor of any spiritual visitation; and therefore thou dealest justly with me, when thou leavest me poor and desolate. For though I could shed a sea of tears, yet should I not be worthy of thy consolation" (À Kempis, *The Imitation of Christ*, III:52:1).
13. Teresa of Avila, *The Interior Castle*, II:1:7.
14. John of the Cross, "The Dark Night," in *Selected Writings*, I:6:6.
15. Fénelon, *Christian Perfection*, 48.
16. Scupoli, *Spiritual Combat*, 163.
17. Teresa of Avila, *The Interior Castle*, VI:9:18.
18. Ibid., VII:3:8.

Chapter 39: Seasons of the Soul: The Passages of the Spiritual Life
1. Hugh Davidson, *Blaise Pascal* (Boston: Twayne, 1983), 3, 21.
2. Pascal, *Pensées*, 245.
3. Ibid., 35.
4. Ibid., 55.
5. Tauler, *Sermons*, 72.
6. See my book *Sacred Pathways: Discover the Soul's Path to God* (Grand Rapids: Zondervan, 2002).
7. Fénelon, *Christian Perfection*, 173.

Chapter 40: Spiritual Terrain
1. Ignatius Loyola, *Spiritual Exercises*, 109.
2. Anonymous, *The Cloud of Unknowing*, LXXII:1.

Chapter 41: Stations in Life
1. Law, *A Serious Call*, 208.
2. De Sales, *Introduction to the Devout Life*, 123.
3. 1 Timothy 5:1-3,9-15; 2 Timothy 2:22; Titus 2:2-8; see also John's view in 1 John 2:12-14.
4. Bregy, *The Story of Saint Francis de Sales*, 61. I'm convinced that Francis was able to counsel from his own experience on this one. When he was a young man studying law at the University of Padua, wilder students often resented his ascetic habits. Although the provost praised Francis upon his graduation ("You have lived in the midst of a voluptuous city and preserved your innocence"), Francis understood that we can win the war of personal holiness and lose the war of evangelism if we don't respect our surroundings.
5. Ibid., 62.

Chapter 42: Soul Surgery: A Guide to Spiritual Direction
1. Augustine, *Confessions*, V:23.
2. Ibid., VIII:1.
3. Anonymous, *The Cloud of Unknowing*, VIII:14.
4. Climacus, *The Ladder of Divine Ascent*, 259.
5. À Kempis, *The Imitation of Christ*, I:9:2.

6. Ibid., III:7:2-3.
7. See 1 Peter 5:8.
8. Ignatius Loyola, *Spiritual Exercises*, 119.
9. Ibid., 110-11.
10. De Sales, *Introduction to the Devout Life*, 11.

Chapter 43: Choosing a Spiritual Director

1. À Kempis, *The Imitation of Christ*, I:4:2.
2. Teresa of Avila, *The Interior Castle*, III:2:12.
3. Ibid., VI:8:8.
4. Ibid., VI:8:9.
5. Climacus, *The Ladder of Divine Ascent*, 233.
6. Ibid., 179.
7. Ibid., 119.
8. Ibid., 92-93.
9. De Sales, *Introduction to the Devout Life*, 13.

Chapter 44: Growing Together

1. De Sales, *Introduction to the Devout Life*, 107-8.
2. Climacus, *The Ladder of Divine Ascent*, 107.
3. De Sales, *Introduction to the Devout Life*, 300.

Chapter 45: The Call to Be a Spiritual Director

1. De Sales, *Introduction to the Devout Life*, 12.
2. Ibid., xix.

Chapter 46: Cooperating Christians

1. Bonhoeffer, *The Cost of Discipleship*, 55.
2. Edwards, *Religious Affections*, 164-65.
3. Tauler, *Sermons*, 125.
4. Scupoli, *Spiritual Combat*, 148.
5. Calvin, *Epistle to the Philippians*, vol. 21, *Calvin's Commentaries* (Grand Rapids: Baker Books, 2003), 67.
6. Edwards, *Religious Affections*, 168.
7. Scupoli, *Spiritual Combat*, 148-49.
8. Edwards, *Religious Affections*, 9.
9. Guyon, *Experiencing the Depths of Jesus Christ*, 113.
10. Julian of Norwich, *Revelations of Divine Love*, 57.
11. A.W. Tozer, *The Pursuit of God* (Harrisburg, PA: Christian Publications, 1948), 67.
12. Drummond, *The Greatest Thing in the World*, 114.

Chapter 47: Radical Transformation

1. Tauler, *Sermons*, 71.

2. Edwards, *Religious Affections*, 141.
3. Ibid., 142.
4. Ibid., 151.
5. Tozer, *The Pursuit of God*, 88.
6. Ibid., 37.
7. Edwards, *Religious Affections*, 180.
8. Drummond, *The Greatest Thing in the World*, 114.
9. Ibid., 237.
10. Tozer, *The Pursuit of God*, 58-59.
11. Ibid., 64.
12. Edwards, *Religious Affections*, 179.
13. Tauler, *Sermons*, 128.
14. Edwards, *Religious Affections*, 151.
15. Drummond, *The Greatest Thing in the World*, 88.

Chapter 48: More Love

1. Tauler, *Sermons*, 131, 133.
2. Scupoli, *Spiritual Combat*, 54.
3. Tauler, *Sermons*, 134.
4. Scupoli, *Spiritual Combat*, 103.
5. Julian of Norwich, 22.
6. Drummond, *The Greatest Thing in the World*, 51.
7. Ibid., 51.
8. Ibid., 57.
9. Ibid., 63.
10. Ibid., 52.
11. Ibid., 56.
12. Ibid., 64.

Meeting God in Quiet Places

F. LaGard Smith, illustrated by Glenda Rae

Bestselling author LaGard Smith shares faith-renewing reflections in these inspiring parables drawn from his walks through the magnificent Cotswolds of England. He leads you on a beautiful devotional journey to the stillness and splendor of God's presence.

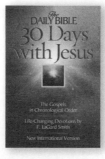

30 Days with Jesus

F. LaGard Smith

This life-changing Bible study integrates the four Gospels into one chronological narrative to highlight the character and attributes of Jesus. Introduction sections give readers an in-depth look into Jesus's earthly ministry.

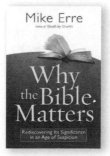

Why the Bible Matters

Mike Erre

Mike Erre, teaching pastor of a large, culturally relevant church in Southern California, offers intelligent answers to questions emerging generations are asking about the Bible. He upholds the Bible's authority in creative, engaging, and intellectually satisfying ways. Erre's contagious enthusiasm and deep respect for the Scriptures match his first-rate scholarship.